Y0-DJQ-797

Play for America

Much of the public recreation program we take for granted today is the result of efforts over many years by the NRA and its supporters to convince the American public of the values of recreation.

Play for America

The National Recreation Association 1906-1965

RICHARD F. KNAPP
CHARLES E. HARTSOE

NATIONAL RECREATION AND PARK ASSOCIATION

Arlington. Virginia 1979

Library of Congress Cataloging in Publication Data

Knapp, Richard F   1939–
    Play for America.

    Bibliography:
    Includes index.
    1. National Recreation Association—History.
    2. Recreation—United States—History.
    I. Hartsoe, Charles, joint author.   II. Title.
    GV53.K6   790'.06'173   79–22644

    ISBN 0–9603540–0–X

                        Printed in the United States of America

*To all who have contributed
to the recreation movement
in America*

Contents

Foreword

Despite the growth and development of recreation in the United States very little has been recorded down through the years of the individuals and organizations that have played a major role in organizing and promoting the recreation movement. There are few scholarly books on the subject of the contributions of national service organizations such as the National Recreation and Park Association. Many professional recreators as well as the general public have neither an awareness of or an appreciation of the difficulties encountered over the years in gaining public acceptance of the importance of recreation in our society. It is no secret that historians have paid little or no attention to the significance of recreation in American culture.

The National Recreation Association, the forerunner of NRPA, was established in 1906 as an outgrowth of the progressive movement for improvement of urban conditions. For sixty years the NRA was the major institutional influence on the development of public recreation in the United States. *Play for America* is an account of the ideas, personalities and circumstances involved in the evolution of the Association.

From 1927 to 1935 the NRA sponsored the National Recreation School which was the first educational institution to establish graduate study in the administration of public recreation. As a graduate of the NRS, I can testify to the effectiveness of the School's well-rounded curriculum. Many of the graduates went on to prominent positions in the park and recreation field. When colleges and universities eventually started to provide courses in recreation, the NRA closed the School.

It is appropriate and timely that two distinguished educators joined forces to fill this void and to record the development of recreation which covers the span of services of the NRA from its inception until it was merged with the professional organizations; namely, The American Institute of Park Executives, The American Recreation Society, The National Conference on State Parks and the American Association of Zoological Parks and Aquariums in 1965 to form the National Recreation and Park Association.

The authors are uniquely qualified to write this book which will no doubt be a valuable resource for students, practitioners and those interested in the history of public recreation. Dr. Richard F. Knapp is a historian with the North Carolina Department of Cultural Resources specializing in American history since 1800. Dr. Charles E. Hartsoe worked closely with NRA executive director Joseph Prendergast and the Association's board of directors in the period leading up to the merger to form the NRPA. Dr. Hartsoe is Chairman of the Department of Recreation at Virginia Commonwealth University.

As the authors have pointed out, the NRA over the years has effectively fostered the acceptance of municipal responsibility for the provision of organized recreation. Its leaders promoted an ever broadening concept of recreation and leisure. As an organization it championed the importance of training and professionalism in the field. In a personal sense, the NRA has contributed richly to my own career as it has to countless other professionals and citizen leaders throughout the country. Americans owe much to the NRA for its contributions over the years.

The National Recreation Foundation provided a grant to make the printing of this book possible. As Executive Secretary of the Foundation and on behalf of its board of trustees, I would like to acknowledge our gratitude to the authors for this splendid account of *Play for America* and to the NRPA for their assistance in making the publication of this study possible.

ROBERT W. CRAWFORD
Commissioner
Department of Recreation
Philadelphia, Pennsylvania

Preface

As a graduate student at Duke University Richard F. Knapp became interested in the beginnings of municipal recreation in New York City. Upon recognizing the close relationship of that topic with the founding of the Playground Association of America, which later became the National Recreation Association (NRA), he began a study of the latter group and completed a dissertation about the NRA from 1906 to 1950. Thus Knapp is responsible for the first seven chapters of this new volume. Charles E. Hartsoe, associated with the NRA during its later years, produced the eighth and ninth chapters and coordinated the process of publication. The remaining pages resulted from a mutual effort.

This book is more than a history of the NRA, which for half a century provided the most continuous institutional impetus for the growth of municipal recreation in the United States. The study reveals part of the struggle to establish and maintain a major voluntary association and a new occupational specialty. The narrative also explores cooperation and competition among various public and private organizations serving the same field. Other elements of the story are the hasty expansion of centralized government in national emergencies and the process by which separate federal agencies attempt to define jurisdiction in an area already occupied in part by local government and private organizations. Yet the central argument of our essay is that the NRA was the primary enduring institution promoting the physical and conceptual rise of municipal recreation in America. In this capacity the Association successfully fostered the increase of municipal responsibility for provision of organized recreation, an expanding definition of recreation and leisure, as well as training and professionalism in the vocation.

The most important sources for our work are the surviving records of the NRA, which have endured several moves in the custody of the successor National Recreation and Park Association (NRPA). When the authors initially examined the documents, the archives included nearly complete minutes of the board of directors of the Association, correspondence, reports, publications, and the professional files of Howard Braucher, chief executive of the NRA for forty years. A sizable bulk of material has been transferred to the Social Welfare History Archives at the University of Minnesota in Minneapolis. The NRPA files, now in Arlington, Virginia, also contain substantial historical data on the American Recreation Society and the American Institute of Park Executives, both merged into the NRPA. In the National Archives the records of the Commission on Training Camp Activities and the Office of Community War Services are revealing. There is a body of literature on American recreation, leisure, and related topics, but little of it is strictly historical in nature. Among periodicals *Recreation*, official publication of the Association, is by far most significant.

As authors we are indebted to a number of individuals and institutions. The Woodrow Wilson Foundation, Duke University, and the National Academy of Sciences each provided fellowships enabling Knapp to complete the major portion of this study. The National Recreation Foundation furnished funds for publication. Its president, Mrs. George T. Francis, Jr., and other board members, especially Susan M. Lee and Mrs. James H. Evans, have been very supportive of this project. The National Recreation and Park Association extended to us full use of its library and historical records and permitted various staff members to type, read, and proofread parts of the manuscript. The staff of the James Branch Cabell Library at Virginia Commonwealth University were most helpful as were faculty members in the Department of Recreation. The World Leisure and Recreation Association was generous in making its records available.

Many people, some now retired or deceased, helped us in a variety of ways. The following correspondents, all of them with years of service in the Association, supplied personal recollections, hitherto often unavailable in written documents, and evaluations in answer to our queries: George Braden, Mrs. Howard Braucher, Mrs. A. O. Brungardt, Reynold E. Carlson, George E. Dickie, John W. Faust, Virginia Musselman, George A. Nesbitt, Marion Preece,

Charles E. Reed, William G. Vinal, and Arthur Williams. Other recreation authorities who similarly aided us were V. K. Brown, Ray R. Butler, Raymond B. Fosdick, J. Halsey Gulick, George Hjelte, F. S. Mathewson, Mark A. McCloskey, and Allen V. Sapora. Longtime recreation experts Temple Jarrell, Harold D. Meyer, and G. Ott Romney kindly contributed personal interviews. George D. Butler, E. Dana Caulkins, and W. C. Sutherland all with experience on the NRA staff, graciously furthered our research with lengthy interviews and correspondence. In addition Robert W. Crawford, James H. Evans, and Susan Lee reviewed parts of the study. Former NRA executive director, Joseph Prendergast read the entire manuscript and provided a useful critique.

At the NRPA various staff members aided us over the years. Arthur E. Todd deserves a special thanks for his early interest and numerous acts of cheerful assistance and advice. His associates Diana Dunn, Waldo Hainsworth, and Sidney Lutzin (who arranged publication of Knapp's initial essay in *Parks and Recreation*) joined with Ott Romney and Wayne Sommer in a group interview with Knapp. NRPA executive director John Davis and deputy director Thad Studstill coordinated NRPA support in the final stages of preparation of the manuscript. Several staff members, particularly Linda Thorsby Bynum, gave of their expertise in proofreading and other skills.

I. B. Holley, Jr., professor of history at Duke University, was indispensable to initial completion of most of these chapters. He carefully reviewed successive drafts and offered constructive criticism and encouragement during Knapp's labors in graduate school. Holley's colleagues Robert F. Durden, Kazimierz Grzybowski, John Tate Lanning, Harold T. Parker, and Richard L. Watson also read the dissertation or related papers and gave valuable advice.

Three competent people, Ginny Albert, Henri Dawkins, and Dorothy Sapp, typed portions of the manuscript. As the deadline for publication neared, Arthur Menius worked faithfully to finish the index. Vladimir L. Reichl provided design, consulted and assisted us throughout the preparation of the book. Also, at R. R. Donnelley & Sons Company, Guy Scobbie oversaw production and gave assistance.

We now know from experience why so many writers acknowledge that their greatest debts are to their spouses. This is true in our case. Sharon Estes Knapp and Joyce Wright Hartsoe have given countless hours, which they might have used for their own recreation, to assist us in innumerable ways in this study of recreation. And Mary Elizabeth Knapp, in her two short years of life, has lost a considerable amount of her daddy's companionship to this venture.

It is our hope that proceeds from sales of this book will be used to support the Joseph Lee Library at the National Recreation and Park Association as well as to encourage further examination of the heritage of recreation and leisure in America.

RICHARD F. KNAPP
CHARLES E. HARTSOE

Parts of New York in the late nineteenth century were the worst of slums packed with people and buildings. A portion of notorious Mulberry Street later became, however, a city park.

1
Municipal Recreation:
Background of an Era

Recreation today is big business in the United States both in terms of economic impact and mass participation. Citizens spent by one measure over $72.5 billion on a great variety of recreation pursuits in 1976, a sum representing about 6.6 percent of the total money used for personal consumption in that year. Another source, with somewhat different indicators, estimated that expenditures for recreation amounted to $180 billion in 1978, over 12 percent of personal spending by consumers.[1] The soaring leisure market, which has outpaced a decade of inflation in the late 1960s and 1970s, contains a diversity of activities and products ranging from opera and ballet to theme parks and luxurious motor homes, from air travel at discounted rates to cable television and video-cassette recorders. People allocate more money for seeds, flowers,

1

and potted plants than admissions to motion pictures, yet commercial amusements and spectator sports still draw hordes of fans. In 1976 commercial establishments offering motion pictures, amusements, and recreation in America had receipts over $17.4 billion. Major league baseball and college football each recorded approximately 32 million admissions that year, and professional football attracted over 11.5 million to its games. In all, some 255 million spectators attended major sports events in 1978. More active recreation is popular too: during that year researchers estimated there were 96.7 million walkers and joggers; 84 million picnickers; 83.5 million swimmers in pools and 59.5 million users of beaches; 66 million bicyclists; 62 million fishermen; 40.9 million tennis players; 34 million boaters; 28 million hikers; 13.5 million horseback riders; and 9.3 million ski enthusiasts.[2]

Citizens can turn to all levels of government to aid them in their recreation. Perhaps the national parks and forests are the most visible evidence of the multi-faceted federal interest in recreation. The National Park Service counted 210 million recreation visits to its facilities in 1978 and administers 294 different sites including national parks, historic monuments, recreation areas, and seashores with a total of 31,283,517 acres.[3] The breadth of federal recreation interests by 1967 encompassed 263 separate programs in 93 governmental units. A Bureau of Outdoor Recreation (BOR), created in 1962, was charged with promoting coordination among these various agencies and engaged in research, technical assistance, and nationwide outdoor recreation planning. In 1978 the Heritage Conservation and Recreation Service superseded the BOR, adding several historic programs formerly under the park agency to the traditional recreation concerns. The federal government by 1965 aided state and local governments in a variety of ways, using twenty-three different pieces of federal legislation to assist recreation departments seeking land for new facilities.[4]

State and local governments, too, are interested in providing their citizens with opportunities for recreation. A number of states, following the examples of North Carolina and California, have set up recreation commissions or departments with broad powers to advise local governments and furnish recreation. All of the states had park areas by the end of 1955.[5] Many counties, cities, and towns have their own recreation or park agencies. By 1965, the last year in which the National Recreation Association made a complete survey of the topic, American cities and towns claimed to have 24,298 supervised playgrounds; 30,000 local park and recreation areas covered about 1.5 million acres. Cities spent over

$2.5 billion on operation and expansion of parks and recreation in 1976.[6]

From the foregoing statistics, which are, of course, only an illustrative sampling, it is evident that local governmental units in the United States have emphatically accepted responsibility for providing citizens with opportunities for the creative use of leisure. This phenomenon, largely a development of the twentieth century, has not been confined merely to the provision of facilities such as parks and playgrounds. The field of recreation has also expanded to include a host of occupational categories involving supervision and leadership, stretching from part-time workers at summer playgrounds to professors in graduate schools devoted to training professionals. Clearly the value of professional leadership in planning and guiding recreation activities is widely recognized in the United States today.

Along with the rise of this new brand of professionalism has come an enlarged popular definition of the concepts of recreation and leisure. "Recreation" is defined by one recent authority as

> any activity which is not consciously performed for the sake of any reward beyond itself, which offers man an outlet for his physical, mental, or creative powers, and in which he engages because of inner desire and not because of outer compulsion.[7]

At the turn of the century, in contrast, people used the term "play" with much the same connotation that "recreation" would come to hold by the 1930s by which time "play" came to have a popular usage equating it with playgrounds and activities for children. The switch from children's "play" to "recreation" for all ages is indicative of the broadening of the concept which took place over the first three decades of this century.

The evolution of the National Recreation Association has been inextricably wrapped up with these three major themes—the development of governmental responsibility for recreation, the rise of professionalism, and an ever expanding definition of recreation and leisure. The organization was a voluntary, nonprofit, nonsectarian service group devoted to aiding the spread of recreation, particularly urban public recreation. When the last of the early chief executives died in 1949, the Association could look back on nearly fifty years of service during which it had been the most influential institution in the United States fostering the development of recreation as its major objective. The leaders of the Association believed in the gospel of recreation and played a crucial role in winning widespread acceptance of governmental, chiefly municipal, responsibility for the provision of recreation opportunities as well as the need for trained recreation personnel of professional stature. In its final decade and a half as an independent society, the organization continued to furnish service and leadership to the widening recreation movement but ultimately opted to participate in a merger of the significant associations in the field of parks and recreation.

The beginning of the National Recreation Association in 1906 was a direct outgrowth of the industrializing, urbanizing America of the twentieth century. The rise of the new industrial city carried with it the seeds of many changes in American society including fresh approaches to play and recreation. By 1900 conditions in urban America, ranging from the increasing squalor of crowded slums to the beginnings of municipal reform movements, were ripe for the birth of a national movement to cope with the problem of urban recreation. Opportunities for recreation, while severely limited for some slum dwellers, were not entirely absent in the cities of the 1890s. Despite the cramping effects of the Protestant work ethic, which frowned on idle play, and despite the congestion and lack of facilities increasingly evident as urbanization rushed ahead, Americans had a rich heritage of recreation pursuits stretching back to the manly sports popular in the seventeenth-century colonial era.[8]

As cities became increasingly crowded in the late nineteenth century, sports began to achieve a new popularity. By 1890 America had seen a series of organized athletic activities sweep the nation. Baseball became the national game; and croquet, tennis, football, and bicycling all enjoyed surges in public favor. The sports page became an established part of the daily newspaper and made reading about one's favorite teams a new form of recreation. Unprecedented popularity marked both professional and amateur sports; in fact, the first news story reported by wireless was a sports event. The brutality of college football became such a national issue that finally President Theodore Roosevelt intervened.[9]

For those not interested in sports, there were, of course, other diversions. If a man were well-to-do, he might join a country club to play golf, visit one of the five isolated national parks of 1900, or even buy a costly automobile and face the challenge of inadequate roads and frequent breakdowns. Almost anyone, regardless of his income, might find a club or lodge of some sort to attend. Some of the larger cities were developing parks and a few playgrounds; but with additional masses of people crowding into the cities, most middle and lower class residents had to depend on commercial recreation for many of their leisure activities outside the home.

Cities, large and small, abounded with various commercial amusements, ranging from legitimate theater and opera for the cultivated or affluent down through vaudeville, movies, burlesque, and sidewalk peep shows.[10] A notable lack of accessible public parks and playgrounds prompted local trolley companies to fill the void by building imitations of the gaudy Coney Island amusement park, which one observer in 1905 called "the tom-tom of America."[11] Far more common than trolley parks were neighborhood saloons. Lists of corner saloons in some city directories exceeded the combined total of clergymen and teachers. Despite the objections of prohibitionists, saloons rendered valuable services by providing social centers and free meeting places. The saloons helped make up for the lamentable paucity of municipal toilets and drinking fountains on the hot streets. Even policemen on duty had to rely upon saloon restrooms, although it was generally illegal for officers to stop at a bar while on duty. Often saloons were the only public places available for escape from the bustling streets.[12]

The urban masses spent much of their increasing leisure in the streets. Although a few groups of citizens in several cities were groping for alternatives to life on the pavement, the typical situation was simply an absence of any municipal recreation facilities. And, as an astute observer noted at the time, the people generally used their leisure poorly on the vulgar and commercialized streets.[13]

Among the factors behind the growth of leisure were technology and shrinking hours of labor. Consumers discovered early versions of such time-saving inventions as the automobile and the telephone, along with gas and electric home appliances. Weekly hours of labor in agriculture and industry had been contracting since the mid-nineteenth century. The average work week in all industries in 1850 was 69.7 hours. This had dropped to 61.7 hours by 1890 and 54.9 hours in 1910.[14]

As the American work week diminished and potential hours for recreational use rose, the term *leisure* appeared increasingly in public discussions. As early as the 1870s Horace Greeley had recognized the importance of using leisure wisely and asked: "Who will teach us incessant workers how to achieve leisure and enjoy it?"[15] The Puritan work ethic was clearly coming under fire. Presidential candidate James A. Garfield continued this attack when he declared at Chautauqua in 1880 that man's two greatest problems were, first, the struggle to obtain leisure and, then, the question of what to do with it. By the 1890s magazines such as *Scribner's* and *Atlantic Monthly* were publishing articles on "the new leisure." In the next decade social workers Florence Kelley and Mary McDowell carried the assault on the traditional work ethic still further by proclaiming the "right to leisure."[16] Reform-minded scholar Delos F. Wilcox in his book *The American City* (1904) epitomized the growing recognition of the need for constructive use of free time. Recognizing that leisure could bring both good and evil results, he recommended that the nation's spare hours be used to positive advantage in programs of wholesome public recreation and civic work. He saw the possible implications of a leisure society:

> The difference between virtue and vice as characteristic of a community, which means the difference between the success and failure of democracy, lies principally in the use that the people make of their leisure. Work, even under disagreeable situations, causes few moral wrecks. It is pleasure-seeking run amuck that threatens the integrity of a race and the performance of free institutions. The changes that are being wrought in modern life emphasize more and more the importance of the right use of leisure, for with the shortening hours of industry, the minute division of labor, and the transformation of workmen into machine-tenders, the real significance of work in the formation of character and the development of citizenship is becoming less.[17]

Yet such advanced views, which no doubt impressed some thoughtful civic leaders with the need for action in the field of urban recreation by voluntary groups or perhaps local governments, were not typical. To many people there was still a stigma attached to leisure and recreation. A specific example of this lingering attitude was maverick economist Thorstein Veblen's influential book, *The Theory of the Leisure Class* (1899). Veblen emphasized the connection of the wealthy, leisure class with wasteful, "conspicuous consumption" and thus gave leisure a bad connotation.[18] Major support for the attacks on leisure came from the common praise of work. The glorification of work had been reinforced by the gospel of success which evolved in the prospering materialistic America of the late nineteenth century. Quantity often seemed more important than quality in life; if a thing was

All too often the most common urban recreation was simply idleness with little positive potential. With vacant lots gone, streets became crowded, dangerous playgrounds. Relatively few people, and hardly any of the poor, could enjoy the limited active recreation at large landscape parks such as New York's noted Central Park.

bigger, then to many it appeared better. Numerous intelligent Americans believed that work was the serious part of life and that play was a waste of time, or at best, as Franklin D. Roosevelt once said, "a polite form of indolence."[19] Few Americans in 1900 had a positive conception of the social and educational values in recreation and play.

Some individuals, however, were aware of challenges to the traditional view of recreation.[20] For example, the widely read Herbert Spencer, purveyor of Darwinism to America, saw play, among other things, as a device for using up surplus energy not required for the essential maintenance of life. Other writers, such as William James in *Principles of Psychology* (1890), classified play as an instinct; this "instinct-practice" theory culminated in the work of Karl Groos of Switzerland in *The Play of Animals* (1898) and *The Play of Man* (1901). Groos saw instinct as the principal motivating factor behind play and considered play to be an important element of training and preparation for life as an adult. German educator Guts Muth emphasized the recreative value of play; after work and toil, play refreshed a person. G. Stanley Hall of Clark University maintained that a growing child at play experienced a recapitulation of the earlier cultural epochs of man; play instincts were inherited. There were other theories of play and recreation in the late nineteenth century, but such thinking meant little or nothing to millions of Americans in growing urban slums who were daily experiencing the effects of urbanization and a pitiful lack of recreation opportunities.

Urbanization and problems related to it were among the major phenomena of late nineteenth-century America. By the last decade of the century 29 percent of all Americans lived in 448 urban areas, and 9,700,000 citizens dwelt in the 28 cities with populations of over 100,000.[21] With this increase in urban numbers came such problems as lack of adequate sanitation and housing. Urbanization and congestion disrupted the patterns of relaxation for Americans; the new industrial society did not provide sufficient physical facilities or social organization for recreation of the masses.[22] City governments themselves were weak and incapable as a result of several factors, including corruption and inflexible charters which did not fix clearly the axis of official responsibility. Such conditions caused English observer James Bryce to characterize American city governments in 1888 as "the one conspicuous failure of the United States."[23]

The biggest city in America, and one which exemplified most of the problems of urbanism, then as now, was New York. A brief review of conditions in New York between 1880 and 1900 may make clear some of the many related problems faced by American cities of the era which intensified the need for recreation facilities and programs. New York had the worst tenement problem in America by 1900. Even the city's finest mansions stood side by side, but congestion was far more acute in the slums.[24] One investigating committee found 360 people, including 40 children, living in a single tenement building; the death rate for children under five there, whose play yard was 5 feet 10 inches wide and 12 steps below street level, was 325 per 1,000. New York south of Harlem had the greatest density of population in the world; one 32-acre section had 986.4 persons per acre.[25] Many of the tenements housed 26 families in a five- to seven-story building on a lot 25 feet wide by 100 feet deep. By 1900 two-thirds of New York's 3,400,000 people lived in 82,600 tenements.[26] Closely related to the tenement house problem were the perils of life in the streets and flourishing crime. With vacant lots gone, the wagon and trolley-filled streets became dangerous playgrounds. Central Park was miles away and inaccessible; only three of forty-eight boys interviewed in a downtown public school in the 1880s had ever been in the park. Public health suffered in the crowded city. Ordinary diseases easily approached epidemic proportions in the slums; and for many, malnutrition was a normal way of life.[27] Police often disrupted harmless street play, and children drifted into gangs of delinquents.[28]

Institutions such as schools and parks seldom adequately relieved these problems. Although a sizable number of youths worked in factories and tenements and evaded ineffective child labor legislation, the schools lacked room even for those who did try to attend. In the school year 1888–1889, 14,085 applicants were turned away for lack of facilities.[29] With crowding on the rise in the next years, proper play areas adjacent to the available schools were a luxury.[30] The educational system was hindered by lack of an adequate compulsory attendance law and shared with the park board the common problems of shortages of money and a plethora of politics.[31] The park board was more interested in large landscape parks, such as Central Park, than in recreation spots spread throughout the city. These landscape parks helped fulfill the desire of the upper classes for carriage drives and evening strolls but hardly touched the plight of the teeming slums.[32] Provision for organized sports and play in the parks was pitifully inadequate. The park board in 1891 winked at devious tycoon Jay Gould when his elevated railway encroached on parkland but refused permission for the New York Athletic Club to play football on a Central

Park ball ground. "Keep off the grass" was the dominant philosophy of park use.[33] The Tenement House Commission of 1900 found that greater New York had 6,776 acres of parkland, only 40 of which directly served the 1,585,000 people in the tenements of Manhattan who lived several thousand to a block without backyards. The notorious tenth ward, one of the city's smallest and most densely populated wards, with 10,000 children under five, had no park wholly within its bounds; the 190-acre thirteenth ward, with a total population of 55,000, had 9,400 such children and no parks whatsoever.[34]

If the tenements of New York were representative of the worst of life in America's rising urban, industrial areas, the deplorable conditions themselves called out for improvement. In addition, other forces and ideas were at work across the nation in the 1890s which promised a constructive response to the factory and the slum. Such notions stimulated urban reforms on a host of fronts, including attempts to alleviate some of the effects of congestion with new recreation facilities.

The reform-conscious 1890s were a watershed of American history, dividing a rural, self-contained, confident America from a predominantly urban, industrial nation with more than a trace of skepticism.[35] Scholars seem to agree on the importance of the decade or two after 1890 in the molding of twentieth-century America.[36] It was the time of the Populist revolt and the armageddon of the agrarians, but the future of the nation already lay with the industrial city. Technology, bigness, organization, expertise, and a host of impersonal economic forces threatened the world of the once self-reliant individual. Community and collectivism became viable alternatives again. The downfall of Darwinian determinism meant that a man no longer was dependent on the philosophy of laissez-faire. Concepts of environment and nurture challenged ideas of heredity and nature as determinants in an individual's life. Leaders in fields such as economics and sociology increasingly stressed the idea that man could be a significant power in his world. Some of the impersonal forces of the universe could be altered by the expert, the professional, and the scientist. Society could be improved; democracy, revitalized.

From the agrarian Populists and municipal reformers of the 1890s to the leaders of the next decade's so-called progressive movement, men felt that society could be improved if only people would act.[37] As the Populist party fell apart, leaders in various reforms tended increasingly to come from the business and professional classes of the cities and to share common ideas, prejudices, and characteristics. According to leading historians, the urban progressives were often from established American families, economically secure, and educated. Such people were frequently ready to tackle city problems by supporting increased public or private action in areas such as the education, recreation, and welfare of less fortunate neighbors. A large number of these well-bred progressives were ambitious, with a strong sense of individualism and desire for power and influence. Many set themselves apart from the masses and felt, as did Theodore Roosevelt and Woodrow Wilson, that progress originated with a few effective, benevolent leaders. The reformers knew where talent and righteousness resided and spoke out in moralizing tones. They looked to efficient professionals, frequently themselves, to help bring a beneficial order in a democratic society. The progressive mentality combined a strong ethical strain with a sense of moral superiority and respect for the dynamic individual. A significant number of these tendencies marked the key pioneer leaders of early attempts at national coordination of urban recreation.[38] The progressive had great faith in leadership and could look to both an individualistic, democratic America and an efficient, centralized state.[39] But progressivism, with its belief in social justice, the expert, and governmental responsibility for society, was only part of a matrix of positive responses, including the push for adequate urban recreation, to the problems of industrialism and urbanism.

A number of institutions and agencies of urban America were undergoing drastic changes by the 1890s. Such modifications helped them adjust to the spirit of reform in the environmentalist, man-centered philosophies of the twentieth century and prepare for a role in supplying leadership, support, and some competition for the rise of public recreation. A significant number of private groups concerned with social justice—churches, settlements, and charity agencies—were experiencing similar developments. Public and private movements were considerably interrelated. By 1894, when the National Municipal League was founded, there were eighty citizen-led municipal reform groups, sixty of them new since 1890. The reformers' twin avenues of attack were improvement of city government and humanitarian, social service reform.[40] While the new ideas and practices of reform did not make great headway immediately against the overwhelming problems of urban life, many such developments proved to be catalysts which quickened the evolution of a number of phases of city life. The beginnings of urban public recreation were bound up with several related fields such as education and social work, and certain changes in each of these areas hastened the growth of municipal recreation.[41]

Some educators in both public and private circles, who gave significant leadership to the early push for urban playgrounds, paid increasing attention to new ideas in the 1890s. Changes in technology, population, and psychology began to affect the nation's urban schools, which were still often inadequate and also victims of overcrowding and politics. Yet education was expanding and making progress toward a system of universal, free public schools.[42] Innovations—kindergartens, health examinations, nurses in the schools—spread out from their origins in large cities.[43] Educational psychologists, particularly G. Stanley Hall of Clark University, began to emphasize scientific study of children and play. Educators increasingly tested, measured, and compared the health, aptitude, and even recreational habits of large numbers of children.[44] Scientific testing was but one indicator of a rising sense of professionalism in the administration and operation of education.[45] The National Education Association (NEA) provided a base for the growing forces of public education as did the federal Office of Education. But the teachers' society was generally conservative in both political and social thought, and, while isolated voices of social protest were raised even within the organization, the most exciting educational developments of the era were led by individuals rather than the NEA.[46]

Perhaps the most important educational trend of the period was the beginning of "progressive" education. Often linked with educational philosopher John Dewey, this school of educational theory sprang from the same urban, industrial conditions as the push for adequate recreation facilities and the general reforming interest of the time.[47] The central thrust of progressive education was to broaden the school's function in society and, through a more child-centered approach, better prepare citizens for life in the American democracy. Dewey once expressed his philosophy of education in a single sentence. "Education is the fundamental method of social progress and reform."[48] In 1899 Dewey's seminal little volume, *The School and Society*, appeared. In it he expressed the need to make social organization grow naturally in schools, as it might on playgrounds. The school was to be a "miniature community" in which children might "really live and get a life experience. Relate the school to life, and all studies are of necessity correlated."[49] With such philosophy, educators easily justified broadening the schools' programs to include a great many new activities such as vocational education and recreation.[50] Thus teachers in some large cities became deeply involved in using the

Various approaches led to improved recreation opportunities in New York. Reporter and gadfly Jacob Riis exposed the evils of the slums and fostered playgrounds as part of general reforms. Educator Seth Stewart promoted playgrounds at schools for years before becoming the first director of a new progam of summer vacation schools and playgrounds. The Union Settlement cleared the center of a block for a playground.

schools to provide facilities and leadership in recreation for children and adults.

Physical education was another developing field which supplied considerable aid to the initial growth of twentieth-century recreation. By about 1900 leading American physical educators were starting to favor the use of sports and games as opposed to formal gymnastics. At the same time, physical education, then also called "physical training" or "physical culture," was moving increasingly into the public school curriculum. Meanwhile, a professional organization, the American Physical Education Association, had been founded in 1885, and innovators such as Dudley Sargent and Luther Gulick were pushing special training and recognition of the significance of physical education. Thus the field was prepared to supply a corps of leaders to the emerging forces of urban recreation.[51]

Municipal parks, like city schools, were generally incapable of meeting many pressing needs for varieties of urban recreation in the 1890s. The very existence of such parks, however, provided a seedbed for initiating and refining ideas and facilities for serving the growing leisure of the urban population. Imitating New York's 840-acre Central Park, major American cities created large parks which, however, were often miles away from crowded slums. In 1898 New England park superintendents organized a professional association which eventually became the American Institute of Park Executives.[52] The prevailing idea for parks run by these men was a man-made replica of a pleasing rural landscape designed to provide chiefly for passive recreation, quiet relaxation, and leisurely strolling. Park designer Frederick Law Olmsted expressed the philosophy behind these large landscape parks, stressing the need for considerable open spaces and natural rural scenes to complement and give relief from the city.[53] While some proponents of rural-styled parks recognized the need for smaller parks, and even playgrounds, in the hearts of tightly packed cities, their main emphases seemed to be on peaceful, well-landscaped parks and connecting parkways, usually on the rim of the metropolis.[54]

A number of park designers and landscape architects joined with housing reformers of the 1890s in the changing field of city planning in hopes of finding alternatives to the aimless uncoordinated development of the bustling cities. In 1902 designers drew a plan for Washington, D.C., and a cry for plans went up across the nation. Within a few years, Harvard introduced the first program for university training in planning, and the profession began staging an annual National Conference on City Planning. Notable early city planners, such as John Nolen and Olmsted, recognized the need to arrange for systems of adequate municipal recreation areas.[55]

Meanwhile, a host of private social and philanthropic agencies were organizing new efforts to battle the ills of urban society. Like education and city planning, social work was acquiring a new sense of professionalism, organization, and a wider scope of service, which included urban recreation.[56] Social workers also dealt with other related matters—education, housing, child labor, health, and crime. By the 1890s charitable agencies were banding together into charity organization societies, which endeavored to be "scientific" and coordinate private welfare in given cities. Gradually the specialized caseworker replaced the spontaneous friendly visitor. A sense of professionalism arose as the status and use of volunteers declined. In 1903 the New York School of Philanthropy offered a full year's course in social work. The following year there were 150 cities with organized charities. Efficiency was the goal of organization.[57] Some of the most effective social workers served in settlement houses in great cities and, like social workers in general, moved toward professionalism and organization and also developed a wide variety of programs, including some of America's first playgrounds.[58]

The large number of early settlement house residents motivated by Christianity was but one reflection of urban Christianity's response to the industrial city.[59] Socialism and labor issues had dominated the social gospel of the 1880s, but there had also been interest in problems of immigration, the saloon, the family, housing, and amusements. In the next decade social Christianity experienced its greatest flowering up to that time, and social gospeler Lymon Abbott announced: "The object of Christianity is human welfare; its method is character-building; its process is evolution; and the secret of its power is God."[60] And so adherents of social Christianity, working through institutional churches and religious settlements, were another group who could provide leadership in urban reforms such as recreation.

One major nondenominational organization, with a religious background and an interest in physical recreation, although not an ardent proponent of the social gospel, was the Young Men's Christian Association. By the mid-1890s the YMCA, after four decades in America, was solidly established with 1400 local branches staffed by 1200 general secretaries or supervisors.[61] The program of the YMCA tended to emphasize buildings and included welfare, athletics, education, and youth work. The YMCA had organized leadership and coordination at the city, state, and national levels. The key men in the total system were the local YMCA directors or "secretaries"; the secretaries had formed a professional association as early as 1871 and could receive special training at the schools, later colleges, established by the YMCA in the 1880s. Following the Spanish-American War, the YMCA began its two greatest decades of national growth. With expansion came increases in numbers, specialization, and control of decisions by the secretaries. These skilled secretaries and former secretaries constituted a corps of trained leaders not only for the YMCA but also for the blossoming playground movement.[62]

In addition to trained leadership, social services of all kinds needed adequate funding, and here too a new style of operation developed rapidly during the nineties.[63] Traditionally, private agencies in America had pioneered in new areas of social welfare, and government allocations for such programs were rare in the late nineteenth century. Foundations were also possible sources of funds, but only a few foundations were in existence before 1900. After that date new foundations increased rapidly.[64] Foundation grants were seldom perpetual, however, so fund raising played an important part in social work. Nineteenth-century fund raising had depended mainly on tactics such as personal appeals, bazaars, and "begging letters"; reformers of urban recreation refined these methods. In 1905 two YMCA leaders developed some of the first whirlwind, intensive campaigns. This method, with minor improvements, was to be a major tool of American fund raising for decades. The era also saw a shift from limited, emotional, and religious pleas to professionally run solicitations stressing secular mass appeal.[65] By this time, too, several cities had experimented with the promising community chest approach. After 1900 the number of organizations soliciting nationally increased 300 percent in two decades.[66]

In sum, a significant number of groups interested in various reforms and social work initiated or solidified national organizations about the turn of the century. Spurred by both the negative and positive effects of industrialism and urbanization and by the promises of new technological and philosophical developments, urban reformers plunged into the work of improving their world. Local experiments became national institutions. Social worker Mary Richmond counted thirty-nine new national health or welfare societies in the first decade of the century, more than in any previous decade.[67] In fact, each major reform on the urban scene developed its national association. And, while many institutions, such as schools, parks, and settlements, were interested in and fostered recreation, the playground movement itself moved increasingly toward an independent national status in the turn of the century's encouraging environment of municipal reform. The result would be the National Recreation Association, forerunner of today's National Recreation and Park Association.

Joseph Lee devoted much of his life to philanthropy and social work, especially in recreation and education. By 1904 he had a national reputation as a leader in recreation. He later served as unpaid president of the National Recreation Association from 1910 until his death in 1937.

2
From Ideas to Association: Founding and Early Years

In the quarter century after 1885 leaders of the playground movement in the United States nurtured their interest to such an extent that they succeeded in forming a national organization, the Playground Association of America, which they hoped would encourage and guide the local impulses. By the end of this period, the Association had tasted some success both in aiding the rise of municipal recreation and in building a permanent organization. The chief leaders of the Association transferred to the national level ideas which they had developed in cities such as New York and Boston.

Although the American playground movement had roots in several communities, its primary impulse came in the summer of 1885 in Boston. Dr. Marie E. Zakrsewska, who was visting in Germany, sent a letter describing the inexpensive sand piles used as highly effective play areas for children in the most congested parts of Berlin to the Massachusetts Emergency and Hygiene Association, a Boston charity group. Following this lead, the Boston association set up two sand pile playgrounds for local children.[1] Over the years the group enlarged this program, replacing its volunteer staff with paid matrons and in 1893 appointing a general superintendent for its ten summer playgrounds. Convincing demonstrations of this privately supported service helped to educate city officials to the need for expanding the work with public resources. The city moved gradually from merely supplementing the private play areas to furnishing supervised municipal facilities. By the end of the decade, city funds accounted for significantly more of the expenditures for playgrounds in Boston than individual contributions, and Mayor Josiah Quincy had even pushed a bill through the state legislature permitting the use of up to $500,000 for a "comprehensive system of playgrounds" in the parks of the city.[2]

Activities in Boston helped influence the establishment of playgrounds in other cities on the sand garden model. By 1895 private groups had founded similar playgrounds in at least four additional cities: New York, Chicago, Philadelphia, and Providence. Before the new century began, the roster contained seven more cities.[3] Boston, then, was a fountainhead of the American playground movement. As the movement began to spread both geographically and conceptually, that city provided a training ground for Joseph Lee, later to become president of the National Recreation Association for almost three decades and one of the half dozen most influential men in American recreation.

Joseph Lee was born into the wealthy Boston aristocracy in 1862, the son of a leading merchant and banker. Both an old family nurse and Lee's father instilled in young Lee a sense of social responsibility. After a happy childhood, Lee went to Harvard, where the teacher who reportedly influenced him most was philosopher Josiah Royce. Following graduation, Lee entered the Harvard law school after a year of travel and study in Europe.[4]

Upon the completion of his legal studies, young Lee, assured of independent wealth but troubled by the prospect of unearned riches, felt a great desire to serve mankind. Casting about for a suitable career, he started what became a ten-year study of juvenile delinquency in Boston while engaged in work with numerous other social issues. This led him to join the board of directors of Associated Charities of Boston in 1894. Feeling that democracy might be destroyed by certain effects of industrialism, he decided that education and improvement of the environment of the poor were the most effective roads to social progress. Lee had a strong sense of noblesse oblige and wished to use himself, as well as his money, to aid the underdogs of society. He emphasized not mere charity but a positive, curative program. This was evident in the title of his first book, *Constructive and Preventive Philanthropy* (1902). By the late 1890s Lee, influenced by his parents, his up-bringing, and especially his growing philanthropic activities, was well on the way to a life dedicated almost exclusively to social work.[5]

Lee's experience with social work in the 1890s taught him the importance of both governmental and private responsibility in social improvement and the necessity for planning, organization, and perseverance in campaigns of reform. In 1895 and again in 1898 he was a leader in the legislative fight for a Massachusetts Children's Bureau. The failure of both these attempts convinced him of the futility of merely promoting a recognized need without planning carefully for the effort. So Lee deliberately set out to create a nonpartisan, nonsectarian reform group free of obligation to anyone. The result was the Massachusetts Civic League, established in 1898 to:

> inform and organize public sentiment in matters pertaining to the charitable and reformatory interests and institutions of the Commonwealth and to promote the study, careful framing, and systematic agitation of measures of social improvement.[6]

Lee's legal knowledge, ample personal resources, and free time made him an ideal leader for the League. His work with the League helped him to perfect methods of fund raising, organization of voluntary associations, and dealing with voters and officials. The League, which Lee served as president or vice-president for the rest of his life, recognized the value of private research as a stimulus to legislation aimed at obtaining governmental responsibility for social conditions.[7]

Lee used the League and other means to express his opinions on a broad spectrum of related social reforms. He often spoke of such improvements as being like a piece of sod with intertwined roots; wherever a reformer began he was soon connected with all of the issues. Lee, however, divided the problems of society into two great classes: "who shall be born and . . . what shall happen to people after they are born."[8] "Who shall be born" was the key issue; thus Lee believed in birth control, sterilization of the insane, and immigration restriction. For those already living, the solution involved constructive reforms in areas such as housing, health, and especially recreation and education.[9] He agreed with John Dewey on the basic importance of the school in a democratic society and served nine years on the school board of Boston. Since Lee wanted skilled teachers, he aided what eventually became the graduate school of education at Harvard University by giving $25,000 to establish a professorship in 1900 and also by paying the salaries of two faculty members for a number of years. Recreation and education eventually became Lee's dominant interests, but he continued many of his related activities and his general conception of the two key questions in social work throughout his life.[10]

In addition to his concept of social work, Lee's views on man and society appear to have crystallized in the 1890s. He saw the need for both individualism and collectivism. Individualism was central to much of his thought, as with many others of his generation. So he pushed self-help in philanthropy. "Money, bread and butter, or a suit of clothes will only pauperize a man, but make him a gift of opportunity and he will make himself rich."[11] Lee recognized the great creative power of individuals and argued that the key element in a municipal recreation system was the one man who headed it.[12] Another of his emphases was the importance of the individual's wants in recreation. A few years before his death, Lee lectured the directors of the National Recreation Association on the relationship of strong individuals to a healthy society and the value to this connection of competitive games.[13] If Lee emphasized individualism, he also supported cooperation and the community of individuals. Before 1902, he wrote that philanthropy had shifted from one class aiding another to a cooperative activity open to all for ". . . the building up of the better life of the community. It is no longer what I can do for you, but what we can do for ourselves and our country."[14] If people would just get together and work for the common good, Lee urged, all of the individuals too could benefit.[15]

In both individual and community efforts, said Lee, quality was more important than quantity. Like many progressives, he believed in efficiency. It was better to meet a few needs effectively than to obtain mediocre results on many fronts. The key to quality was through fixed goals, organization, and expertise.[16] Lee's belief in quality was reflected in both his philanthropy and his distaste for the mere things of his materialistic society. The goals of man, he once remarked, were loyalty, contest, nurture, service of the beautiful, and the search for truth.[17] Lee seldom talked about religion but, perhaps influenced by the Unitarianism of his father, seemed to emphasize God as Truth and Beauty and Life rather than follow any specific creed.[18] These ideals, coupled with self-expression, were for Lee the components of the good life. His aim was to help himself and others to achieve such a full existence.

> To make people by education capable of living at all—on any amount of money, large or small. Very few Americans are capable of doing this. . . . The hackman points out to you the beauty of the sunset. He isn't paid to do it, he just can't help it. He hasn't any money . . . but he does know a little how to live.[19]

Thus Lee increasingly emphasized education for the wise use of leisure as the means to help people achieve happy, creative lives. But before ideas such as these were complete in Lee's mind, he had begun to move directly into playground promotion in Boston.

Beginning in the early 1890s, Joseph Lee gradually became more active in the playground movement in Boston. He first recognized the value of play when working with the Associated Charities.[20] Playgrounds, he felt, were a constructive service to society. By the end of the decade Lee set up his own experimental playground in Boston to determine the best types of administration, leadership, design, and program for play areas. For several years this research was his major preoccupation. He took photographs and wrote daily reports of his observations. Having seen unsupervised playgrounds degenerate into breeding grounds for petty tyrants, he hired and trained leaders for his experiment. He also included a variety of activities from sand gardens for small children to handball courts for adults. From all these many activities, Lee developed standards for the operation of playgrounds. Stressing quality over quantity, he refused to lower his new standards simply to lure in municipal financial support.[21]

Out of his efforts to develop a model playground early in the new century, Lee formulated his philosophy and views on children's play.[22] The educational ideas of the German Friedrich Froebel, who developed the kindergarten, greatly influenced Lee, whose instinct psychology depended largely upon William James and Karl Groos. Lee postulated three basic groups of human instincts: reflexes, hungers, and achieving instincts. Most important of the achieving impulses were the seven play instincts: creation, rhythm, hunting, fighting, nurture, curiosity, and team play. Learning was implied in play instincts. Play, Lee argued, was the serious activity in children's adjustment to life.

Lee felt recreation had vital significance not only for children but also for everyone who wanted a meaningful life. Organized recreation thus had to take many forms, such as art museums, night schools, parks, athletic fields, and music. Even work was recreation to a lucky few. Play, "the architect of man," might even provide for others an antidote to the boredom of the assembly line.[23] Lee always emphasized the positive value of recreation for its own sake and felt that any benefits it might give in improving citizenship, diminishing delinquency, and fostering health were but valuable side effects.[24]

By 1904 Lee had spread his ideas well beyond the Boston area and achieved a national reputation as a leader in recreation. He mailed reports of his Boston experiments to leaders of playgrounds around the country and drew considerable response. In addition, his book *Philanthropy* and an increasing number of articles and speeches in periodicals and newspapers helped diffuse his message of play. Lee frequently visited the leading recreation reformers of New York and also kept in touch with progress in Chicago.[25]

Another Midwestern city, St. Louis, provided the opportunity for Lee to move into a position of leadership with a national civic group interested in playgrounds. In 1904 the young American League for Civic Improvement built a model street at the great exposition in St. Louis celebrating the purchase of Louisiana. On the street Lee designed and financed a model playground.[26] When the League became the American Civic Association that same year, Lee took charge of its Department of Public Recreation and established a national information service and an advisory committee of experts on recreation, which included social worker Charles F. Weller of Washington, D.C., educator Luther Gulick of New York, and several others.[27] Lee and the American Civic Association, however, did not develop the field of national playground promotion very actively because Lee was still much involved in his Boston work, and a stronger impulse for national development soon came from New York.

New York by 1905 had taken a leading position among American cities with public recreation programs.[28] After several abortive attempts, recreation reformers in the city had joined the general movement for social and political reform which in 1894 had brought William L. Strong into the office of the mayor. Under Strong, the city had moved forward with both small parks in con-

By 1905 thirty-five American cities had supervised playgrounds. The South Parks District of Chicago then opened ten pace-setting recreation parks at a cost of $5 million. The parks, praised by President Theodore Roosevelt as "the most notable civic achievement of any American city," included large recreation centers, indoor and outdoor gymnasiums, swimming pools, sand gardens, lecture rooms, and libraries.

gested areas and school playgrounds. A few years later nineteen private groups interested in playgrounds had coalesced into the Outdoor Recreation League, which had run its own model playgrounds and also convinced a newly active school board to open summer playgrounds as part of the vacation school program. Once established, the progressive educators' bureaucracy, with annual tax funds and popular support, had expanded the summer recreation program so rapidly that nearly 1,000 teachers had become involved after a mere four years. Meanwhile the creation of supervised playgrounds on costly park land was expanding too, although at a slower rate. By 1905 the summer program of the schools had a budget of $381,000 and over 100 play sites, including 23 evening recreation centers in school buildings.

Three educational administrators in particular provided significant leadership in planning and organizing recreation in the New York school system and shortly were to rise to prominence in the national recreation movement. Superintendent Seth Stewart for years had recommended school playgrounds and had been the first director of the vacation schools and playgrounds.[29] Stewart had also been partly responsible for the selection of Henry S. Curtis as director of child study of the school system. Curtis, a Yale graduate with a Ph.D. from Clark University, had made a number of investigations dealing with children and had also visited Germany where he had studied several recreational activities. By 1905, Curtis was supervisor of the East Side school playgrounds of New York.[30]

Perhaps the most important of the educators was the director of physical education in the school system, Luther H. Gulick. Born in Hawaii, Gulick was the last of five children of a missionary couple. He had experienced an erratic formal education before earning an M.D. degree at New York University. Undoubtedly both his religious background and an interest in physical education made service with the YMCA seem an attractive career. Therefore Gulick joined the faculty of the YMCA college at Springfield, Massachusetts. By emphasizing training of leaders and professionalism, he transformed physical education in the YMCA from calisthenics, used to lure boys to religious classes, into a recognized, independent program dominated by sports and games.[31]

Gulick developed most of his fundamental ideas on physical education while working with the YMCA. He saw a close relation between body, mind, and spirit and invented the familiar triangle symbol of the YMCA to express this connection. To Gulick, physical education had educational, recreational, and therapeutic aims.[32]

His chance to spread his ideas further came in 1903 when he became director of physical education for the public school system of New York, with the largest professional staff in the nation.

While building the citywide program, Gulick initiated an athletic association for boys, the Public School Athletic League, first such group in the country. Wealthy citizens supported the work of the League, which considerably broadened opportunities in athletics for students. Gulick organized interscholastic competition but also, in order to serve the average boy, developed tests which all boys could take to win badges of athletic proficiency. Both professional and financial support for the League could be seen in its board of directors, which included the city superintendent of schools; a wealthy member of the board of education; the president of City College, John H. Finley; lawyer and promoter of athletics Gustavus T. Kirby; and two leaders of the local playground movement. Soon the League convinced the city government to build four new high school athletic fields.[33] Thus by 1905 Gulick had attained considerable success in widening physical education in both the national YMCA and the New York city schools. At the same time, the thoughts and actions of the backers of Gulick's League provided a prototype for the imminent national playground organization.

During his years in New York, Gulick refined his concepts of play and recreation.[34] Play, he said, was based on both animal instincts and tradition but was also doing what one wanted to do simply for the fun of it:

> Play is more than a name applied to a given list of activities: it is an attitude which may pervade every activity. . . .
> Play as free expression of the self, as pursuit of the ideal, has direct bearing on the ultimate questions of reality and worth. The spirit of play has value as a philosophy of life.[35]

He maintained that both individuals and nations were most truly revealed in their use of free time and, similarly, that leisure activities had a great formative power, either positive or negative, over the "character and nature" of man.[36] Gulick coupled these views with his notions of progressive education and decided that school playgrounds and recreation were vital to a democratic order and the socialization of individuals.[37]

Gulick himself was a capable, unusual individual able to develop ideas into institutions. He was pragmatic, perhaps even a bit eccentric, and willing to attempt almost anything once. Known for his impulsive actions, he tried out all sorts of theories on his chil-

dren and once persuaded his whole family to become vegetarians.
One day he even jumped out of his moving automobile in hopes
of forcing his wife to learn to drive.[38] An adverse effect of his
quick, impatient manner was that it sometimes antagonized others. In addition, Gulick was not afraid to criticize men who fell
behind his rapid pace or held to what he felt were weak concepts.
Nevertheless Gulick was a highly effective organizer who could
draw out the best efforts and ideas of his fellows. With an ability
to recognize and promote budding ideas, he was much more the
innovator than the long-term manager and builder of institutions.[39] He had vitalized physical education in the YMCA, established the Public School Athletic League, and would soon be a
founder of still more organizations. In the meantime, however, he
was becoming increasingly aware of the expanding playground
movement.

By 1905, twenty years after the first public sand garden had been
established in Boston, thirty-five American cities had founded supervised playgrounds, although not all of these were municipally
operated. Among the leading cities with municipal provision for
active recreation and playgrounds were, of course, Boston and
New York. Los Angeles had already appointed the first trend-
setting board of recreation commsisioners as a municipal arm
separate from both parks and schools. In 1905 Chicago opened ten
small recreation parks in crowded areas at a cost of $5,000,000.
President Theodore Roosevelt hailed this move as "the most notable civic achievement of any American city."[40] Nor was this
simply political rhetoric, for these parks, with indoor and outdoor
facilities for varied year-round recreation by people of all ages,
represented an important conceptual advance beyond mere playgrounds for children.

The more or less random development of municipal playgrounds
in an era when many other urban social interests were forming
national organizations did not go unnoticed. Some recreation innovators recognized a need for a permanent, professional organization and staff, on a solid institutional basis, in order to obtain
effective implementation of municipal recreation. The New York
public school system supplied a model for such an organization.
A group of New York school officials led by Curtis, Gulick, and
Stewart held a series of meetings in 1905 to discuss the local playground situation. After some deliberation, Gulick, fresh from his
recent triumphs with the Public School Athletic League, suggested
a national playground association.[41]

Gulick's proposal raised the issue of whether such an independent organization was necessary at all. On the positive side was the fact that by 1905 a large number of leaders interested in education, sports, parks, physical education, settlements, and social reform had an active interest in the play movement. On the other hand it was entirely possible that the burden of establishing a new national organization might be avoided by making use of an association or agency already in existence. It was not unreasonable to assume that the National Education Association could set up a department of recreation education and playground promotion. Another possibility was to build upon the section of the American Civic Association (ACA) headed by Joseph Lee, the only extant body directly involved in any formal propaganda for play on a national basis.

The impulsive Gulick wasted no time, however, in considering such alternatives; after a brief discussion with Curtis, he wrote a letter, which they both signed, asking Lee to be president of an entirely new organization. Lee replied that there were already too many organizations and suggested that the proposed group become a committee of the ACA. Gulick and Curtis, nevertheless, decided to go ahead with a separate association. Curtis compiled a list of prospective founders and asked them to attend a meeting in Washington, D.C., in the spring of 1906. Then, as Curtis' arrangements began to crystallize, the ACA renewed its interest in the scheme. Clinton R. Woodruff, secretary of the ACA, urged Lee to reiterate the desirability of having the new group join the ACA. A conference of leaders of the ACA, which Lee did not attend, proposed that the ACA expand its work in recreation. Meanwhile Lee, who was doing little real work with the ACA, offered to resign his post and suggested that Gulick head the recreation section of the ACA. Gulick apparently refused, however, and Woodruff acquiesced to the plan for a separate organization.[42]

Meanwhile Curtis was completing his plans for the formation of the new group, which would be named the Playground Association of America[43] He had also moved to Washington as supervisor for the local playground group, whose leaders included social worker Charles F. Weller. Curtis expected the local and national groups to lend each other mutual support. With Weller's help he raised money to finance the founding conference of the PAA in April 1906. He then wrote a constitution for the proposed PAA and incorporated ideas copied from Germany for an annual congress and a magazine.[44] Weller secured President Roosevelt's promise to host a reception for the founders when they gathered in Washington to set up the Playground Association of America.[45]

Curtis, Gulick, Stewart, Weller, and fourteen other playground advocates, mainly from New York and Washington, created the Playground Association of America to provide national coordination, guidance, and promotion of the spreading local movements for public recreation then found in about forty cities. By occupation, the group included laymen, educators, social workers, physical education specialists, and settlement workers; eight of the eighteen present were women. Joseph Lee, hard at work in Boston, was notably absent and apparently indifferent.[46]

At the opening session on April 12, 1906, the founders met at the YMCA and passed Gulick's motion to establish the PAA. Curtis read his proposed constitution, which the assemblage tentatively accepted.[47] The purpose of the Association, according to the constitution, was to:

> . . . collect and distribute knowledge of and promote interest in playgrounds throughout the country. It shall also seek to further the establishment of playgrounds and athletic fields in all communities, and directed play in connection with the schools. It shall aim . . . to establish . . . a national Playground Museum and Library, which shall have models of every form of playground construction and apparatus, a library of all published books and articles relating to play, pictures of games and playgrounds throughout the world, and an information department which shall furnish cities and towns with lecturers, pictures, articles, or advice on any phase of the work.[48]

After an afternoon reception at the White House, social worker Mary McDowell of Chicago presented the nominating committee's slate of officers. The group accepted the slate, which included: Luther Gulick, president; settlement head Jane Addams and Joseph Lee (both absent), vice-presidents; Henry Curtis, secretary; and Seth Stewart, chairman of the executive committee. On subsequent days the founders selected an "executive committee," in reality a board of directors, of twenty-seven members from ten cities; dealt with a multitude of other administrative details; and heard a series of speeches on play and related topics. The final session adjourned on April 14, 1906, with plans to meet again in Chicago a year later. Leaders of the group then staged three public meetings to promote playgrounds for Washington.[49]

This early support of recreation in Washington, which leaders of the PAA hoped would be a model for other cities, foreshadowed several later policies of the Association. In its *Prospectus* the group favored three major objectives: systems of recreation centers after the Chicago model rather than haphazardly scattered playgrounds, support by tax funds, and trained professional leadership.[50] The PAA intended to demonstrate the validity of these concepts in the national capital. Gulick, Curtis, and Stewart drew a plan for the city to provide playgrounds, athletic fields, and recreation centers. Every school district was to have a playground with at least 1 acre of land for each 2,000 children. A year later Congress appropriated $75,000 to begin such a recreation system.[51] The plan attracted enough interest for the PAA leaders to have Curtis make a detailed inventory and map of all potential playground sites in the city. Curtis, recognizing the possible value of such inventories to city planning, tried unsuccessfully to persuade several agencies of the federal government to finance similar surveys in a number of major cities.[52] Meanwhile both the local group and the PAA had frequent occasions, in the process of lobbying for appropriations bills for Washington playgrounds, to learn of the opportunities and frustrations involved in securing Congressional action.[53] Neither Curtis' work in Washington nor federal action was, however, the primary concern of the young PAA.

The fledgling PAA, confronted with the increasingly rapid spread of public playgrounds in America after 1906, had only meager resources to accomplish its self-appointed goals of guiding national development while at the same time building an effective organization. By the end of its first year the PAA counted 408 members who had contributed $2,006; total receipts for the year were only $2,164. As the PAA had neither adequate funds nor staff, secretary Curtis personally wrote 3,690 letters in response to inquiries.[54] He also, with some assistance from the other officers, continued soliciting contributions. Gulick served on a volunteer basis and traveled, made contacts, and tried to stimulate municipal interest in play. Stewart took charge of establishing a monthly periodical, *The Playground*, later renamed *Recreation*, and published the first issue, consisting of a scant sixteen pages, in April 1907.[55] Other members helped too; the PAA early established committees to study publicity, financing, and various recreation activities.[56] Yet the lack of financial support and the absence of a paid, full-time staff seriously hindered the new organization. Nevertheless, Curtis laid ambitious plans for the convention in the coming year.

The play congress of 1907 which was finally held at Chicago in June was to be the first of a long series of annual conventions. Besides attending to numerous matters of business and making an on-site inspection of the pace-setting recreation centers of Chicago, the congress listened to papers by several leaders in the play movement. These addresses revealed both the highly practical bent and widening scope of the movement. About 200 delegates from 30 cities heard speeches on the relation of play to democracy, health, citizenship, and social morality. Several speakers felt, as did Curtis, Gulick, and Lee at the time, that municipal boards of education offered the most promising agency to administer recreation. Indeed, the United States Commissioner of Education, Elmer E. Brown, was a featured speaker.[57] Of more significance to the immediate future of the PAA than the speakers was the presence of New York reformer Lawrence Veiller, representing the Russell Sage Foundation.

Veiller's subsequent report to the foundation, newly established and with assets of $10,000,000 second largest in the country, helped to persuade the trustees to back the playground movement.[58] The foundation appropriated $20,000 for playground promotion and hired Gulick as chairman of its new Playground Extension Committee. With his salary thus paid, Gulick could devote almost all of his time to the PAA while still continuing in his capacity with the foundation, a dual role he performed for nearly three years. For secretary of the committee, Gulick chose Lee F. Hanmer, an inspector of athletics in the New York public schools. The foundation assigned Hanmer to work full time as the field secretary of the PAA, visiting cities across the nation to foster public recreation. The foundation also made a special $5,000 grant for the play congress the next year and gave additional funds for the PAA to hire a financial secretary to build membership.[59] The rate of contributions to the PAA soon increased sixfold. The PAA received $12,670 during the first year of aid from the foundation besides the services of Gulick and Hanmer. There were, however, some strings attached. A foundation committee, consisting of Gulick and two Sage representatives, directed the expenditures of all funds given for playground extension. And this committee was responsible to the foundation, not to the PAA. The PAA had power only over the lesser amounts contributed directly to the Association from other sources. This lack of absolute autonomy did not deter the Association from effective work since, during the first year of Sage aid, the number of American cities initiating and continuing playgrounds actually doubled.[60] If this was any indication

Three men active in the public schools of New York were key leaders of the young Playground Association of America. Luther H. Gulick, head of physical education, conceived the idea of the PAA and served as first president from 1906 to 1910. Henry S. Curtis, author and director of playgrounds, collaborated in founding the PAA and was its secretary from 1906 to 1909. Lee F. Hanmer, inspector of athletics, became the first traveling field secretary of the Association from 1907 to 1909.

of increased effectiveness by the PAA, then the start of the Sage support was an event as important as the founding of the PAA itself.

With a monetary base and the beginning of a paid, full-time staff provided by the foundation, the PAA promptly expanded its activities. In November 1907 the organization opened a headquarters in New York. The same year Gulick and Curtis, perhaps recalling the fair at St. Louis, arranged for an exhibit and model playground by the PAA at the Jamestown Exposition in Virginia. Such publicity apparently paid off, for the PAA received many requests for advice after the affairs at Jamestown and Chicago. Field secretary Hanmer wrote to all of the registrants at the Jamestown exhibit and began collecting data on playgrounds in cities of over 5,000 population. Hanmer and Gulick, in their first year as paid staff members, made 77 trips to various cities to aid local playground groups. As field secretary, Hanmer went only* where asked but frequently expended considerable energy to obtain an invitation.[61]

Meanwhile the PAA continued collecting and distributing all sorts of information about playgrounds. Curtis, looking toward more breadth, municipal responsibility, and professionalism in the movement, began such projects as the formation of national committees, one of which formulated a course in play for use in normal schools and colleges. This endeavor, headed by physical educator Clark W. Hetherington of the University of Missouri, aimed to provide a start toward systematic training of leaders to various levels of competence for service in the expanding field of public recreation. After two years the committee produced its lengthy report outlining three graded courses. About the time the report was finished the Joseph Fels Endowment gave Hetherington, who had done most of the work, a grant for a year to publicize recreation and physical education. He traveled to some 30 states stressing play, athletics, and the new course, practically the first such training available. A few months after its initial appearance, the course was in use in 60 cities.[62]

Although the publicity of the PAA spread to many cities, New York was of special concern to leaders of the Association. Thus Stewart took charge of trying to unite the several factions of the parks, schools, and private societies in that city to strengthen support for public recreation. The first major device used was a dinner to honor Mrs. Humphry Ward, English authoress and noted friend of children's play. The lavish banquet attracted extensive newspaper coverage and about 475 guests, many of them wealthy New Yorkers.[63]

New York was also the site of the annual PAA congress for 1908. In preparation, Curtis sent letters signed by Theodore Roosevelt, honorary president of the PAA, inviting the mayors of major American cities to send delegates. Besides the usual addresses and discussion groups there were exhibits of scale model playgrounds by the Association and demonstrations of folk dances by school children. The congress drew 408 delegates from 31 states as well as 397 registered visitors.[64] Much of the success of the convention, as with other activities of the PAA by 1908, could be attributed to the imagination and resourcefulness of Curtis and Gulick.

During the period 1906–1910, especially after the Russell Sage Foundation's financial support, Gulick succeeded in implementing most of his initial plans and policies for the PAA. Stressing quality over quantity, he wanted to upgrade existing playgrounds and foster organized local support only in a few pilot cities until the coordinated national movement was well underway. PAA aid was to supplement this local initiative, carefully tailored to the needs of individual cities rather than standardized. In addition to field work, Gulick introduced a variety of other activities. The PAA, or the Sage committee via the PAA, held several short training institutes, published manuals, and fostered organized athletics and badge tests for physical skills on the model of Gulick's Public School Athletic League.[65] Gulick also knew the value of publicity in the mass media and endorsements from famous people.[66] Thus he was of prime influence in the early development of the organization.

By 1908 the PAA, under Gulick's leadership and the generous support of the Russell Sage Foundation, had achieved a certain degree of stability. The corps of leaders included officers and a board of directors as well as a council of some 130 persons. In addition, there were twenty-nine local affiliated playground associations. The Association also had about a dozen national study and advisory committees consisting of experts from various cities. These committees dealt with topics ranging from folk dancing to play in institutions.[67] Despite all this impressive activity, finances remained a weak point, partly because the board of directors was dominated by professional social workers and educators, few of whom could be expected to make substantial financial gifts to the Association. In addition, the PAA still depended considerably on Russell Sage Foundation support which was admittedly temporary.

In spite of financial weaknesses, the board late in 1908 took steps to find a full-time professional executive secretary for the PAA. They authorized Gulick to seek out as first choice Howard S.

Braucher, highly successful secretary of the Associated Charities of Portland, Maine. In April 1909 Braucher, who was to serve the Association for forty years, agreed to begin work the next September.[68]

Howard Braucher (1881–1949) was born in New York State and had considered several related careers before joining the PAA. A graduate of Cornell University, his first choice of a calling had been the ministry. After a year at Union Theological Seminary, however, he gave up the ministry for social work and soon joined the Associated Charities. As a student he had served at church settlement houses. He not only had worked with a boys' club, at a school recreation center, and as an organizer of play for crippled children but also had attended the first congress of the PAA and become a member that same year.[69] Thus Braucher brought to the PAA an interest in both social work and the social gospel.

Religion was a leading motive of Braucher's entire life. Far from being a denominational zealot, he emphasized social Christianity and service to mankind.[70] He spoke of recreation as "life more abundant" (John 10: 10):

> Some day in the not too distant future—if we are ready to will it—we shall think and talk more of beauty, sport, adventure, art, literature, of life, and of God.
> And work and machines like the breathing of air and the drinking of water will be taken for granted in their proper place.[71]

The work of the PAA was for him a "spiritual movement," and when recruiting prospective staff members he was always careful to consider their basic motives in life. He saw recreation and religion as two of the major areas of living and sought to maintain a close relationship between them.[72]

In addition to his religious motivations, Braucher maintained his faith in the worth and dignity of the individual. Freedom to fulfill one's own leisure desires was the very essence of recreation. Leaders could expose people to more creative forms of recreational activities but, he believed, never had the right to mold or force individuals' tastes with undemocratic means. At the same time freedom required a certain degree of cooperation and planning, but bureaucratic regimentation was taboo.[73] Braucher's democracy of individuals, like that of Lee, Gulick, and others of the progressive era, had room for experts to guide the masses. Along with this respect for professional leadership, Braucher, again like Lee and Gulick, preferred high standards to hasty results.[74]

Unlike Lee and Gulick, Braucher spent little time studying the biological aspects of play and recreation but dealt mostly with psychological and sociological implications. Recreation was an answer to materialism and the work ethic, two factors detrimental to the quality of American life.[75] Americans in general, he believed, would need to make wise use of the new leisure arising from technological developments and shortening hours of labor.[76] Braucher recognized that recreation was not only a wide list of activities for all people but also an attitude, a way of looking at life. This creative, satisfying spirit of play was for Braucher a vital part of the whole man.[77]

Since leisure was so important in society, Braucher felt that government, especially on the local level, had a responsibility to provide supervised recreation. There ought to be no imposed national scheme which might violate the freedom of the individual community to develop a recreation system best for local conditions.[78] Thus, even as he was building the PAA into a stable, national institution, he resisted uniformity in local recreation and sincerely maintained that the Association, which he apparently equated with the broader movement, was a "nonmechanical, noninstitutional, nonself-seeking service."[79]

Meanwhile, Joseph Lee, who was to share most of Braucher's forty-year tenure with the PAA, was moving increasingly into its most active circles. At the first congress, he had become head of a committee to write a model state enabling law for municipal recreation. Back in Boston, aided by his Massachusetts Civic League, he had secured passage the following year of such a law, which required a referendum in each town over 10,000 population on whether or not to establish municipal playgrounds. Then Lee joined with the PAA in a campaign for a positive vote. This effort resulted in twenty-three of twenty-five cities opting for playgrounds.[80] Grateful for the aid supplied by the PAA, Lee played an even larger role in the group the next year.

The PAA was indeed fortunate that able new leaders such as Lee and Braucher were moving into the heart of the organization in 1909 just at a time when serious internal problems had begun to destroy the then-current leadership of Gulick and Curtis. Curtis himself reportedly was one of the problems. There was no doubt that Curtis gave significant service to the young PAA and had a mind fertile with ideas. Several of his co-workers, however, were antagonized by his excessive concern for receiving credit for virtually all of the policies and projects developed collectively by the Association. Early leaders such as Gulick and Stewart felt Curtis' actions seriously injured the play movement.

The difficulty came to a head when Gulick and his supporters became so irritated with Curtis that they lined up solidly against him on key issues which he vigorously espoused. First they resisted his determination to reject advertising in *Recreation* by manufacturers of playground equipment; then they successfully opposed his plan to set up a southern regional office of the PAA in Washington; and finally they refused to publish a book he had prepared for the PAA. Ultimately, just after Gulick hired Braucher, Curtis was passed over for a full-time salaried post. He thereupon quit as secretary and accepted a far less important position as second vice-president.[81]

More serious than Curtis' departure was the relation between the PAA, Gulick, and the Russell Sage Foundation. There was a definite resentment by some members of the PAA over the fact that Gulick was president of the Association but drew his salary from and made his headquarters at the foundation. At the congress in 1909 the matter dominated a long night meeting of the PAA council. Several members questioned the control of the field work by the foundation rather than the PAA and suggested a complete separation of the two organizations. This touched off a lengthy debate in which it became evident that the leaders of the foundation independently had under consideration a partial withdrawal of support from the PAA. Finally, despite hours of discussion, the issue appeared still undecided.[82]

Within a year the termination of foundation support and a change of leadership resolved the matter. In June, Gulick told the directors that the time had come for the PAA to "stand on its own feet." Faced with the loss of crucial foundation support, the board temporarily discontinued the costly office of field secretary. Hanmer continued his work directly for the foundation which, after having spent $60,000 on playground extension and the PAA, eventually established its own department of recreation. Gulick, however, stayed with the PAA until the end of another year at which time he too returned to the foundation, and Lee became president of the Association.[83] Gulick's resignation could perhaps be explained by his unpopular, sometimes dictatorial methods of leadership; his financial connections with the foundation; and his desire for pioneering rather than administration of details.[84]

When Braucher and Lee, who were to prove expert at administration, assumed the major positions in the PAA in late 1909 and mid 1910, respectively, the young organization was faced with a host of challenges. The playground idea was spreading with uncontrolled rapidity. Of the 900 American cities with a population of more than 5,000, only 90 had playgrounds in 1907. This figure had jumped to 187 cities in 1908 and 336 cities by the end of 1909.[85] Despite the great need for guidance of this mushrooming phenomenon, there was more duplication and confusion than effective cooperation between the now-independent PAA and the foundation. Once out of the PAA, both Gulick and Hanmer suggested that the Association concentrate only on children's playgrounds while the foundation tackled the far broader field of general public recreation. Of course Braucher opposed this, but Gulick and Hanmer went ahead with limited recreational work under the foundation. Braucher was frustrated by what he felt was the indecisive policy of the foundation which neither directly supported recreation via the PAA nor expanded its own efforts to cover the field adequately.[86] Meanwhile the PAA had great difficulty trying to raise funds from other sources to support the bold expansion of program desired by Braucher. Finally the organizational structure of the PAA itself, as set by the constitution, was impractical, lacking a clear-cut division of authority among national council, board of directors, and officers.

New leaders Braucher and Lee found, however, that although they inherited some knotty problems, several key changes had already begun to take place in the PAA before 1910. For instance, Braucher himself had made it a condition of his employment that the PAA place more emphasis on varied recreation for all people. Before his departure Gulick had made several similar recommendations and, as most of the key leaders concurred, the directors decided that the topic of the next congress would be "Public Recreation;" Seth Stewart went so far as to urge substituting the phrase for "playground" in the name of the Association.[87] Committees were already at work drafting revisions in the constitution to alter the organizational structure and seeking incorporation to strengthen the Association. Thus when Lee and Braucher began their joint leadership of the PAA in June 1910, the Association, born in response to local developments, had, despite some severe internal problems, already achieved no little success in establishing itself as a national organization. The great task remaining before them was to build a PAA capable of serving the rapidly growing national interest in municipal recreation while at the same time perfecting a stable organization and an aggressive program so that public recreation throughout the United States would become a quality institution rather than a passing fad.

Howard Braucher had joined the PAA staff in 1909 as executive secretary, a position he held until 1941. He then served as president until
his death in 1949.

3
Achieving Institutional Stability, 1910–1916

In 1910 Joseph Lee, then almost fifty years old, yielded to the persuasion of Luther Gulick and Howard Braucher and accepted the presidency of the PAA, thus beginning a happy partnership with young Braucher which was to last nearly three decades.[1] The two men worked well together since they shared not only an intense devotion to the promotion of recreation but also a common set of values. These included a concern for the importance of religion as well as faith in the unlimited potential of the free and responsible individual in a cooperative and democratic society which, through education and the cultivation of experts, would bring not only social justice but also a life abundant in happiness and meaning. Between 1910 and 1916 Lee and Braucher established many of the permanent operating policies of the PAA and achieved considerable success in building a solid institutional framework for the organization. The two leaders also carried further the definition and acceptance of the three major concepts promoted by the PAA. These were governmental, primarily local, responsibility for providing wholesome public recreation; a broader definition of *recreation*, including varied opportunities for the use of leisure by all people and not merely playgrounds for urban slum children; and the development of recreation as an independent, professional field.

Lee brought to the PAA twenty years of experience with public and private social agencies, a gift for public speaking, a legal background, the prestige of his name, a sense of mission, and creative ideas. He delegated much of the administrative responsibility to Braucher and built a sound organization within a few years.[2] Fund raising was one of the difficult tasks at which Lee worked not only diligently but successfully. While serving without remuneration as president, he personally contributed over $360,000 to the Association and year after year obtained about 40 percent of the budget in the form of donations from members of the board of directors. An active chairman of the board for twenty-seven years, Lee missed only a handful of meetings until sickness restricted the final years of his life. Mindful of his earlier experience with organized recreation in Boston, Lee know the importance of close attention to administration; he therefore never was too busy to work on matters of organization, personnel, and policy formation.[3]

Lee's influence on the philosophy, policies, and activities of the PAA was surely significant. Tireless in promoting his ideas to members of both staff and board, he was ever careful to assure himself that those who were to carry out policies understood them. He continually emphasized the importance of maintaining high quality by starting a limited number of projects and developing them effectively. The general guidelines laid down by Gulick for spreading the recreation movement made sense to Lee, who recognized a need to guide, not push, the diffusing play idea to obtain a broad, popular concept of public recreation with local leadership.[4] In the early years he personally investigated a number of key issues and then made decisions in the name of the organization. For example, he decided in 1910 that the PAA would support, but not actually administer, the new Boy Scouts of America.[5]

As the years passed, however, Lee usually worked jointly on major decisions with Braucher, the actual functioning head of the Association. Although Lee lived in Boston, the two men maintained close contact.[6] Braucher's aide, Arthur Williams, who served the

Association for fifty years, subsequently observed that Lee and Braucher were ". . . colleagues working together, freely exchanging ideas, and jointly planning. . . ."[7] Braucher described his close relation with Lee:

> . . . I never had consciously to adapt myself to Mr. Lee because we had both of us the Froebelian philosophy [of play], we both naturally believed in individualism, in freedom, in democracy, in the things that count. It was natural for me to wish to give wings to Joseph Lee's ideas and try to give them practical expression. Neither Mr. Lee nor I ever tried to distinguish where one left off and when the other began. We just naturally worked together.[8]

While Braucher, with his managerial and executive ability, did "give wings" to Lee's ideas, Lee found Braucher a source of ideas too. The partners cooperated closely even on trivial matters such as the color of the letterhead Braucher used for general correspondence.[9]

Before this strong and persuasive combination of personalities and ideas, the board, if not always agreeing, seems usually to have acquiesced in matters of policy.[10] The directors as early as June 1909 authorized Lee, then only one of several vice-presidents, and Braucher to select chairmen for the national committees of the PAA. Eighteen months later, the board voted that Lee, Braucher, and treasurer Gustavus T. Kirby of New York be "authorized to make such arrangements as are necessary to conducting the work of the Association providing the funds of the Association warrant such arrangements."[11] These three men soon became the nucleus of the small but active executive committee. Eventually the board decided that "on matters of lesser importance," two members of the executive committee could authorize official action by written recommendation at the request of secretary Braucher.[12] Thus Braucher and Lee, continually in touch with operations of the PAA, dominated formation of policy.

In the office of the PAA in New York the everyday attitudes, habits, and personality of Braucher played an increasingly decisive role in ongoing operations. For years he took considerably less salary than was offered him and dutifully carried a full briefcase home at night.[13] He had a deep compassion for others and was unfailingly kind and generous to his staff; in return, he expected them to follow his example of dedication to the cause of recreation as personified by the PAA. Imbued with a missionary-like zeal, Braucher could be so immersed in his work as to be somewhat aloof. He also tended to be shy if not actually secretive, rarely making speeches of any sort. His office door was always closed so he could concentrate on his work.[14] Braucher was not self-seeking but had a high regard for his own talents and seemed to consider himself as the unsung, top professional executive.[15] Few decisions and probably no policies resulted from staff meetings. He reportedly did not take advice easily and was, as even his loyal associates admit, "paternalistic" and "something of a dictator."[16]

Braucher's intense individualism and dominant leadership were not restricted to the office of the PAA. Just as Braucher himself served as the resident expert within the PAA, so he tended to regard the Association as the sole guide for the expanding recreation movement. At times he even seemed to equate the institution with the movement. This role became increasingly difficult to continue as other confident new leaders in recreation matured independently of the Association.[17] Nevertheless the PAA, with its vital contributions to the course of public recreation in America, remained nearly unchallenged as the principal representative of recreation for two decades after Braucher and Lee took the helm of the young, growing organization.

Lee and Braucher were a more successful leadership team for the PAA than Gulick and Curtis had been. To begin with, Braucher and Lee as personalities were much more compatible. They also had more hours to devote to the PAA, which was certainly the major time-consuming interest in life for Braucher and perhaps also for Lee. Wealthy Lee, with his contacts in the best social circles of Boston, had access to potential financial support which educators Gulick and Curtis were far less able to tap. Gulick founded several voluntary associations and frequently changed jobs; Lee and Braucher appeared more suited to the management of an ongoing, stable institution. Finally, in the developing occupational field of recreation, which experienced an initial shortage of high-level administrators, Lee and Braucher supplied the PAA with loyal, effective, and continuous leadership for decades.[18]

When Lee and Braucher took command, they needed immediately to revitalize the PAA so it could effectively serve and guide the rapidly spreading interest in municipal play and recreation. In 1909, and each year thereafter, more cities reported supervised playgrounds initiated than in the whole period from 1899 to 1906. By mid-1910 as many as fifty letters daily poured into New York asking for aid from the PAA. Lee and Braucher recognized the critical state of this unexpectedly rapid upswing of interest in municipal recreation. The PAA desperately needed field representatives, but to place additional men in the field would also require a stronger supporting institution.[19]

One event symbolic of the growing and broadening role of the PAA was a change in name from *Playground* to *Playground and Recreation* Association of America (PRAA). *Playground*, which seemed to connote no more than children's play, was simply too narrow a term to suit the increasingly dynamic conception of recreation held by the leaders of the PAA. Accordingly the directors adopted *PRAA* on May 10, 1911. A year later some members of the board even suggested *Recreation Association of America*.[20]

In addition to the new name, the PRAA obtained a revised constitution as part of the administrative reorganization undertaken by Lee and Braucher. The original constitution rather awkwardly had divided authority among various officials. Since in practice the system proved cumbersome, in 1910 a committee chaired by tenement house reformer Lawrence Veiller of New York, and including Lee, Braucher, and treasurer Kirby, prepared a new document in hopes of making the PRAA both as democratic and efficient as possible. The new constitution, adopted in June 1910, created a national board of directors with staggered three-year terms. Any member of the PRAA, not just the officially constituted nominating committee, might nominate officers at the annual meeting. In this and many other respects the new document was greatly simplified.[21]

Another scheme, which matured under Lee and Braucher but had originated earlier, was the attempted incorporation of the Association. After uncertainty about the merits of state versus federal incorporation, the directors in 1911 finally opted for federal action.[22] Apparently the matter rested for several years, although Braucher drafted some sample bills. Then Lee secured the introduction in Congress of two such bills. Both, like most bills, died in committee, partly because the House Committee on the Judiciary was determined to stop a flood of similar requests resulting from the incorporation of the Boy Scouts of America by act of Congress. Braucher's attempts to push the bills appeared amateurish; there was not even a companion bill for the Senate.[23] Nonetheless Lee and Braucher, sensing both the legal and promotional value of incorporation by Congress, were not about to abandon the endeavor entirely.

Meanwhile in the years between 1910 and 1916 Braucher and Lee were perfecting the basic institutional infrastructure, policies, and procedures of the PRAA. These forms and methods would last,

with but slight modification, as long as the Association itself endured. During these prewar years the PRAA became an established
institution. It worked with some success to foster national trends
toward widening the concept of recreation and leisure; it promoted
greater governmental, especially municipal, responsibility for furnishing recreation opportunities; and it developed professionalism
among leaders in the field.[24]

To promote these three basic objectives, Lee and Braucher built
a national board of directors and a professional staff. At least
through 1911 up to half of the directors were drawn from occupations such as social work and education; but within a decade the
typical director was a well-to-do businessman with side interests
in recreation, social work, and civic affairs. The directors met
quarterly with an average attendance of perhaps eight at any one
meeting; only rarely were more than fifteen members present.[25]
Carrying on the daily functions of the PRAA were a rising number
of office and field workers. Some of the principal lay and professional leaders of the PRAA, among them not only directors but
also staff and field secretaries, served for decades; such loyalty
obviously helped preserve continuity within the organization.[26]

Meanwhile the Association had to secure increasing contributions if it were to keep pace with requests for assistance and the
spreading interest in public recreation. Lee and Braucher groped
for methods to insure adequate financing, a problem which inhib-
ited the fullest expansion of the services of the group for decades.[27]
Since the PRAA lacked strong local units, it was precluded from
employing two highly successful new techniques of fund raising:
short, intensive drives and joint campaigns such as those conducted by local community chests or united funds. The Association
instead adopted a local sponsor system of fund raising, which was
to serve well for several decades although it was essentially an
updating of the old individual solicitation method of the past
century. Sponsors, usually board members or other prominent
local citizens, lent their names to the PRAA which, by a technique
innovative in its day, produced what appeared to be personal
letters of appeal written on sponsors' private stationery. By March
1914 contributions were coming in at about eight times the rate
of 1909–10, the last year before Lee's presidency.[28] The PRAA was,
however, finding new demands and opportunities for its services
at an even faster rate, reflected in the increased staff of eight field
secretaries. Braucher, hired on the understanding that he would
not need to solicit funds in person, found himself extremely over-
worked after a few years when, besides his routine managerial
tasks, he had to raise as much as $3,000 each month.[29]

The PAA fostered both supervised municipal playgrounds and a stronger financial base for its work by seeking businessmen as board members. Three such directors joined Howard Braucher for a walk at Atlantic City: (left to right) Gustavus T. Kirby, Otto T. Mallery, Braucher, and Walter May. Age did not prevent active fun, as Kirby showed when he played leapfrog over Joseph Lee.

In 1914 and 1915 the financial problems of the PRAA were com-
pounded by a slackening of the growth rate in contributions. A
major factor appears to have been the depression of 1913–15. The
outbreak of war in Europe at first fueled the depression and probably intensified the loss of income to the PRAA. By May 1914
Association efforts at fund raising had lost fully half of their effectiveness.[30] A more fundamental and enduring hindrance to financing was, as Braucher recognized, the dominance of the work ethic
in American culture. Many people still felt recreation centers were
luxuries, not necessities. Another problem was that to numerous
individuals the crucial organizing work of field secretaries seemed
to be merely talking rather than sound technical advice.[31] The
weakened PRAA held neither institutes nor congresses in 1914 and
1915 and cut back on staff in the latter year.

Braucher and Lee looked desperately for ways to renew the
upward climb of financial support. In early 1914 they were even
ready to discontinue the PRAA if the federal government would
take over the work. This action should perhaps not have been
surprising since the directors four years earlier, with Braucher
and Lee present, had gone on record supporting a proposed $75,000
federal appropriation to provide field agents for the Office of Education. In addition the new Children's Bureau, with interests overlapping those of the PRAA, was in operation. Lee and Braucher
conferred with California Congressman William Kent, a vice-president of the PRAA. Kent said there was no chance of securing federal funds for the work of the PRAA and warned that agitation
of the issue would further hamper fund raising. Braucher and Lee
dropped the idea, and never again did the directors consider such
action.[32]

By 1916 the depression was largely over, and the financial problems of the PRAA eased. The Association was expanding again and
had achieved stability as an organization. Although contributions
had been only about $12,000 in 1910, receipts had risen rapidly for
several years; and, even after the rate of increase slowed, the PRAA
counted about 5,000 members and an annual income of $115,000
after the tenth year of operation. In 1910 the PRAA, after Hanmer's resignation, had been temporarily without any field secretaries; their number reached eight before the United States entered
World War I. Late in 1916 the total PRAA staff numbered some 40
men and women.[33]

Along with the building up of this staff came increased contacts
with other voluntary and professional groups interested in recreation and a corresponding determination by Lee and Braucher to

maintain the integrity of the PRAA as an organization. They were eager for the Association to serve and cooperate actively with other groups. For example, Braucher and Lee helped found the Boy Scouts of America and were even ready to annex the infant scout organization. Nevertheless when Gulick, having left the PRAA, suggested a "recreation corporation" to merge several interests in recreation, including the PRAA, into a federation, Lee vetoed the scheme.[34] Certain elements within the professional American Physical Education Association also at one point desired to merge with the PRAA, but the Association retained its independence.[35]

Successful in preserving the independence of the Association, Lee and Braucher by 1916 had perfected the chief operating procedures of the PRAA. There were basically seven areas of operation: a central office, national committees, the periodical *Recreation*, other more specialized publications, regional training institutes, annual recreation congresses, and field work. Since the main changes which took place over the years in these activities of the Association were for the most part quantitative rather than qualitative, they may be discussed without reference to chronology.

The central office, in addition to its obvious functions as an administrative and coordinating center, also had a more direct connection with the clientele served by the society. The office staff worked as an information clearinghouse which collected and classified data about recreation. Employees used this information in correspondence and consultation with thousands of people yearly. In sending replies to inquiries the PRAA followed the trend toward professionalism which characterized the Progressive Era and referred to the leading authorities on the matters in question.[36] Staff members in New York were also responsible for publishing the literature of the society and maintaining a nationwide employment service for professionals in the recreation field. Much of the information flowing from the central office was, however, dependent on the work and reports of the national study committees of the Association.

These committees also reflected an interest in expertise and professional knowledge. They dealt with matters such as rural recreation, games, physical fitness, badges, Boy Scout activities upon the playgrounds, folk dancing, playground equipment, and amateur athletics.[37] Top leadership of the Association and prominent experts in recreation from across the country staffed the committees, which helped to broaden the scope of the recreation movement by their practical reports on many subjects. For example, the Committee on Badges developed a brief, standardized series of tests which boys and girls could take to meet certain levels of physical fitness and win a badge. The tests, resembling those promoted by the government-sponsored "President's All-America Team" fifty years later, involved muscular coordination in running, throwing, and jumping. Over one hundred towns participated in the badge tests in 1916.[38] Other committees studied diverse topics including commercial recreation and play in institutions such as orphanages. Most of the committees seemed to find a convenient vehicle for publicizing their reports in *Recreation*, the monthly periodical of the PRAA.

Braucher served as editor of *Recreation*, the deficit-laden major informational service of the PRAA. The monthly journal, which reached leading advocates of public recreation across America, consisted chiefly of items such as addresses from the annual congresses, stories of hometown activities by local recreation leaders, technical reports, and semi-scholarly articles.[39] Braucher recognized the enormous value of photography, so the magazine frequently carried illustrations on such varied subjects as swimming pools and blind boys using special equipment to run the 100-yard dash. Advertisements were only a minor source of revenue. The journal normally contained the yearbooks of the PRAA, compiled from questionnaires mailed to cities across the nation to determine the statistical growth and trends of the national recreation movement.[40] *Recreation*, the most important of the several publications sponsored by the PRAA, helped broaden the concept of recreation and leisure by its variety of subject matter and at the same time provided a useful medium for the exchange of professional information. Nonetheless the editors seldom emphasized potentially great problems facing recreation and rarely subjected their aims to critical analysis.

In addition to *Recreation*, the PRAA, or its members and leaders on their own, issued a considerable range of other printed material. Besides leaflets aimed specifically at potential contributors, the Association turned out a flow of original pamphlets, bulletins, committee reports, and reprints from the PRAA *Proceedings*, *Recreation*, and related periodicals. The first book of the PRAA had been *The Normal Course in Play* (1909), a manual for instructors. Lee, ex-officers Gulick and Curtis, and field secretary Lebert H. Weir, former Cincinnati social worker and juvenile probation officer, wrote a number of additional volumes which the Association had published. Several leaders of the PRAA wrote articles on recreation for magazines other than *Recreation*.[41]

Some of this printed material proved useful in connection with the interest of the PRAA in professional training and regional recreation institutes. Besides promoting its own *Normal Course* in schools and colleges, the PRAA tried to secure the introduction of additional instruction in recreation at Columbia University. Lee personally also provided funds for educator George E. Johnson to initiate courses in recreation over a period of sixteen years at Harvard University.[42] More widespread in impact than this early search for a professional college-level curriculum were the regional institutes of the PRAA. These training sessions each lasted several days and provided an opportunity for local recreation leaders to meet in groups with experts to discuss technical matters, such as the equipment and administration of playgrounds. The early programs included papers, discussion groups, demonstrations of play activities, tours of public recreation facilities of the host cities, and reports of practical ideas used in different towns. Some of the institutes attracted many delegates and thereby provided excellent opportunities for spreading the objectives defined by Braucher and Lee for broadening the concept of recreation, urging the acceptance of municipal responsibility for provision of basic recreation facilities, and fostering professional development.[43]

The annual national conventions, or recreation congresses, held by the Association were less technical than the institutes and on a larger scale. The PRAA combined its yearly meeting with these congresses. The conventions were similar to the earlier sessions before Lee became president; the meetings held October 2–6, 1916, at Grand Rapids, Michigan, were typical. A total of 717 delegates, 211 of them from Grand Rapids, attended the congress; the delegates included mayors, park commissioners, school superintendents, teachers, members of chambers of commerce, social workers, and playground leaders. The schedule contained both general sessions and also seminars on practical aspects of topics such as swimming pools, rural recreation, budgets, adult recreation, and summer camps. For their own recreation, the delegates sang songs, played games, danced, and enjoyed a banquet. As publicity, the Association sent information about the congress to a list of 22,000 people, and had 14 important figures, 10 of them state governors, send out letters.[44] Typically, the PRAA used the convention, which drew delegates from 178 cities, to spread both propaganda and technical knowledge.

Perhaps the most successful method used by the Association to disseminate the concept of public recreation was the work of the traveling field secretaries of the society. Field services, resumed soon after Lee took office, were modeled on the earlier work of Lee Hanmer. In addition to Hanmer, Lebert Weir and Rowland Haynes, erstwhile seminarian and psychology teacher at the University of Minnesota, were among the notable early field secretaries.[45] Their goal was to persuade key city leaders to establish a comprehensive recreation system headed by a professional administrator at municipal expense. The secretaries' tactics involved convincing town leaders to accept a public responsibility for play, securing a definite plan, connecting the responsibility and the program to a local personality, and obtaining city funds. The field secretaries stressed the need for capable, persevering local play advocates as well as municipal dollars to support the recreation system and superintendent.[46]

Reflecting the emphases of both Lee and Braucher on quality and individualism as well as the Progressive cult of efficiency, field secretaries were the professionals who combined salesmanship with expertise to prod local leaders toward effective municipal recreation. Braucher required the field men to submit daily reports of their work. With a limited number of agents, the PRAA did not encourage the casual and unplanned spread of municipal recreation. In fact, the Association soon learned that repeat visits were often necessary to maintain or improve the quality of established recreation systems.[47] Adapting their tactics to individual situations, field secretaries had neither standard solutions nor set time limits for visits to cities; they stayed until all feasible possibilities for current progress were exhausted. Even in the financially difficult year ending in May 1915 field secretaries were instrumental in establishing year-round recreation systems in almost thirty American cities, ranging from Portland, Oregon, to Raleigh, North Carolina, and Providence, Rhode Island. The next year 174 cities benefited from field work.[48]

One of the major tools developed by the early field secretaries was the recreation survey to learn what people did for recreation and discover the available public, private, and commercial facilities. The last step was to submit an individualized plan for obtaining municipally supported recreation. The aim of a survey, said Rowland Haynes, was to secure efficiency in recreation.[49] An effective survey was the result of detailed socioeconomic data. Haynes produced an innovative and able survey of Milwaukee, which *Recreation* publshed in detail to facilitate its imitation in other cities. The PRAA and its field secretaries effectively pushed the survey idea, and in the half decade ending in 1916 sixty-two communities made such surveys.[50] These surveys probably were the most significant weapons used by field secretaries to jolt cities into recognition of their inadequate facilities for recreation and into action leading to acceptance of municipal responsibility for provision of a broad program of public recreation.

To understand further the several means used by the PRAA to foster the spread of municipal recreation, it may be useful to have some idea what emphasis the Association placed on each activity. The distribution of money spent by the PRAA was one indicator of the importance which Lee and Braucher attached to their various projects. In a year during which the PRAA spent in all $82,506, a sum of $1,655 went for general printed matter, $1,726 for national committees, $4,134 for *Recreation*, $10,543 for central office correspondence and consultation, and $60,979 for field work. In two other periods the organization devoted $48,230 of $73,765 and $37,186 of $58,557 to field service.[51] Even without travel allowances, the remaining costs of the field secretaries still far outdistanced any other category of expense. Braucher and Lee valued field work above all other actions, perhaps because of its continued direct contact with local recreation movements. All of these techniques, however, interlocked in promotion of the major concepts of the Association, which were all-encompassing and endured for many years to come.[52]

The actions undertaken by the PRAA to broaden the definition, scope, and concept of recreation included the introduction of new activities providing more varied recreation for a greater number of people, the development of the social center, rural recreation, the beginnings of industrial recreation, considering the problems of commercial recreation, discussion of the need and significance of recreation, increasing public recognition of rising leisure time, and an interest in play in other countries. Some of the activities growing more popular with the help of the PRAA involved large groups of people. The society promoted music and dancing, especially folk dancing, as healthful recreation for both sexes and several age groups. Community pageants might serve as recreation and foster local pride and spirit as well. The dramatic instinct in people could also be filled by other forms of drama both on the playground and in the community.[53] Athletics obviously opened a major opportunity for group activity. The PRAA encouraged proven games but also fostered development of new games, such as softball, for the average child. Finally, still another variety of mass-participation activity which the PRAA felt worthwhile was the use of public celebrations and festivals to mark holidays on the playgrounds.[54]

The Association also aided the diffusion of activities which offered more occasions for development of individual and small group skills. Play and games were not to be left at the recreation center but also were adaptable to home use.[55] Arts and crafts in which citizens actually constructed things with their hands had many possibilities. Finally the PRAA recommended a long list of additional diversions, such as storytelling.

The PRAA stressed the need for recreation by people of all ages, classes, beliefs, and races in America. Its leaders, nevertheless, apparently recognized the prudence of not endangering general progress in recreation by great stress on recreation for "special" interests and remained initially silent on the possibilities of factors such as segregation denying equal opportunity for recreation to Negroes.[56] A committee of the PRAA, however, studied play conditions in institutions such as orphanages, mental hospitals, and homes for the blind and crippled, whose residents also needed recreation to relieve the monotony of their lives.[57]

A favorite means of providing recreation for a wide spectrum of people was the recreation center or social center. These facilities often used the equipment of school buildings to provide both active and passive recreation and many kinds of clubs to interest a large proportion of the nearby population. The use of school buildings after regular hours eliminated the need for costly new facilities. In addition to providing wholesome recreation, school social centers not only encouraged neighborhood spirit and pride but also aided the assimilation of immigrants.[58] Social centers had all of the beneficial qualities of playgrounds plus added activities for more groups of people.

The PRAA was, however, hardly alone in its interest in and support of social centers. Certain elements within the National Education Association, for example, had been interested for years in the wider use of schools. In 1907 Rochester had opened its schools as social centers, and four years later the first national conference of social centers was held in Wisconsin. The National Community Center Association came into being in 1916. Indeed, social centers were a part of the so-called "community movement" within the ranks of social workers whose leaders believed the neighborhood or community was the natural unit for man's social relations. To these people all sorts of communal activities, and particularly the use of leisure, might best be organized by institutions such as settlements and social centers operating on a neighborhood level. In addition, social centers kept alive the idea of making recreation a subdivision of education and placing local recreation programs under the control of the schools.[59]

Lebert H. Weir, first field secretary hired directly by the Association, served nearly forty years. Regional training institutes, such as this one in which school teachers in Michigan learned to play games, were another effective tool. Abbie Condit edited many of the hundreds of publications produced by the PRAA over the years.

Social centers could also be used for recreation in rural areas, a collateral interest of the PRAA.[60] Factors such as agrarian decay, monotony, and loneliness appear to have influenced the decision of the PRAA to expand the urban concept of recreation into the countryside. The Association gave considerable effort to developing rural recreation by such means as employing a special field secretary for a time in rural New England. In the absence of municipal governments, the PRAA encouraged private agrarian institutions, such as churches, schools, and granges, to develop recreation programs. Many of the activities and techniques used in cities, such as athletics, were entirely suitable for rural adaptation. Industrious farmers were encouraged to recognize that they, like all people, needed play.[61]

The PRAA did not give as much attention to recreation in industry as to rural recreation. Braucher did recognize, however, the relation between industrial efficiency and proper recreation programs for employees and their families. The Association accomplished little in the relatively new area of industrial recreation, but it did make some attempts to popularize the concept.[62] Even before Lee's presidency, Curtis had recommended a study of recreation in industry. In 1916 Weir surveyed welfare work and recreation provisions in 150 firms in Indiana. Early the next year the directors voted for a special man to develop industrial recreation if funds became available.[63]

Another aspect of recreation which, like industrial recreation, was linked to the rise of the city was commercial recreation. Much commercialized recreation appealed to people's basic emotions. Amusement enterprises, the leaders of the PRAA recognized, were not inherently bad, but there appeared to be evidence connecting some such establishments, particularly movie theaters and dance halls, with lewdness and vulgarity.[64] With this in mind, the PRAA characteristically formed a committee which looked into the matter in several large cities and recommended municipal regulation of nine aspects of commercial recreation. The Association recognized that businesses such as movie houses and dance halls were within the broad realm of recreation and felt that certain standards of morality and safety should be maintained.[65] In the long run, however, Braucher preferred to ignore commercial recreation rather than compete on its often low terms.[66]

The PRAA would later be considerably more active in its interest in recreation in foreign nations than in commercial recreation. Member C. M. Goethe of San Francisco took a trip around the world promoting playgrounds and donated $2,500 toward a training school for recreation workers in Korea. By 1915 the directors had been through two abortive attempts to arrange international recreation congresses. Short of money for new ventures, they decided to limit their international efforts temporarily to inexpensive actions such as assistance by mail to overseas play enthusiasts.[67] By showing recreation to be a global phenomenon the PRAA hoped to expand the American concept of the term.

One indicator of the widening American view of recreation was that both perceptive citizens and leaders of the PRAA increasingly recognized the growing importance of leisure in American life. Such well-known public figures as John Dewey and Herbert Croly joined with the new Federal Council of Churches in identifying the vital significance of the expanding leisure and its use.[68] Braucher, Lee, and some of the field secretaries spoke out publicly on the same topic. As industrialization fostered repetitive labor with its boredom and working hours fell, organized recreation attempted to offset this monotony through the wise use of leisure. To achieve this goal, the PRAA sought adequate facilities for wholesome and enjoyable recreation. Men would need to make efficient use of their free hours, the PRAA leaders argued, to obtain self-fulfillment. Recreation could utilize leisure to add meaning to life.[69]

Besides broadening the concept of recreation, Lee and Braucher also wanted America to recognize a governmental, especially municipal, responsibility for providing at least basic recreation facilities. The elements of municipal responsibility were year-round programs, supervised recreation with trained leadership, a comprehensive recreation system rather than merely a collection of playgrounds, and decent standards of commercial recreation. Efficient administration and professionalism in recreation also were related to municipal responsibility. It was not enough for a town simply to accept a vague obligation for public recreation; to be adequate a municipal recreation program had to meet certain criteria. Lee and Braucher felt, for example, that one requirement of a worthwhile recreation program was to have facilities available for use both day and night throughout the year.[70]

Although Braucher and Lee were primarily interested in securing governmental action for recreation on the municipal level, both state and federal governments were beginning to show a minor interest in recreation before World War I. In addition to statutory support, state and national agencies in a limited way were moving into both technical assistance and direct provision of recreation facilities. Only a year after the birth of the PRAA, the University of Missouri had hired a field representative to help local schools organize recreation and physical education. Several states, such as New York, New Jersey, and Massachusetts, had enabling acts for municipal recreation. California under progressive governor Hiram Johnson undertook a statewide survey of recreation needs.[71] A few states established state parks and forests with provisions for recreation use. Nevertheless Braucher and Lee did little to promote state-level interest in recreation. Their philosophies of individualism and of recreation as a personal experience inclined them to prefer that recreation activities of government normally be kept on a local level, as close to the people as possible. In addition the expanding PRAA, concentrating its field work on cities with favorable chances of success, simply lacked the funds to lobby effectively in state legislatures.[72]

Recreation interest at the federal level of government resembled the situation in the states. Before World War I at least four federal agencies dealt with recreation in one way or another, but their total impact was not great. The Forest Service was already opening up some land for private recreation use by renting sites for resorts. Meanwhile pressure from several sources by 1916 led to the creation of a National Park Service to coordinate and expand the small number of existing national parks into a nationwide system. Under Stephen Mather, first director of the Service, active recreation and sports began to creep into the parks, although beauty of scenery rather than mass recreation remained the primary concern of the Service for several decades.[73] Two other agencies, the Office of Education in the Department of the Interior and the Children's Bureau in the Department of Labor, undertook minor services in research and advice for movements close to recreation, such as the widening use of schools. Lee and Braucher were aware of these activities, and in 1914, the reader will recall, they had actually been ready to turn over the work of the PRAA to the federal government. Braucher had even considered a four-year campaign for a "Bureau of Recreation."[74] But any such scheme for turning the PRAA over to permanent federal control was no doubt born chiefly of expediency; after the financial plight of the Association eased, and even later when dollars were again scarce, the notion of dissolving the PRAA vanished. In general, Braucher and Lee were not opposed to federal activity in recreation but were very skeptical of federal control at the expense of local private and governmental initiative, individualism, quality, and freedom.

To be effective, the leaders of the PRAA believed, governmental programs of recreation had to supply organized play and trained professional leaders. Playgrounds in Duluth, Toledo, and Baltimore had been closed as nuisances for lack of supervision.[75] Many children simply did not know how to play a variety of games, practice good sportsmanship, or properly use playground equipment; yet with proper leadership, delinquency might be curbed on the playground. Municipal recreation could utilize trained leaders to teach not only children but people of all ages new activities and interests, higher values, and good citizenship.[76] Workers in recreation needed the special education they could get through the publications and local training sessions offered by the PRAA. The PRAA encouraged professionalism with this emphasis on training and also made studies of titles, qualifications, and salaries for positions as executives in local recreation. At the highest level of administration, large cities ought to have such professional recreation secretaries, experts with skill in executive actions, proficiency in recreation, and some knowledge of social work.

The recreation secretary, or superintendent, functioned best as director of a comprehensive recreation system which provided a continual variety of opportunities for play and leisure under professional leadership. A committee of the PRAA tentatively recommended that commissions independent of partisan political control have charge of municipal recreation; such a commission could efficiently combine resources of city parks and schools.[77] This arrangement might offer a multitude of activities at parks, playgrounds, school social centers, and other facilities.

The Association continually stressed the importance of efficiency in municipal recreation to obtain optimum use of public funds. The PRAA thus reflected the Progressive yen for efficiency; for instance, committees and congresses dealt with topics such as expertise and professionalism in recreation. The congress in 1911 had even employed "Efficiency in Play" as its theme. Programs of recreation could not be operated haphazardly; rather, they were to utilize the advice of experts and adapt proven methods to local conditions. While not wishing to create a national stereotype at the expense of local initiative, the PRAA made such expert knowledge available.[78]

The effectiveness of the PRAA in spreading information and stimulating public recreation was evident in comments of individuals, changes in specific towns after visits by field secretaries, and statistical data found in the yearbooks of the PRAA between

1910 and 1916. America had begun to take play seriously, said Julia Lathrop, head of the Children's Bureau. For example, Hanmer visited Pensacola, Florida, and within a few months the city had four year-round play centers in operation. The PRAA held a congress in Pittsburgh one year; after the event many prominent local citizens, formerly uninterested, rushed enthusiastically to aid the local playground group.[79] John F. Walsh, president of the national Association of Park Superintendents, felt that sending a copy of *Recreation* to every American park head would "do more to further the playground movement, so ably advocated by your Association, than any other means I know of."[80] The field man, of course, did much to promote local action; a field secretary sent to New Ulm, Minnesota, "took an audience largely composed of stolid, slow-moving German farmers and from the platform practically organized a committee to look into the question of a recreation survey for New Ulm."[81] The use of statistical data from the annual yearbooks furnishes an effective method of obtaining a wide view of rising municipal recreation without the necessity of citing additional examples in particular cities.[82]

All of these gains in public recreation certainly reflected the increasing acceptance in American cities of the need for municipal responsibility, professionalism, and the broader definition of recreation as propounded by the PRAA. Since the Association was the only organized group consciously promoting these purposes as its major objective, it is not unreasonable to assume that a major part of statistical growth in these areas resulted from the efforts of the PRAA. In 1910 some 184 cities had a total of 1,244 playgrounds; of these cities, playgrounds in 62 operated with municipal funds, while 59 received both municipal and private dollars. By 1916 some 414 cities had 3,270 playgrounds and neighborhood centers; municipal funds supported these facilities completely in 171 cities and in combination with private resources in 95 cities. Overall, the figures for total municipal management of recreation programs had risen to 63.8 percent of the 414 cities reporting supervised recreation in 1916.[83] In 1911, 36 cities employed 377 recreation workers on a year-round basis; by 1916 the figures had increased to 110 cities and 1,058 workers.[84] In 1912, 47 cities had training classes for recreation workers; 19 of these cities had student workers. By 1916, 65 cities held such classes, and 39 of the 65 reported 1,405 students.[85]

Between 1910 and 1916 the broad definition of recreation urged by the Association also found rising favor in the culture of the United States. The yearbooks showed an increase in the variety of activities used in city play programs and in the use of schools as recreation and social centers. A list of activities performed in connection with playgrounds in 1910 contained the following events and the number of different cities in which they were used: dramatics, 26; folk dancing, 94; gardening, 43; industrial work, 76; libraries, 52; singing, 72; storytelling, 114; and wading, 51. The same list in 1916 read: dramatics, 110; folk dancing, 229; gardening, 133; industrial work, 180; libraries, 122; singing, 151; storytelling, 243; and wading, 115. The roster for 1916 also included over a dozen activities, such as Boy Scouts, not listed in 1910. In 1910, 31 cities had schools used as recreation centers; 27 of the 31 cities reported 201 such schools. By 1916, 127 cities said they utilized 663 schools as social centers.[86] The Association had clearly helped to guide American cities from informal "play" to public "recreation."

Public recreation, broadly envisioned, was the goal of the Association. Although Lee and Braucher basically believed in municipal responsibility for providing professionally supervised recreation opportunities for citizens and a generously wide concept of the term *recreation*, they also hoped to build a national movement with local autonomy while at the same time increasing the effectiveness of the PRAA as an agency of guidance and assistance. The two dedicated leaders assured the continuance and expansion of the PRAA as an effective institution of service to the recreation movement. Between 1910 and 1916 they perfected patterns of operation of the Association, such as the use of field secretaries and national conventions, and in the same period substantially increased its staff, membership, and budget. Public recreation certainly did grow in the decade ending in 1916 and the Association was a major stimulant of this growth. Meanwhile the so-called community movement, also involved with public recreation, was rapidly bounding ahead; the fusion of this movement with the impact of mobilization for World War I was to result in a dramatic, although temporary, shift of emphasis in the service of the PRAA.

When the United States entered World War I, the PRAA determined to provide recreation for thousands of new recruits in towns near training camps prior to movement overseas.

4
War and Community Service, 1917–1922

Although much of Europe was at war by 1916, certain progressive reformers in the United States were more concerned with improving functional democracy in America than with meddling in affairs across the Atlantic. Indeed, as Edward J. Ward, authority on school social centers, announced, the American neighborhood and community seemed to offer a superb institution upon which to build idealism and unity to fend off the selfishness and savagery of a world at war.[1] Ward's view of the crucial importance of the neighborhood typified the thoughts of a growing band of students of society, including many influential leaders in urban recreation. Advocates of the community movement, including such figures as Jane Addams, founder of Hull House, and sociologist Charles H. Cooley, claimed that technology and other impersonal forces operating on a national scale were destroying close-knit local groups important to the social structure. Such thoughtful observers increasingly stressed the key position of the neighborhood and called for a social reordering of communities as well as a nationwide moral unity which might foster a sense of national community. Literature on community cooperation and organization for such purposes as the constructive use of free time began to appear with increasing frequency. All of these trends, with roots in institutions such as the rising numbers of schoolhouse community centers and settlement houses, constituted the so-called community movement, whose promoters aimed to show the potential for beneficial coordination of neighborhoods and communities.[2] The neighborhood, said Robert A. Woods, a friend of Joseph Lee and leading Boston authority on settlements, was

> large enough to include in essence all of the problems of the city, the state, and the nation . . . [yet] small enough to be a comprehensible and manageable community unit. It is in fact the only one that is comprehensible and manageable. . . .[3]

Thoughts such as these were common in several institutional manifestations of the community movement.

In practice the community movement was not a single crusade but a reflection of the advances of its various interrelated parts. For instance the federal Office of Education initiated its own activities to encourage the use of public schools as community centers, and enthusiasts founded the National Community Center Association. Rural areas, long familiar with institutions such as the Grange, also took a renewed interest in their communities; for example, Osseo, Wisconsin, hired America's first rural civic secretary to organize social and civic affairs. North Carolina established a state Bureau of Community Services in 1916 to foster community activities in its dozens of rural counties.[4] In the same year a group of social workers formed the National Social Unit Organization and undertook an ambitious three-year pilot experiment in organizing a Cincinnati district of thirty-one blocks into a cohesive "social unit" for purposes such as group health care and recreation[5]

Both the PRAA and the recreation movement across America accepted this increasing emphasis on the importance of the community. Howard Braucher set out, therefore, to encourage an attitude of community and cooperation among the users of public recreation. He felt citizens ought to be able to develop a "spirit of neighborliness" and thus feel a part of the municipal recreation center in their locality; when this spirit vanished the center was manifestly too large.[6] The PRAA promoted the community spirit through its field secretaries and by selecting "The Awakening of Neighborhood Life in America" and "Community Building Through Play" as themes for two annual conventions. Within two years the number of municipalities with recreation centers in schools increased threefold to 152 cities. Solid but less spectacular gains occurred in municipal promotion of such activities as corporate songfests, dramatics, and pageants; for instance, Newton D. Baker, recreation-boosting progressive mayor of Cleveland, organized the first municipal dance in his city. New York and Chicago were leaders in developing municipal recreation on a neighborhood basis.[7]

Meanwhile the PRAA was optimistically expanding its general operations. Early in 1917 there were twenty field workers actively promoting recreation in many cities and also in a statewide campaign in Michigan. With all this activity, Braucher and Lee felt that conditions for the spread of municipal recreation were extremely promising. Accordingly the board authorized expansive plans for governors' conferences on recreation in Michigan and Minnesota, a specialist's service to recreation in industry, and a foundation-supported model program of city recreation.[8]

Although the PRAA devoted much of its energy in the first months of 1917 to seeking continued expansion of municipal recreation, Braucher was also watching the ominous pattern of events increasingly drawing America toward war with Germany. Preparedness had been in the air the previous year at the annual convention of the PRAA; indeed, Newton D. Baker, by then Secretary of War, had been a featured speaker. Braucher groped for ways in which organized recreation might aid in national defense. Late in March 1917, with the nation almost at war, the board of directors of the Association approved the suggestion that the Secretary of War appoint a federal recreation commission to provide for the "wise use of leisure time" by recruits in military training camps. The directors also offered the full services of the PRAA to the national government. When war came a few days later, Braucher fully expected the War Department to federalize the entire staff of the PRAA to act as the principal vehicle for providing wholesome recreation for troops in training camps.[9]

Lee and Braucher were not alone, however, in recognizing the necessity for looking into the military trainees' recreation activities. The previous summer President Wilson had mobilized some

100,000 national guardsmen along the volatile Mexican frontier. As troops poured into small border towns, which had virtually no recreation opportunities, complaints of prostitution and venereal disease flooded into Washington. Secretary Baker asked Raymond B. Fosdick of the Rockefeller Foundation, a close friend of Braucher and brother of preacher Harry Emerson Fosdick, to inspect the area. Fosdick found uniformed soldiers and obvious whores roaming the streets as well as houses of prostitution filled to capacity.[10]

Fosdick's investigation convinced the government that there was indeed a serious social problem caused by a sudden influx of troops into unprepared communities. Since the military lacked both plans and policies for meeting the situation, Baker himself began to cast about for solutions. The YMCA, which had begun to provide a few services, including books and writing paper, for servicemen, offered another organizational vehicle but little had been accomplished before the declaration of war in 1917. Faced with the prospect of millions of recruits in new training camps, Baker and Fosdick began to explore the various ways in which civilian welfare associations might best serve the camps and nearby towns. Braucher, Lee, and other leaders of voluntary groups offered ideas to Fosdick.

With the coming of war, swarms of citizen groups wanting to aid soldiers forced Baker and Fosdick to turn from discussion to action. They drew plans for a Commission on Training Camp Activities, or CTCA, to coordinate the work of voluntary associations in creating a wholesome social environment for soldiers in camps and adjacent communities. On April 18, 1917, Baker, with the approval of President Wilson, officially established the CTCA and asked Fosdick to serve as chairman. Some ten individuals, including Joseph Lee of the PRAA, John R. Mott of the YMCA, and Lee Hanmer of the Russell Sage Foundation, comprised the CTCA. Other groups working closely with the Commission were the Knights of Columbus, Jewish Welfare Board, American Library Association, and, of course, the United States Army.[11] As Baker saw it, the main task of the CTCA would be to rationalize as far as possible the activities of the several competing, overlapping social service groups and the bewildering environment of war camps.[12]

The CTCA not only coordinated the work of voluntary associations but also operated its own programs both inside and outside the training camps. Baker believed that most young men would prefer decent recreation activities to saloons and brothels. Thus, besides waging a campaign of propaganda and law enforcement against all forms of organized vice, the CTCA was also to provide each training camp with athletic directors, song leaders, theaters and dramatics, adult education, and post exchanges. Three religious voluntary organizations—the YMCA, the Knights of Columbus, and the Jewish Welfare Board—provided most of the facilities and services for the troops' on-post leisure. The YMCA program was by far the largest and set the pace for the other groups. Each major unit in training was to have a YMCA building and staff to provide the troops with a multitude of free recreation opportunities such as games, movies, and professional entertainment as well as religious services.[13]

Baker and Fosdick knew, however, that no matter how attractive the CTCA and YMCA made the opportunities for spending leisure hours inside camp, the average soldier would go to town if he got the chance. To meet this problem the leaders of the PRAA decided that its wartime mission would be to help camp towns organize to serve soldiers with wholesome community activities. Influenced by previous experience with the community movement and realizing that towns suddenly inundated with military visitors would encounter many acute problems in all phases of life, not just recreation, Braucher and Lee opted to broaden the war services of the PRAA. Their thought was to furnish local groups with expert advice to meet the many changed social conditions caused by the military presence. In effect, the PRAA would "create a massive settlement house around each camp" to foster voluntary community cooperation in towns near military bases.[14] Although several private groups received the sanction of the CTCA to operate within camps, Lee convinced the Commission to endorse only the PRAA to be

> . . . responsible for the work of stimulating and aiding communities in the neighborhood of training camps to develop and organize their social and recreational resources in such a way as to be of the greatest possible value to the officers and soldiers in the camps.[15]

Early in May 1917 the first agent on this assignment arrived in Chattanooga, Tennessee. By June community organizers, often field workers of the PRAA diverted hastily to the task, had reached a dozen other cities near training camps.[16]

With the YMCA war budget up to $5 million in its first two months, Lee and Braucher realized that the normal sources of PRAA revenue, which yielded at most only $100,000 a year, would be entirely inadequate for the expanded services of the Association. Emergency loans and grants supported the initial work in camp communities, but the two leaders soon decided to engage professional fund raisers skilled in the mass soliciting tactics pioneered by the YMCA a decade earlier. Within four months, the American people, reacting to the appeal of patriotism, gave $2,200,000 to the "War Camp Community Recreation Fund."[17] One particularly generous contributor, secured through Fosdick's influence, was wealthy John D. Rockefeller, Jr., who took an active interest in helping raise funds for Braucher's cause.[18]

By December 1917 the war efforts of the PRAA, backed by far greater support than the prewar. Association had ever enjoyed, were crystallizing into standard policies and procedures. For example, different names for the program around the country had led to confusion, so Braucher and the board, on the advice of Fosdick, asked all local committees to unite under "War Camp Community Service," or WCCS. The substitution of "community service" for "playground and recreation" in the new name was indicative of the broader function of WCCS as compared to the prewar PRAA and also placed the organization firmly on record as a major participant in the community movement. The new national headquarters of WCCS, officered and staffed primarily from the ranks of the PRAA, later became, on paper, an independent corporation.[19] The mushrooming growth of WCCS, which at its peak reportedly had a national staff of some 3,000 workers who had organized 755 cities in 47 states with the help of over 500,000 volunteers, obviously required an enlarged central administrative organization.[20] Braucher and Lee proved capable of directing the vastly expanded operation; Lee did much of the promotional work while Braucher ably served as chief administrator of the entire program. In his office in New York he eventually developed ten functionally defined departments to serve local areas in eight geographic divisions.

Believing in the primacy of local citizen initiative and responsibility, and probably wanting to maintain direct contact with individual cities, Braucher did not establish state-level committees of WCCS. Instead he sent out district representatives who advised local community organizers in much the same way as had the field secretaries of the old PRAA. The community organizers, key figures in local operations of WCCS, went into camp towns, studied needs and resources, and recommended voluntary members for local citizen committees of WCCS. The skilled organizers then served as executive officers of the committees, which were to be representative of the various religious, philanthropic, and civic elements of the towns. The task of the committees was to pool local resources, coordinating public and private organizations, to provide soldiers with as many as possible of the normal amenities in life, such as social and recreation activities which were limited or unavailable in camps.[21] Working together, local committees and community organizers appointed operational subcommittees to carry out programs with the aid of volunteers and paid staffs.

Braucher kept close track of the organizers, requiring daily and weekly reports, and encouraged them to be as liberal as the spirits of individual communities permitted regarding such sometimes controversial programs as dancing and organized activities on Sundays. Local budgets had to pass careful scrutiny in New York before receiving national funds. Once approved, however, municipal committees handled all monies and tailored operations to fit particular requirements rather than a national stereotype.[22] Although individually planned for local conditions, the programs all had to meet certain national standards of quality, could benefit from expert advice available from WCCS headquarters, and were designed to meet basically the same needs.

The local community-wide services of WCCS, then, all contained a significant proportion of the same ingredients, as had the municipal recreation systems formed in prewar days with the aid of the PRAA. Lee and Braucher wanted the varied offerings of WCCS to duplicate the best qualities of American home towns; indeed, a criterion for any activity was whether it helped soldiers feel at home in the community. Volunteers learned soldiers' interests and guided the men to clubs and churches of their choice. A soldier might obtain a bed in town for as little as 25 cents in one of hundreds of WCCS servicemen's clubs, which ranged from a few rented rooms to commodious six-story buildings. Millions of troops used WCCS information booths, went home for dinner with local families, and attended community dances with respectable local girls. Officials of the WCCS provided soldiers on pass with tickets to entertainment of all sorts and opportunities for a variety of recreation. Citizens opened their homes to families visiting Army sons and loaned their cars to soldiers' tour groups. Committees protected transient troops against profiteering by local merchants. In one typical month WCCS events included parties for 208,000 military men; dances for 345,000; on-post entertainments for 223,000; auto rides for 32,000; singing festivals for 1,321,000; rooms for 142,000; and meals for 613,000. The employees of WCCS, of course, depended greatly on local volunteers to staff these services. WCCS, like the PRAA, initiated systematic activities run by home folks themselves; the function of WCCS was to send community "organizers," not "superintendents." Thus, while recreation events were an important part of WCCS, the total program covered a wide range of social services to soldiers.[23]

In many cases facilities and good will to support the broad WCCS program for white soldiers away from home already existed and needed merely to be coordinated and supplemented. Suitable facilities were scarce, however, for the first great masses of some 400,000 black American soldiers arriving at training camps late in 1917. Only a few churches offered hospitality to Negro troops in towns such as Petersburg, Virginia, and Chillicothe, Ohio, although thousands of blacks were in camps nearby. Although unequal treatment of blacks was a part of American life, Braucher resolved that WCCS ought to give the Negro soldier equal opportunities; he did not, however, launch a frontal attack on cultural and legal segregation. Instead he pragmatically utilized Negroes as community organizers to set up essentially the same WCCS programs for black troops as those offered to white soldiers. Many of the facilities for blacks were of the very best quality. An example of those outstanding facilities was the cafeteria in the WCCS club at Columbia, South Carolina, to which federal health officers awarded a mark of 97 for cleanliness, the highest rating then given any hotel or restaurant in the city. At its peak, WCCS operated one hundred clubs for blacks in ninety-seven communities in thirty-one states.[24]

In mid-1918, Lee and Braucher initiated an experimental expansion of WCCS programs to reach workers in war industries, another segment of the population which, like black and white soldiers, often found itself an outside group in a strange community. Boom towns with new war plants experienced the same taxing of community resources as cities near huge military camps, and the response of WCCS to both situations was essentially the same. The "War Workers Community Service" initiated programs including civic activities, recreation, and educational services in thirty-two war production centers such as Chester, Pennsylvania, and Rock Island, Illinois.[25]

By the time Braucher was deploying WCCS to serve workers in war industries, the programs of the organizations working under the CTCA, already a year old, were in need of vastly increased funding to continue their expanding momentum. The first year had been marked by no little confusion and rivalry among the organizations at work inside the camps. Some of this competition spilled

War Camp Community Service gave aid such as information, lodging, and recreation in cities and towns near military bases across the nation. A major goal of WCCS was that local residents befriend servicemen.

After the war Community Service provided recreation from playgrounds to dramatics in various localities.

over into the independent fund raising of the groups and engendered jealousy of the WCCS, officially alone outside the camps.[26] Although several hundred cities adopted combined war drives as a local expedient, the national leaders of these organizations resisted a unified campaign. WCCS had been willing, although not eager, to enter a joint fund since January 1918. Finally public opinion, pressure from government leaders such as Baker, and the promise of an efficient canvass, led to a United War Work Campaign by seven associations, including WCCS. The well-oiled solicitation, coming ironically in the week of November 11–18 as the shooting in Europe ceased, proved highly successful and collected $190 million, of which over $16 million went to WCCS.[27]

The signing of the armistice with Germany signaled a shift toward demobilization, but WCCS and other groups serving under the CTCA found many needs to be met in aiding the transition of nearly five million individuals from military to civilian status. In addition, these organizations, like all segments of American society, had to decide upon aims for their long-term roles, if any, in the postwar period. The CTCA, reportedly considered by Baker to be an outstanding achievement and acclaimed by *Survey* magazine as "the most stupendous piece of social work in modern times," had nevertheless had its problems, notably the competition and duplication of services by the groups operating in the camps.[28] Consequently, upon the recommendation of Fosdick, leaders of a number of national welfare societies, and many Army officers, the War Department transferred the functions of the CTCA to the War Plans Division of the General Staff.[29] Meanwhile Braucher and Lee redirected the work of WCCS to aid in demobilization. As military installations closed down, WCCS increasingly phased out its services. At the same time, however, Braucher asked local committees of WCCS to welcome troops home, aid servicemen in re-entering community life, and help ex-soldiers to find employment.[30]

Lee and Braucher were no doubt as much concerned with the question of how to conserve nationwide gains in civic cooperation made under the WCCS as with the problems of returning soldiers. The exposure of millions of Americans to the possibilities of public recreation and community betterment via WCCS in over seven hundred cities had created a tremendous potential demand for continuation of such activities. The WCCS had been highly successful during the nineteen months of war when patriotic spirit ran high, and Braucher and Lee were determined to draw further benefit from the experience before that spirit waned.[31] The two leaders also had to decide on the future of the PRAA, parent of the

WCCS. Although municipal recreation in general had held its own during the war, the prewar upward momentum of the PRAA itself had obviously been lost. In fact, the Association, limping along with the remainder of a staff mostly loaned to WCCS, had seen nearly a 70 percent decline in contributions from 1917 to 1919, when its income fell below that of 1912.[32]

Faced with the need to set courses of action for both the floundering PRAA and the seemingly robust WCCS, Lee and Braucher had decided by early 1919 to found a third society, Community Service, or CS. They hoped it would consolidate and make permanent the broad pattern of community cooperation laid out by WCCS. Fosdick and Baker, who both feared that Braucher would trim the functions of WCCS back to the old recreation-centered work of the PRAA on the prewar scale, also vigorously backed the proposed Community Service organization.[33] Braucher and Lee formally established CS as an independent corporation on March 4, 1919, and intended to have it take over the assets of the PRAA. The PRAA, however, had a number of loyal supporters, such as board member Charles W. Eliot, president emeritus of Harvard University, whose protests persuaded Braucher and Lee to continue both organizations. Thus the two men were simultaneously president and secretary, respectively, of three separate associations—PRAA, WCCS, and CS. The three groups, although they had separate finances and identities, had almost identical boards of directors; and, as Braucher later admitted, "the real control in the three organizations was practically the same."[34]

Not only Braucher and his associates but also a number of other men and organizations promoting voluntary community cooperation planned ways to renew the community movement in peacetime. In fact, progressive social reform groups of all sorts emerged from the war apparently confident that the millennium was near; strategy-minded reformers even held a National Conference on Social Agencies and Reconstruction to consolidate their plans.[35] Meanwhile a number of writers, including some trained sociologists, produced an increasing flow of literature advocating community organization as the best means to obtain goals such as citizenship, vital grass-roots democracy of the sort so admired by the Progressives, and the wise use of leisure. Joseph K. Hart, a social worker and former employee of WCCS, spelled out the importance of "community spirit" in his book, *Community Organization*, for which Braucher had read the manuscript. Clarence Rainwater, an early historian of the play movement, announced that "neighborhood organization" and "community service" were in practice the latest stages in the evolution of urban recreation.[36] With such ideas in the air, groups new and old tried to implement different schemes of community organization. The neighborhood-based social unit experiment was still underway in Cincinnati. Social centers in schools had received a tremendous boost from the wartime Council of National Defense, which organized local community councils in schools and hoped to develop such activities further. In addition private organizations such as the YMCA, American Red Cross, and National Catholic War Council had new community-centered programs to conserve wartime gains in various stages of development.[37]

Despite the possibility of competition and duplication between Community Service and any number of these organizations, Lee and Braucher, flushed with the wartime success of WCCS, felt their conception of Community Service was sound. Certain national conditions in 1919, such as acute inflation, a wave of violent labor strikes, numerous race riots, and a growing paranoidal fear of a domestic bolshevik revolution punctuated by several bombing plots, also boded ill for any such liberal reform schemes. Lee believed, however, that this unrest was merely a symptom of the depersonalized, meaningless lives created by modern industrialism.

> The causes of unrest are not economic, but spiritual; not physical, but moral. What we are witnessing is the revolt of men who see life passing away without their having ever lived, who face the prospect of carrying their ideals and their aspirations unfulfilled and unspoken to the grave.[38]

Fortunately, although men might find little fulfillment in their work, CS might teach Americans to help themselves utilize their leisure for worthwhile, constructive, and creative activities such as art, music, games, athletics, and civic activities. As Lee phrased it, the purpose of Community Service was to "liberate the power of expression of people and communities."[39] The new Community Service was to build not merely wholesome leisure activities but also to foster a community spirit. In short, the vision of CS which Lee and Braucher spread was broad enough to encompass almost any sort of public or private social work or leisure time program leading to individual and community betterment. In practice, however, much of the program was to center on the use of leisure and to be a continuation of the kind of activities sponsored by WCCS but expanded to serve the entire community.

By mid-1919 Braucher was busily implementing the policies and operations of Community Service in hopes of establishing it on a firm foundation. Since legal complications restricted use of the funds of the well-heeled WCCS, he initiated a separate drive to secure $2,000,000 for CS. Although John D. Rockefeller, Jr.'s Laura Spelman Rockefeller Memorial appropriated $200,000 toward Braucher's goal, the overall campaign faltered and only brought in some $300,000 by the end of the year. Braucher reminded the directors that lack of funds caused the loss of "unusual opportunities," such as the opportunity to obtain the entire staff of dramatic experts from the CTCA.[40] Meanwhile he started a month-long training course for workers in CS and sought out the best employees of the gradually disbanding WCCS to ensure a corps of skilled specialists.[41]

Cities having experience with WCCS were logically the most promising targets for these community organizers. Using techniques learned from the PRAA, CS secured from responsible groups of local citizens formal invitations and agreements to try a CS program for a year. Often the nucleus of this effort was the local committee of WCCS. Then followed the arrival of the community organizer, supplied free of cost to the city for up to three months. During this time the agent was to stimulate community initiative in creating a local committee of CS, getting operations underway, and raising funds to pay an executive director for a year. When the organizer finished his work, the program became completely independent. National CS, however, continued to supply ideas, information, and expert aid; Braucher developed a system of bulletins and periodic visits by geographically assigned district representatives to guard against stagnation in isolated cities. A committee selected its community activities and recreation programs according to local needs rather than a standardized national plan. Committees in some cities developed a variety of educational, recreational, cultural, civic, and social activities utilizing citizens' leisure time. Such programs ranged from playgrounds and cooking classes in Columbus, Georgia, to an opera club and organized recreation periods in the factories of Cincinnati. Many of the services either directly continued or resembled the work of WCCS. In order to qualify for the use of the official emblem of CS, a red circle, each local group generally had to comply with certain national guidelines and policies such as confining projects to the broad field of leisure time and recreation, promoting the municipalization of suitable parts of that field, and offering services to all of the community and not just to specific ethnic groups.[42]

Braucher recognized that cooperation with other voluntary groups both nationally and locally was necessary if Community

Service were to survive in individual cities. Having witnessed the wartime friction among the societies supposedly cooperating inside the training camps, he was wary of formal alliances which might restrict CS nationally, but nevertheless he encouraged local committees to cooperate with all other associations in their communities to avoid duplication and competition. To foster good will and its own expansion, Community Service even worked jointly at greater cost than elsewhere with state-level confederations, such as the Ohio Council of Social Agencies.[43] The most challenging example of work with another national group was the aid rendered, using funds of the WCCS, to communities through the new American Legion, the yet untried but potentially powerful veterans' group formed in 1919. The membership of the Legion represented to Lee and Braucher nearly a million potential volunteers for local social work. Lee exerted considerable effort in hopes of persuading Legion posts across the country to sponsor programs of CS. The Legion stood for "100 percent Americanism." Lee's aim was to make that "Americanism" center on voluntary cooperation and friendship through sharing leisure activities rather than the flag-waving, book-censoring brand of patriotism.[44]

Despite the alluring possibilities in mutual support with the American Legion, neither the expansion of Community Service into local communities nor the fund raising to cover further development approached the high hopes of Lee and Braucher. The American public, which had given so generously to WCCS, had had enough of war and its social innovations. By December 1919 contributions amounted to no more than 15 percent of the sum sought in the national financial campaign of CS. Distressed by this poor showing, Lee and Braucher decided to continue the campaign on a tentative week-by-week basis. Nevertheless returns dwindled increasingly in 1920, and by May only sixty-five local committees of CS had actually become permanent, funded operations whereas WCCS had once operated in over seven hundred cities.[45]

By May 1921, after two years of life, Community Service had taken hold in 120 cities, but the national financial picture was bleak, and a host of local conflicts with other groups were more troubling than ever before. In New York, CS, already subsidized by Braucher's office, was about to fail. In a number of other cities, such as Washington, D.C., local units of other voluntary groups, fearing possible competition, helped kill the idea of CS. Rumors that CS was a Catholic agency seemed to Braucher to damage the organization in small rural communities. Meanwhile, funds contributed to national CS had dropped to approximately $70,000 annually, and Braucher had to discontinue the attractive policy of three months of free organizational work in cities new to Community Service. Finally in September 1922, by which time contributions to the old PRAA were nearing twice their record prewar rate, Braucher and Lee asked the directors to consider making CS a department of the PRAA. The board agreed, and on December 1, 1922, the staff and operations of Community Service quietly became a part of the more durable PRAA.[46]

In retrospect, the final collapse of Community Service resulted from the hard fact of increasingly unsuccessful fund raising as well as a consequence of the inevitable postwar letdown. In its initial and best year, Community Service had secured only a small fraction of its financial goal, and most of that had come from one generous source. Many other social organizations also had found fund raising difficult after the war; even the American Red Cross, which late in the war had raised $70 million more than a requested $100 million, had obtained only a bit over one-half of its modest $25 million goal the next year. A proliferation of new national fund-seeking groups and a full-fledged depression by 1921 had added still more problems for any new organization such as Community Service. Furthermore, Lee and Braucher, like many American leaders, had done little if any postwar planning during hostilities and thus had been forced to implement CS far too hastily in the months following the unexpected armistice. Although the sponsors of Community Service had to capitalize on public support for WCCS, planning for this new permanent organization had not begun in earnest until mid-1919.

By that time a helter-skelter general demobilization was well underway, and a reaction against the patriotism, idealism, and fervent energy of wartime had set in. The wave of violent strikes and race riots, along with the bolshevik-hunting national paranoia of the "Red Scare" and a growing hostility to aliens, had done nothing to help the cause of social reform, and Community Service suffered in consequence along with many other reform agencies.[47] In this climate, Lee had refused to consider the more extreme requests of the super-patriots but also had allowed CS to become involved in a number of projects sure to excite controversy. He declined to accept contributions with political conditions attached; insisted that foreign folk dances done by local groups of CS were not subversive; and encouraged the participation of CS in work with Negroes, migrant farm laborers, union coal miners, and cooperative buying experiments.[48] Much of the reaction and unrest of the demobilization era disappeared within a few years, but Community Service had also vanished by then.

Conditions in the United States immediately after the war had hastened the demise of Community Service as well as of the entire spectrum of community organization, of which CS was but one manifestation. The social unit plan tried in Cincinnati ended without prompting any imitations. School community centers entered a decade of decay although they tended to shift offerings from lectures and civic meetings to more popular recreation activities. "Community organization," so much touted as an ideal of cooperative democracy by many workers in WCCS and CS, increasingly became merely an efficient method for combined fund raising by community "chests," notwithstanding the fate of hundreds of "war chests" which had fallen apart at the armistice. The old closely knit, self-contained American community itself lost strength as social, technological, and economic changes increased the mobility of citizens and the interdependence of many geographic areas. More and more people lived in one neighborhood, worked in another, and shared special recreation interests with residents of still other areas.[49]

Despite the decline of the movement for community organization and the end of Community Service as an institution in 1922, the wartime experience with community cooperation and recreation left a legacy of no small import to the PRAA, which had narrowly escaped termination during the initial enthusiasm for CS. Millions of American soldiers and civilians, many for the first time in their lives, had participated in recreation programs run by WCCS in hundreds of cities. Similar activities had been continued on a reduced scale by CS. All of this activity created a huge corps of citizens who, having once enjoyed organized recreation, might well be inclined to taste it again. Moreover, WCCS was decidedly solvent. The wartime agency had raised and spent over $15,000,000 in three years. And on December 31, 1922, WCCS still had $1,480,000 in unspent funds while the PRAA war fund raised in 1917 contained an additional $1,690,000. When the war ended, the exact purpose for which the funds had been raised no longer existed. After months of debate, Lee and Braucher finally decided to use the money to promote organized recreation chiefly in towns across America to which servicemen returned. The fund of 1917 was invested in securities. WCCS continued as a corporation and in effect spent its capital, mainly raised in the joint campaign of 1918, to supplement the service and leadership training of the PRAA. The resources of WCCS lasted until 1930 and significantly added an average of over $250,000 yearly to the support of the PRAA programs. With peace restored, however, Braucher and Lee emphasized the PRAA and rarely made public mention of WCCS. The influence of programs of CS, generally privately funded, increasingly resulted in a broadening of the scope of municipally run recreation.[50]

The war years, then, while they caused a temporary decline in certain phases of municipal organized recreation as reported in yearbooks of the PRAA, had a positive overall effect on the PRAA and its field of activities. With Community Service gone by December 1922, Lee and Braucher once again turned nearly all of their energies back to charting a course to conserve and expand the normal work of the Association. For support they had, besides some of the men and resources left over from the war experience, much of the long-term staff of the PRAA, which had been quietly undergoing a rapid postwar growth and was now operating on a budget of nearly twice the prewar high.

NATIONAL RECREATION SCHOOL

CONDUCTED BY

THE PLAYGROUND AND RECREATION ASSOCIATION OF AMERICA

THE HECKSCHER FOUNDATION BUILDING   NEW YORK CITY

Where The National Recreation School Is Located

In 1926 the PRAA established a National Recreation School to train college graduates as municipal recreation executives to fill numerous new positions created by the expansion of public recreation in the decade.

5
Prosperity Decade:
The 1920s

Immediately after World War I Lee and Braucher had to decide how to adjust the operations of their several organizations to meet the needs of peacetime. Flushed with the success and patriotic support of their war work, they, along with numerous other social workers, misjudged both the rapidity and the effects of the post-war letdown. Consequently the alternative the two leaders initially favored, Community Service, failed as an institution despite much idealism and great effort. Simultaneously the old, deemphasized PRAA made an amazing, unplanned financial comeback. In 1919 when Community Service began its operations, receipts were ten times as large as gifts to the PRAA. A mere three years later, however, funds were flowing to the PRAA at a record-breaking rate to produce three times the amount of income of the then rapidly expiring Community Service.

The experience with Community Service was not, however, the only wartime legacy received by the growing, postwar PRAA. Wartime revelations of a lack of physical fitness among Americans created an opportunity for the PRAA to strengthen physical education in public schools. By this time progressive leaders in the field increasingly had followed the advice of men such as Luther Gulick and Clark Hetherington and turned from formal gymnastics to recreational sports and games. Although promoters of physical education and the PRAA had made some attempts to secure mandatory physical education in public schools as a part of the general campaign for preparedness, only eight states yet had required physical education programs in the schools. Existing legislation had been ineffective as well as scarce. The American public, while generally unconcerned about these inadequacies, had been shocked by a War Department announcement that one-third of the men examined by the Army were physically unfit for full military service.[1] In 1918 Willard S. Small, a promoter of state legislation for physical education who recognized the potential value of public exposés as a means to reform, had persuaded the federal commissioner of education to call a conference on health and physical education. Representatives of some forty interested national groups attended the meeting and asked that a committee be formed to foster federal as well as state legislation for mandatory physical education in public schools. The committee shortly decided that an established organization might best handle the task and approached the PRAA to do it.

Lee and Braucher recognized the request as an unexpected opportunity to expand substantially a hitherto underdeveloped interest of the PRAA; the directors appropriated $10,000 for the initial year of the work, to be known as the National Physical Education Service.[2] To head the new service, Braucher might have selected a prominent leader of physical education or an experienced lobbyist. He preferred instead a loyal member of the PRAA team and chose E. Dana Caulkins, former field secretary and manager of the Washington, D.C., unit of War Camp Community Service. Caulkins immediately encouraged physical educators throughout the country to support the National Physical Education Service itself and to back legislation requiring physical education in schools. He also secured endorsements from a wide range of nationwide associations such as Rotary International, the YMCA, and the American Federation of Labor. Then, with the aid of a number of part-time field secretaries, Caulkins initiated the first of several annual campaigns designed to lobby in state legislatures. The technique proved successful at first glance; soon twenty-eight states had new laws for mandatory physical education in the public schools. Only fifteen of the states, however, had state directors of physical education to implement effective programs. Some states lacked adequate standards, and others appropriated no funds for the legislation.[3]

Late in 1919 after a year of campaigning, Braucher and Caulkins became convinced that federal legislation for matching grants to states with acceptable school physical education would induce all states to adopt satisfactory standards and statutes. Lee, who for years remained skeptical of the use of federal subsidies, backed this decision by Braucher and the directors.[4] Since the Smith-Lever Act of 1914 and the Smith-Hughes Act of 1917 had already established precedents for federal grants to state programs of agricultural and vocational education this bid for federal funds was not unjustified. Caulkins went to Washington and in February 1920, aided by representatives of the various national groups cooperating with the National Physical Education Service, secured the introduction of the first of several bills for federal aid to physical education.[5] These bills, typically appropriating as much as $10 million in matching grants to be parceled out to states working toward universal physical education in public schools, twice advanced to the stage of hearings by congressional committees. Despite at least lukewarm support from numerous organizations including labor and women's interests, a national publicity campaign, and a lack of any real opposition to the bills, all these proposals failed to become law, each one killed by congressional indifference.[6]

Although Braucher was defeated in Congress once again, just as he had been in his earlier attempts to incorporate the PRAA, he still found that the publicity of the move for a national law greatly aided the work of the National Physical Education Service in securing more effective action for compulsory physical education in the states. In fact, the war-born service became one of the most successful ongoing programs of the PRAA and actively helped secure legislation in thirty states. After two decades, by which time thirty-three states with 80 percent of the population of the country had organized physical education in the schools, Braucher was to suspend the service so its director, James E. Rogers, could deal with recreation aspects of national defense.[7]

Another long-lasting new service of the PRAA which grew out of the war concerned recreation opportunities for blacks. Following the war, in spite of a violent wave of anti-Negro riots, some twenty-seven cities continued recreation programs for black citizens begun by War Camp Community Service. Braucher was anxious to see these modest programs succeed and wanted to broaden even further recreation possibilities for Negroes as well as all other Americans. Realistically appraising the segregationist attitudes of many people, he decided that separate, hopefully equal facilities were preferable to no facilities. Consequently in July 1920 he called Ernest T. Attwell, son of a prominent black clergyman of Harlem, to head a Bureau of Colored Work for the PRAA. Attwell had been for years a teacher, football coach, and follower of the influential Booker T. Washington at Tuskegee Institute.

The bureau in effect provided all of the regular help, such as field service and training institutes, of the PRAA to biracial and black groups seeking organized recreation for Negroes. Legally, however, Braucher and Attwell did not promote segregation; they actually gave cautious support to integration when their actions would not hurt what progress had already been made in recreational advantages for blacks. Although such opportunities lagged far behind public recreation open to whites, Attwell's work was successful from the beginning; and within six years almost a hundred cities had established recreation facilities for Negroes.[8] The research director of the National Urban League considered the bureau "the one outstanding organization in the field of recreation for Negroes."[9] Attwell was to continue this work until his death nearly three decades later.

By 1923 Attwell's work was well underway, and Braucher had terminated the operations of the abortive Community Service program so that he and Lee might turn their major energies back to the PRAA. Given the changed mood and conditions of postwar America, no longer so inspired with progressive concepts, and forewarned by the failure of Community Service, they might at this time have reevaluated in depth the basic assumptions, policies, and operational techniques of the PRAA. Perhaps some of the thousands of people who as volunteers had aided war recreation might yet have been organized into local units to support public recreation and the PRAA in various ways. Just as Braucher urged cities to plan for future recreation, he himself might well have undertaken long-range strategic planning for the Association. The two leaders chose without question, however, to return to the prewar policies of the PRAA. With a legitimate, relatively noncontroversial cause, Braucher and Lee saw little gain in changing an apparently successful operation and risking another failure such as Community Service. There was still an obviously great need to be met in the provision of adequate municipal recreation, and the rapidly mounting receipts of the PRAA seemed to indicate satisfaction with its usual services.

In hopes of continuing the postwar upward spiral of the organization, they set out to improve and expand the crucial system of field service. Seeing a need to both upgrade and maintain quality in existing municipal recreation programs, Braucher utilized the once discarded idea of combining groups of these cities into districts. A specific field worker served each of these areas full time and obviously acquired a better knowledge of the strengths and weaknesses of recreation in his district through continual contact. This "continuation" field service was to prevent backsliding in local recreation operations. The district representative functioned as troubleshooter, builder of public opinion, and outside expert for the cities in his area; he also conducted annual district conferences of local recreation staffs for discussions of technical matters. Braucher even tried an experimental district service to Westminster, Vermont, a village of six hundred, although usually the PRAA did not attempt to secure year-round municipal recreation systems in cities with fewer than eight thousand, since smaller communities generally could not finance such operations.[10] The PRAA also set up two districts for cities with nothing but summer programs and in 1923 authorized a separate district for greater New York.[11] Nor did Braucher neglect to continue the older method of promotional field services to cities without recreation systems.

By 1924 both field services and general operations of the PRAA were at record levels and still increasing in the postwar prosperity. In that year Braucher organized the raising and spending of $348,000, of which $250,000, or more than five times the amount available only three years earlier, went for field service to 318 cities. The annual congress that year drew 600 delegates from 196 cities in 35 states, and 255 cities utilized the assistance of the Association in hiring and training skilled recreation workers.[12]

Along with these expanding services of the PRAA came a rapid rise in municipal programs of organized recreation and a general increase in recreation of all sorts. In a decade, four key indicators of municipal recreation—the number of cities with programs, paid workers, playgrounds, and dollars spent—had at least doubled. For 1924 the yearbook of the PRAA reported 711 cities with public recreation. Of these, 662 spent $20 million for recreation services, a sum double the record amount of two years before. These funds went to over seven thousand different playgrounds and indoor recreation centers staffed by nearly sixteen thousand salaried employees.[13] Only some twenty-eight hundred of these workers were year-round professionals, whose salaries were generally considered adequate if comparable to those in public education.

At the same time technological advances, decreasing hours of labor, rising incomes, and further decline in the bias against recreation as flagrant idleness hastened the upward trend of many forms of leisure activity. Golf boomed in popularity while amateur as well as professional sports and athletics attracted new record numbers of participants and spectators. Americans increasingly moved from simpler to costlier apparatus for recreation; autos and motorboats replaced bicycles and rowboats. Movies drew still more fans, while fraternal lodges declined. Despite the sudden advent of radio, the PRAA, preoccupied with its ongoing program, virtually ignored this much used new device while yet continuing to promote community singing which had decreased greatly in popularity since the war.[14]

Coupled with these increases in recreation activities and facilities was a growing attention in public discussion to the importance of the wise use of leisure. Lee, chief spokesman of the PRAA on this issue, called for studies of how people actually used free time. Agreeing with numerous observers that such activities as movies were often less than imaginative forms of recreation, he advocated a program of education in the public schools for the creative employment of leisure. Convinced that expressive leisure was necessary to combat the boredom of life on industrial assembly lines, he brought the issue to public notice in the publications and congresses of the PRAA.[15]

Others joined Lee's crusade; newspaperman Arthur Pound, for instance, both at a congress and in a book entitled *The Iron Man in Industry* (1922), echoed Lee's ideas. Nicholas Murray Butler, educational reformer and president of Columbia University, in his presidential report for 1924 also asked guidance in the right use of leisure. George B. Cutten, head of Colgate University, followed with his pleas to face *The Threat of Leisure* (1926) and improve the quality of spare time in America.[16] Writers such as these perceptively recognized not only problems inherent in industrialism, such as workers' boredom and loss of craftsmanship, but also opportunities for bettering man and society through the use of additional leisure. They found, however, that identifying a problem is often easier than solving it; few if any of these authors made workable, concrete proposals by which to implement systematic public education for leisure.

Nevertheless the PRAA as well as a host of other organizations, public and private, were enlarging or initiating actions in the field of public recreation. City park executives increasingly accepted active sports and games as a valid use of parks which had hitherto often been reserved for leisurely strolling but unavailable for organized games. Improved transportation via the automobile meant rapidly rising numbers of visitors each year to state and national parks and forests despite the relative inaccessibility of most of the national parks. Given this new interest in state recreation, the PRAA might have encouraged formation of state agencies specifically to assist municipal recreation. Braucher felt, however, that most public recreation belonged primarily on a local level, as close to the people as possible. In addition state agencies might duplicate services of the apolitical PRAA. Similar comments applied to the unlikely possibility of a federal bureau of recreation. All the same, Congress annually appropriated limited funds for campsites in national forests. Meanwhile both the federal Children's Bureau and Office of Education added specialists in recreation to their staffs. More and more people began to call for a nationwide outdoor recreation system utilizing federal lands.[17]

All of these governmental activities were complemented by an expanding interest in recreation and leisure on the part of many private groups; the PRAA listed thirty such national organizations in its revised edition of the *Normal Course in Play*. Sensing a need for regular exchange of ideas among executive directors of nationwide social work associations, Braucher played a major part in forming a National Social Work Council, which was to be absorbed decades later by the National Social Welfare Assembly.[18] The PRAA also assisted numerous groups, including the National Congress of Parents and Teachers and the General Federation of Women's Clubs, in promoting public recreation through their local affiliates.[19] Smaller societies interested in leisure, such as the National Conference on State Parks and the Drama League of America, sought to merge with the growing PRAA, but Lee and Braucher chose not to burden their organization by taking on financial responsibility for these groups. The two leaders also naturally opposed plans to create new organizations to take over or duplicate specific parts of the work of the PRAA. They were convinced that the Association was fully capable of serving as the major voluntary society and only clearinghouse of information in the area of recreation and leisure. Similarly they refrained from interfering with projects done by other groups in areas outside of recreation.[20]

Despite Braucher's and Lee's confidence in the fast-growing PRAA as the central organization in American recreation, the rapid upswing of all sorts of recreation following the war led to the birth in 1924 of the privately funded National Conference on Outdoor Recreation, a coordinating group broader in scope in some respects than the PRAA but emphasizing activities in the great outdoors rather than urban outdoor recreation. The conference was largely the idea of Assistant Secretary of the Navy Theodore Roosevelt, Jr. The outcome of his initiative was the conference itself, a three-day affair in May 1924 which attracted 309 official delegates from 128 diverse organizations including the PRAA, YMCA, American Bison Society, American Historical Association, Sierra Club, United Spanish War Veterans, and National Horseshoe Pitchers' Association, all with purported interests in the outdoors.[21] The conference was expected to assist in developing a national policy to coordinate the disorganized activities of all public and private agencies in providing outdoor recreation for America. Among the twenty-two projects of the conference were a study of the recreation value of highways and a campaign for the preservation of elk herds in Yellowstone National Park. The conference also made a series of prophetic recommendations looking toward a definite federal policy on outdoor recreation.

Although the PRAA was one of the more active private associations in the projects of the conference, Lee and Braucher soon came to see the conference as a potential threat to the leading position of the PRAA in municipal recreation. While the conference officially denied any intention to become a superagency capable of assuming services already performed by member organizations such as the PRAA, several key leaders of the conference clearly harbored such ideas. For instance, they desired to publish material on recreation training which in effect duplicated publications of the PRAA. The conference also proposed that the PRAA limit the scope of its work but did not offer any solution for filling the gap which would result.[22] Braucher and Lee privately expressed fear that the conference might wastefully duplicate the actions of existing effective groups. They also opposed the idea of a superagency as did men such as Lee Hanmer of the Russell Sage Foundation; in fact, Joseph Lee secretly hoped that the small but ambitious permanent organization of the conference would die.[23] Publicly, however, the PRAA took a full part in the group by joining in committees, loaning staff members, and undertaking research projects.[24]

The most significant study done by the PRAA for the conference was a comprehensive $50,000 survey of acreage and administration of municipal and county parks. Since the American Institute of Park Executives assisted the PRAA in the work, the project was symbolic of a growing unity between parks and public recreation, which were no longer divided, respectively, into either landscape parks devoid of sports and games or aesthetically barren playgrounds. Braucher chose top field secretary Lebert Weir to direct the two-year study with the support of a national advisory committee of professionals in parks and recreation. Weir was the logical choice since he was especially interested in parks and already served as the chief connection in the expanding cooperation between the PRAA and the American Institute of Park Executives with their somewhat different clientele. Park leaders increasingly followed the example of men such as V. K. Brown, an imaginative pacesetter who introduced a broad range of organized recreation into the parks of Chicago. Weir helped strengthen this interest in recreation and a wider function for municipal parks through a long-lasting special field service developed to follow up his survey and lengthy book, *Parks: A Manual of Municipal and County Parks*, which grew out of the survey.[25] Nevertheless influential leaders in both parks and independent recreation agencies, concerned with their own lines of work, were not farsighted enough to promote a merger of organizations representing parks with the PRAA, which might just as well have come in the 1920s as four decades later.

Weir's detailed study was but one part of a successful effort by Braucher to expand the scope of PRAA activity in research and publication. In addition to *Recreation* and the lengthening lists of promotional and technical pamphlets long a part of the services of the PRAA, Braucher and his staff developed a series of concise bulletins for the rapid dissemination of information to municipal recreation heads. Gradually the bulletins grew more specialized; separate editions served, for example, leaders of recreation for rural people and industrial workers. Bulletins were a way to draw attention to the many handbooks and short technical reports on specific topics which the PRAA issued for use by local groups administering recreation.[26]

Lee and Braucher also saw the need for substantial studies in certain areas such as commercial recreation, city planning for recreation, and recreation in parks. For several years they mulled over plans for a research department in the PRAA. Then, late in

1925, Lee Hanmer, head of recreation for the Russell Sage Foundation, advocated a new organization devoted exclusively to research in recreation. The possibility of such a group, which might take over the research function of the PRAA, spurred Braucher to action; he hastily contacted Lee, and within two weeks the directors of the PRAA authorized Braucher to establish a department of research if funds were available.[27]

Meanwhile, although the PRAA spent increasing amounts on research and produced a number of major studies, several serious shortcomings in planning characterized its research efforts and to some extent the entire operation of the Association.[28] Lee and Braucher, perhaps justifiably, believed that the national lack of public recreation, which persisted despite notable progress, called for action rather than study. Outside the PRAA as well, promoters and administrators, rather than researchers, clearly dominated the recreation movement by the 1920s. Braucher, the self-confident progressive, apparently seldom questioned his basic assumptions or systematically considered the entire range of alternatives for topics of recreation research, the PRAA in particular, or the recreation movement in general.

In the matter of research, for instance, he might have appointed a committee of qualified experts to survey the whole field of possibilities, delineate priority in needed studies, and offer subsidies to the ablest individuals available to undertake the most pressing research. The National Tuberculosis Association, for example, followed this procedure early in the decade. Such a group, not unlike committees of experts employed by the PRAA for various tasks since before 1910, naturally would have included members of the staff as well as others. Instead Braucher personally took charge of aiding scholarly research and obtained a three-year grant to support Professor Clark Hetherington, a leading physical educator long associated with the PRAA, in a scheme to produce an entire series of books on physical education and recreation. Plagued by failing health and numerous commitments, Hetherington was unable to finish any of the proposed books although the PRAA spent $18,000 on his efforts. While this disappointing venture did not kill Braucher's interest in research, he tended to select for new projects more practical topics, frequently descriptive rather than analytical, which could be handled mainly by staff members.[29] This reliance on the staff, instead of an interdisciplinary committee with members of various leading institutions, also raised some question as to whether or not the PRAA was keeping pace with the latest advances in related fields.

The PRAA in the 1920s began various new programs. Ernest T. Attwell joined the staff and spent nearly three decades promoting municipal recreation for blacks. In 1928 Braucher added a female field secretary to enhance recreation for women and girls. Augustus D. Zanzig directed a national study of music in American culture and became the PRAA's consultant on music and recreation.

If the PRAA neglected periodically to secure broad, systematic analyses of research needs in recreation, the same deficiency was generally true of operations and goals of the Association itself. Three times in the decade after World War I, for example, leaders of the National Municipal League, a voluntary association fostering improved city government, critically examined the basic policies and procedures of the organization. Braucher and Lee, however, except for their initial reorganization of the PRAA after Gulick's departure, apparently were so sure of their cause that they never undertook or authorized an organized critical evaluation of operations and policy of the PRAA solely for the purpose of planning. The closest they came to this sort of systematic critique of the PRAA was a self-analysis by the staff completed as part of an appeal for a major endowment. Such an appraisal might have been even more valuable if done by an objective committee of experts in recreation and related fields outside of the PRAA staff. This kind of examination by outsiders who did not hesitate to criticize organization and administration would, understandably enough, not be particularly popular with managers who might well have reason to fear such scrutiny. For instance, such an impartial but critical study of the management and finances of the National Tuberculosis Association in 1924 had been suppressed as a result of strong reaction from the management group.[30]

An example of the tendency of the PRAA to broaden previous policies and react to outside events rather than actively seek creative new alternatives could be seen in its handling of professionalism among recreation administrators. The PRAA might well have taken the initiative in founding a professional association for such executives in the 1920s. Indeed similar associations had existed in physical education and park administration, two lines of work increasingly involved in organized recreation, since the late nineteenth century. Yet Braucher chose to foster professionalism without formal organization. He called, for instance, for the opinions of local recreation executives on matters such as outlining the responsibilities and tasks of a city recreation superintendent. Upon the request of these executives assembled at an annual congress, he established a national committee on a code of ethics for public recreation administrators. The PRAA also published standards of minimum adequacy, such as those required for recreation leadership and facilities in a city of one hundred thousand against which individual cities might compare themselves.[31] The major contribution of the PRAA to professionalism in public recreation in the

1920s was, however, in training executives capable of administering the growing local systems of municipal recreation.

Braucher and Lee both recognized that one of the greatest problems facing municipal recreation in the 1920s was a shortage of trained professionals which developed as city after city added recreation workers to municipal payrolls. The supply of experienced professionals that did exist seemed concentrated in cities with well-established municipal recreation or in the staff of the PRAA; it was not unusual for cities to try to hire the field secretaries of the PRAA. To help fill this void directly after the war Braucher had utilized his earlier experiences in training hundreds of community organizers for War Camp Community Service. He established a month-long training program in Chicago to prepare leaders for organized recreation. The course, dealing with many phases of executive and administrative operations in community recreation, was taught by the best experts Braucher could find and provided valuable education to some nine hundred individuals in its six-year history.[32]

Braucher realized, of course, that a month of training could not possibly produce an executive fully qualified to fill the higher positions in municipal recreation systems. Nor did another alternative, university training, appear very promising. Lee had personally paid the salary for five years of a professor at Harvard who taught several courses in recreation, but this experiment neither matured into a full-fledged course of study nor produced many active workers in recreation. Other colleges offered only a number of scattered courses. Not only Braucher and Lee, but also many local recreation officials, who turned to the PRAA for hundreds of recommended workers annually, agreed that the need for better training of new local staff members was of fundamental importance. Local executives of large systems were themselves able to train workers for lower positions, but preparation of higher level administrators was another matter. Faced with this intensifying problem, Braucher first tried to raise funds to convert the month-long course into an advanced, one-year program.[33]

Although the money was not forthcoming, Braucher, Lee, and the directors of the PRAA in October 1925 agreed that a separate National Recreation School ought to be established the following year if at all possible. After conference with representatives of several leading universities, Braucher and Lee decided that the school, in order to maintain maximum cooperation and contact with local leaders of public recreation, ought to be run directly by the PRAA rather than by a university. Accordingly the board voted in December 1925 to establish a graduate National Recreation School in New York to begin classes the following September. So concerned with the school were the directors that they authorized funds for its operation even if this meant restricting other work of the PRAA.[34]

The school, more a technical institute than a graduate school, opened its doors for the first class of forty students in September 1926. Each student took a thirty-four week course of study which was refined and enlarged from the instruction given at Chicago. In addition to formal classes, students spent twelve hours each week in practice work as recreation leaders. The curriculum was mainly of a practical nature and frequently emphasized solutions to the variety of problems encountered by a municipal superintendent of recreation. Over thirty topics, among them directing group music, drama, games, and camping; developing a balanced program of public recreation for all citizens with a variety of facilities; and meeting problems of personnel, finances, and cooperation with other agencies, received attention. In short, Braucher designed the school to produce professionals trained in all aspects of the organization and administration of municipal recreation. As faculty and special lecturers the school had Lee, other staff members of the PRAA, university professors, leaders in voluntary groups dealing with recreation, and outstanding heads of local recreation systems. Each of the instructors presented both his own expert knowledge and the best serviceable ideas on a given topic flowing in to the PRAA from the field.[35] With systematic training thus available for the first time to prepare able candidates for top-level executive positions, Braucher and his staff believed that the school was one of the most fundamental advances thus far in the evolution of the administration of public recreation as a profession and a service. Experience was to reveal that their confidence in the school was fully justified.

With the school well underway and contributions to the PRAA again at new record heights by early 1927, Braucher inaugurated a long-needed series of short training institutes for rural residents. For years the PRAA in its field service had neglected small towns and rural villages simply because experience had shown that such areas generally lacked the numbers and resources to support board programs of organized recreation. Meanwhile the federal Department of Agriculture, followed by the states, had been rapidly increasing its rural extension services, chiefly in technical matters but also in social organization to alleviate the isolation of farm life. After half a decade of pleas by men from the Department of Agriculture for special rural service and following unsuccessful attempts to raise funds specifically for the work, Braucher managed to include rural leadership institutes in the regular budget.[36]

Only two states were doing anything to develop rural recreation on May 1, 1927, when field secretary John Bradford began his service to farm areas. The need for his work was evident, since within two weeks requests poured in to fill his schedule two years in advance. Bradford's popular institutes, given in cooperation with federal and state extension agencies, provided training to teach local volunteers how to organize a variety of recreation activities, including many of the same kinds of events promoted in urban areas. Eventually five men were simultaneously giving rural training in what became one of the most successful programs of the PRAA, resulting in some seventy thousand trained volunteers and much more governmental activity in rural recreation. After thirteen years, the demand was to become so great that twenty-seven states employed experts in rural recreation.[37]

The popular rural institutes, which expanded the scope of operations of the Association, were only one of several special programs Braucher was able to bring to fruition during the record prosperity of the PRAA in the late 1920s. As income mounted, he gradually cut general field work back to around half of his budget and also initiated new, intensified services in a number of areas dealing with particular groups or activities long recognized but little served by the PRAA. One such problem was the securing of land for parks and playgrounds as cities expanded. The problem of high land prices, seen at its worst in crowded cities, might have been solved by obtaining sites for recreation prior to development of plats. With this matter in mind, Seattle recreation promoter and PRAA director Austin E. Griffiths had several times had a bill introduced in the state legislature of Washington which would have required 10 percent of all newly subdivided land in or near cities to be donated to the public for recreation sites. None of Griffiths's bills became law, however, nor did similar tactics in other states lead to effective action.[38]

William E. Harmon, wealthy New York real estate developer and supporter of the PRAA, offered other alternatives to Griffiths's condemnation proposals. Harmon had created the Harmon Foundation which, with the aid of the PRAA, had made grants and loans to help some seventy-seven towns purchase playgrounds by 1927. He also decided that convincing developers voluntarily to set aside sites for public recreation would yield better results than the ill-fated attempts to secure mandatory legislation. Harmon knew from his own business experience that the cost of donating land for recreation could be easily offset by the resultant rise in value of the remaining salable lots. To implement the plan, the Harmon Foundation beginning in 1927 financed a special field worker of the PRAA in a campaign of persuasion, publicity, and awards to convince both the public and land developers of mutual benefits from the scheme.[39] The project was, however, only partially successful; and within a few years economic problems at the Harmon Foundation, as well as quarrels with the PRAA over control of the work, caused the demise of the service.

Braucher secured funds in the late 1920s to initiate special full-time service in other areas besides the work with land developers. For many years the PRAA had wanted an éxpert on the particular problems of athletics and recreation for females. With women and girls increasingly moving into public athletics as well as other areas of society, Braucher announced in January 1928 that a new feminine field secretary would begin work in this hitherto neglected area.[40] At the same time the PRAA augmented its efforts in the promotion of music. In March a special field secretary, funded by a two-year grant from a leading foundation, started an experiment aimed at developing greater governmental support of music education in small towns and rural areas. The representative operated first in upstate New York, where she convinced numerous local school boards to appropriate funds to employ music teachers who could by law receive part of their salaries from the state. Meanwhile the PRAA, after a year's wait, secured Augustus D. Zanzig of Harvard University to direct a comprehensive national music study in ninety-seven cities and towns to learn the current and potential state of musical activities in American communities, homes, and schools. After completing his study, *Music in American Life*, Zanzig joined the permanent staff of the PRAA as a music expert.[41] Still another special field secretary added near the end of the decade provided assistance in development of organized recreation in institutions such as orphanages. These new special field services were in keeping with the general expansion of the PRAA throughout the 1920s.

Had Braucher more systematically evaluated possible services of the PRAA, he might well have begun still other special work. As it had in the past, the PRAA generally ignored commercial recreation. Industrial recreation, also a long-standing interest, was another matter. During the 1920s it frequently became a tool of paternalism and anti-union efforts by management. Government studies showed many companies discontinuing recreation programs since workers suspected ulterior motives by management, and the movement seemed past its peak by 1928. The PRAA accordingly elected to emphasize instead participation by factory workers in normal municipal programs.[42] In other areas, notably recreation in hospitals and programs for the elderly, the PRAA had wide-open opportunities to become a pacesetter, yet these fields were not extensively developed until several decades later.

All of these expanded activities naturally had to be paid for. While the fund-raising efforts of the PRAA produced record returns almost every year of the decade, the solicitation of the Association was not entirely on a firm foundation. The PRAA confidently depended for fund raising almost completely upon its own staff and the local sponsor method although it might have benefited from the services of professional fund-raising concerns emerging in the 1920s.

In the face of this apparent success, Braucher nonetheless found increasing difficulty in attracting new donations. More and more local and national charities, as well as educational and medical institutions, annually joined the scramble for the philanthropic dollar in competition with one another and the PRAA. Another problem was the very nature of the appeal of the PRAA, which often seemed nebulous when compared to such concrete, immediate needs as aid to victims of disaster. Then, too, the PRAA had no uniform local branches, as did the YMCA and numerous other organizations, which provided obvious evidence of their work. Instead, public recreation, geared to individual towns, might be available under the auspices of women's clubs, parks, schools, or playground commissions, none of which bore the insignia of the Association. In addition the alleged benefits of supervised public recreation, as well as the operations of the PRAA other than field work, seemed for the most part intangible and difficult to measure. A number of one-time PRAA fund raisers later were unusually successful with professional fund-seeking concerns and testified that it was much easier to secure gifts to institutions such as colleges and hospitals than to the PRAA.

The rising budget of the PRAA did not keep pace with soaring local budgets for public recreation in the decade, and Braucher was unable to extend the annual list of contributors much beyond 15,000. The PRAA reportedly had a reputation for efficient money

raising among national social work organizations, but this is difficult to assess since it has been traditionally hard to obtain accu-
rate data on such operations from voluntary health and welfare
associations. Although the number of large individual gifts to the
PRAA rose significantly and it collected a record $386,000 in gen-
eral contributions during 1929, the rate of growth had tapered off
and did not meet Braucher's expectations.[43]

No doubt one important outside factor affecting this rising
budget was joint solicitation by groups in community chests. In
the 1920s the chest idea increasingly spread and raised great sums
of money, but the PRAA as a rule joined chests only as a last re-
sort. Braucher and Lee opposed centralized control by chests over
funds of independent groups. Since numerous chests allocated
funds mainly to local operating agencies and many givers felt their
duty done after a lump gift to a chest, the PRAA often found its
returns lessened in cities with chests regardless of whether or not
it participated in such joint drives. Mindful of these factors, the
two leaders preferred independent fund raising by separate organizations.

The PRAA was scarcely alone in this dilemma over chests. Like
the PRAA, national health associations without local branches had
either to raise funds nationally on their own, a difficult task at
best, or join chests and accept usually stable but small quotas
with little possibility for growth. Nationwide causes in general
faced the same problem, and many of them, such as the YMCA and
Boy Scouts of America, opted to join chests. Contributions to
chests overall and to the PRAA rose at about the same rate in the
decade, but increasingly after 1929 the advantage was to be clearly
with the chests.[44]

In contrast to their experience with chests, Braucher and Lee
persevered in attempts to gain support from foundations and were
significantly successful with one notable institution. The Laura
Spelman Rockefeller Memorial did far more for the Association
than any other foundation, with the exception of the crucial backing of the Russell Sage Foundation in the early years of the Association. Ever since the outbreak of World War I, the Memorial had
generously aided War Camp Community Service, Community Service, and the PRAA and also had funded most of the special projects of the Association in the 1920s, such as Weir's study of parks.
Finally the heads of the memorial, convinced of the genuine value
of the PRAA, appropriated an unrestricted $500,000 to the Associa-
tion for the dozen years beginning in 1929. Total Rockefeller funds

given to Braucher's three groups equalled $1,749,000 within a decade.[45]

Buttressed by the gift from the Rockefellers, Braucher and Lee made 1929 one of the most active years in the history of the PRAA. Expenditures for regular and special services reached $428,000. The PRAA provided field service on request to 316 cities in 44 states and sent special organizers of activities such as music, drama, and surveys to aid 228 cities in broadening their programs of public recreation. Citizens from some six thousand different areas received specific answers to nearly twenty-four thousand queries through correspondence or consultation. Besides striving to secure increased municipal acceptance of responsibility for public recreation and a growing scope and knowledge of recreation, the PRAA added significantly to the training and professionalization of leaders for organized recreation. For instance, the Association helped fill over seven hundred positions in recreation leadership across the country. More than seven thousand rural leaders received training at seventy-eight institutes held in thirty-four states, and thirty-three students completed the course at the National Recreation School.[46]

Surely such work of the PRAA, guided by Lee and Braucher, must have been a major factor behind the record levels attained by public recreation in the 945 cities which reported in the yearbook of the PRAA for 1929. The returns for that year showed $33.5 million, almost entirely from governmental sources, spent for public recreation, including operation of over thirteen thousand separate recreation sites by nearly thirty-three thousand paid workers and seven thousand four hundred volunteers. Of these persons, fourteen thousand were enrolled in training classes. In five years the number of cities with public recreation supported entirely by municipal funds had risen from 302 to 586, whereas the corresponding numbers funded only with private dollars had declined from 195 to 134.[47]

Despite the real progress being made in the field, public recreation in America as a whole was still woefully lacking when compared to standards of adequate leadership and facilities suggested by the PRAA. One estimate in 1930, for example, guessed that less than one-fifth of school-age children had access to playgrounds. Public recreation was faced perhaps not so much with opposition in the 1920s as with inertia. In short, as a key aide told Braucher, the PRAA had not put its message across to many Americans. Numerous citizens still thought of play and recreation only in

terms of summer playgrounds for children; even people seeking
out the office of the PRAA were surprised at the group's wide
range of activities.[48]

Although the growing PRAA concentrated on improving and
enlarging municipal organized recreation, nearly all phases of recreation and the use of leisure, whether public, private, or commercial, ranging from local to national activities and agencies, had
undergone a decade of marked expansion by 1929. Not only golf
and camping, but also automobile travel and the use of radios had
soared in the 1920s. To meet the rising demand for recreation
services, new facilities, including national parks, tennis courts,
stadiums, and motion picture palaces, had become part of the
American landscape. No doubt segments of this general upswing
of interest in recreation and leisure provided both competition
and encouragement to the record-breaking progress of municipal
recreation and its prime national instigator, the PRAA. One authority estimated that Americans spent perhaps $10.2 billion an-
nually on all sorts of recreation by 1930. Notwithstanding the work
of the PRAA and its supporters, individuals expended three times
as much on the pleasure use of motorboats as cities used for public playgrounds.[49] The permanence of all of these developments
was, however, soon to be tested by an economic disaster which
would influence every phase of American life, including those goals
so ardently desired by men such as Braucher and Lee.

The Great Depression created enforced leisure for millions of unemployed Americans.

6
The New Deal and the National Recreation Association

Late in 1929, as the PRAA was finishing a record year, the stock market crash plunged the nation into the worst depression it had ever experienced and signaled the arrival of a fateful decade for the Association as well. The Great Depression was to affect several generations of Americans and nearly every aspect of life in the United States. Within a few years the gross national product would shrink to half its former size, and one-fourth of the civilian labor force would be unemployed. As state, local, and private resources were to prove incapable of meeting the soaring relief rolls, an energetic new president and administration would channel massive federal aid to the unemployed.[1] In these circumstances the PRAA, weakened by reduced contributions and aging leadership, increasingly would have to share its role as self-appointed spokesman for public recreation in America with a host of new faces. These were to represent not only federal agencies but also rival private interests in an area where the Association had once enjoyed almost unequaled national leadership.

Meanwhile early in the 1930s much increased leisure, which the PRAA had long been warning the nation to prepare for, had finally arrived, even though it came in an entirely unexpected way. Ironically, the drop in average hours of labor and the gain in spare time were to come as much from the harsh conditions of the depression as from technological advances and legislative restrictions, such as the National Industrial Recovery Act (1933) and the Fair Labor Standards Act (1938), both of which were to provide for the forty-hour workweek.[2] At any rate, people did have significantly more time free from work, and Braucher and Lee hoped Americans both on and off relief would now accept the opportunities promoted by the Association for a truly creative use of leisure. Although many unemployed citizens used public recreation facilities more than before, the work ethic was still far from dead, even among the jobless. Given their enforced idleness, such people could hardly be expected to approach free time with the same healthy attitude as those regularly employed. This situation presented public recreation advocates with a challenge to adapt recreation to help meet the physical and psychological needs felt by millions of jobless people unhappy with their spare time.

As unemployment mounted, leaders of the Association seemed at first to feel that encouraging words might successfully assist people in adjusting to the new leisure, just as President Herbert Hoover apparently believed public declarations of faith in the economy would restore general confidence. The PRAA took several actions to gain wider public support for a positive, broader concept of recreation and leisure. Among the first of these moves was the long-needed name change to National Recreation Association (NRA). While this switch in mid-1930 finally removed the by-then restrictive term "playground" from the title of the Association, the transfer itself was hardly enough to remold convincingly the image many people had of the NRA as a child-centered group.[3]

A few months later the directors authorized Lee to appoint a National Leisure Time Committee to explain to the nation the importance of training for the wise use of idle hours.[4] Lee chose, however, not to carry out this proposal for publicity. As an alternative he secured Lawrence P. Jacks, British advocate of adult education and professor of philosophy at Manchester College, Oxford, for a nine-month lecture tour in America. Jacks took his own message, in large part the gospel of creative recreation and leisure fostered by the NRA but developed independently in a similar industrial society, to an estimated twenty thousand local leaders throughout America. The plan of his successful trip, which began in 1931, was to emphasize the philosophy and deeper meaning of recreation rather than the role of the NRA as an institution.[5]

Jacks was not the only foreigner to draw the attention of the NRA, which expanded its operations to the point where a promising beginning was made toward permanent international cooperation among recreation organizations from numerous nations. Director Herbert May, an internationally minded Pittsburgh businessman, had made contacts with several dozen people and agencies in nine European countries during a study of leisure on the continent. Then in 1932 the NRA hosted the long-desired first international recreation congress in hopes of further spreading its ideas abroad. The congress, held in Los Angeles just before the Olympic games in the same city, drew more than one hundred foreign delegates. They discussed worldwide implications of leisure and found the meeting so worthwhile that they called for a second such event to coincide with the 1936 Olympics in Berlin. In the meantime, however, Hitler was to rise to power. Sensing that the affair would be used for Nazi propaganda, the NRA, firmly placing the principles of freedom and democracy over mere expediency, would refuse to participate, although this decision was to retard development of international services by the Association for decades.[6] The Nazi-manipulated German recreation movement, *Kraft durch Freude*, also was to provide Braucher and Lee with a graphic example of what might happen to local public recreation under the standardized control of a national government.

Braucher was continually on the lookout for domestic alternatives which the NRA could employ to help Americans make better use of the increasing free time of the early 1930s. Since true recreation was chosen voluntarily by individuals, he decided to undertake a study of possible differences in what people actually did and what they would like to do for recreation if given more opportunity. Such a check might enable the NRA and public recreation to mold their services more along the lines of what Americans said they wanted for recreation rather than in line with arbitrary decisions as to what they ought to desire. There was, of course, the danger that respondents might prefer fads, whereas public recreation had to spend municipal funds in programs of enduring merit. The survey of leisure activities and desires of five thousand representative citizens completed by the NRA in 1934 revealed that reading and listening to radio were the most common American pastimes. Nevertheless, out of a list of ninety-four activities, people indicated that they actually preferred tennis, swimming, and other outdoor sports favored by the NRA—activities in which there was considerable scope for the provision of public facilities and programs.[7] But Braucher did not overlook the popularity of other inexpensive varieties of outdoor recreation. In the late thirties he secured approval from the directors to hire specialists to set up services for training, publication, and field work in such areas as arts and crafts, nature lore, and gardening.[8]

The NRA was, of course, not alone in desiring constructive use of leisure in America. Few individuals and other organizations could escape noticing the new free time generated during the depression. Otto T. Mallery, an economist and long-time director of the NRA, bluntly told Braucher: "The National Recreation Association has staked out one of the richest gold mines in the United States. For years to come others will be mining it."[9] Mallery was right; the flow of books and articles dealing with leisure more than doubled the record rate set in the previous decade. In addition, a wide variety of organizations, ranging from the newborn Leisure League of America, which produced booklets on hobbies, to the White House Conference on Child Health and Protection called by President Hoover, asked for and received advice on leisure and recreation from the NRA.[10]

One group in which Braucher was especially interested, and which he may well have initiated, was the short-lived New York Committee on the Use of Leisure Time. Both Braucher and educator John H. Finley, vice-president of the NRA, served on this citizens' committee, which was chaired by Braucher's good friend Raymond Fosdick. Aided particularly by the staff of the NRA, the committee studied opportunities for the use of leisure in the city and, in a report written primarily by Braucher, recommended a series of steps by municipal and private organizations to improve the situation. Nonetheless the committee was soon to fold as a result of poor planning; it did not include adequate representation of municipal recreation agencies and lacked either the power to compel or the influence to persuade various groups to take effective action on its proposals. In addition the whole idea was somewhat irrelevant to the severe times of the depression since most jobless New Yorkers were more interested in employment, food, and shelter than in enjoying their enforced leisure. Several days of hearings held by the committee attracted national attention and considerable derision, which did not, however, lessen Braucher's enthusiasm for the idea of similar hearings in other cities to draw publicity and cooperative attacks on the problem of leisure. Fosdick was more realistic. Skeptical of the whole scheme, he had assumed the chairmanship reluctantly and years later was to recall the project as "a waste of time—a piece of showmanship."[11]

The interest in recreation shown by certain leaders of the National Education Association lasted longer than Fosdick's committee. Braucher cooperated with the teachers' group on several important new projects, but because of a lack of funds, he repeatedly had to deny requests that the NRA establish a branch office with the National Education Association headquarters in Washington.[12] Eventually this attention to recreation by educators would lead to a renewal of the debate on whether recreation, with its decades of proximity to the public schools, was a part of education or indeed an independent field.

At this crucial point in the history of the NRA, which was faced with potential challenges and duplication by many outside interests, old age began to overtake key figures in the organization. Joseph Lee was the prime example; in 1932 he was seventy years old and had to curtail his activities as his health gradually failed. He was ready to resign a year later but was still in office four years hence when he died of pneumonia after twenty-seven years as president. Despite repeated urging, his son Joseph, Jr., declined an active role in the Association. Lee's daughter Susan then joined the board of directors, on which she also was to serve to an advanced age.

For some years before Lee's passing, Braucher, who had benefited from Lee's guidance for decades, had been required to manage the NRA by himself. Lee's death cost the NRA not only its president but also an able public spokesman. Braucher, shy and retiring by contrast, rarely made speeches and spent most of his time in his office, hardly a major asset to public relations efforts by the NRA. For assistance he had an able, experienced staff of several dozen workers, which had included fourteen field secretaries in 1930. By 1933 six staff members had served over twenty years, almost as long as Braucher himself; twelve had been with the NRA over fifteen years; and twenty-eight had more than ten years of service. Of ten leading staff members who were to make careers lasting from two to five decades at the NRA, seven were graduates of institutions such as Wellesley, Yale, Cornell, and the universities of California and Wisconsin. Although several of the staff were experienced social workers, many of them gained their special knowledge of recreation while with the NRA.

A majority of the aging board of directors had given more than fifteen years of service, and about one-third of them had served during nearly all of Lee's years as president.[13] Both Braucher and the directors recognized the great need to draw in younger people who would be ready later to assume responsibility for the NRA. This requirement, however, was not notably met in the 1930s. For instance, Vice-President John H. Finley succeeded Lee as president at the age of seventy-four but died within three years.

To compound the problems of the NRA, already faced with mounting external competition and weakened leadership, the depression brought a financial crisis. By 1932 local spending on public recreation declined to $28 million, off one-third from the record set two years earlier. General contributions to the NRA, which offered the average citizen fewer tangible benefits than local programs, fell even faster and plummeted from a high of $386,000 in 1929 to $209,000 in 1932. Six years later these contributions were to shrink to $143,000, a low point which would last five years before recovery began. Moreover the large gifts from the Rockefeller Foundation were scheduled to taper off within a few years. Thus Braucher and the directors, hampered by the loss of generous contributor and skillful fund raiser Lee, searched for rich men or foundations to guarantee support to the NRA. Yet the quest proved futile, and Braucher had to cut back many NRA services, such as promotional field work, to stave off financial collapse.[14]

The situation would have been worse but for the invested resources of the war fund collected by the Association in 1917. By 1930 these assets had amounted to over $2.7 million and formed the capital of a new corporation, the National Recreation School, which had as its best-known function the operation of its graduate school with the same title. Lee and Braucher wisely held the assets of the corporation intact, although they used dividends to follow the precedent of the defunct postwar War Camp Community Service in quietly subsidizing work credited to the NRA. The school spent more than $100,000 annually and was gradually to become a securities-holding corporation which made grants to support operating programs of the NRA.[15] This aid did not, however, come near to offsetting the decline in general contributions.

For various reasons Braucher did not develop several other possible sources of increased funding. He might have secured a net gain in contributions by increasing the percentage of returns spent on fund raising, but he rejected this method as a matter of principle. Apparently he actually decreased the sums allocated to fund raising in the 1930s as compared to the prosperity decade. Al-

The NRA dealt with increased free time in various ways. Lee sent British professor L. P. Jacks on a long lecture tour to stimulate education for leisure. Editor John H. Finley, long a proponent of constructive leisure, became president upon Lee's death in 1937. Finley (right), a contact with President Roosevelt, introduced Mrs. Roosevelt at the recreation congress of 1934. New Deal governor John G. Winant used NRA consultants in New Hampshire and was ranking officer after Finley.

though new federal tax laws in the 1930s encouraged corporate philanthropy, he refused for years to solicit such funds and risk implying endorsement of any product. Had Braucher systematically reevaluated all other alternatives, he might have sought professional fund-raising counsel or considered joining local community chests, which continued to spread and made a far better showing of dollars collected than did the NRA during the decade.

A wealthy Texan presented a final possibility when he offered to finance a campaign for inclusion of the services of the NRA as part of the federal government, a not unreasonable idea insofar as numerous prominent Americans were calling for federal assumption of the heretofore local and private functions of relief. Although the government was soon to be pouring tens of millions of dollars into public recreation, the idea of federalization was heresy to most of the directors of the NRA. In their eyes a cardinal virtue of the NRA was its position as an independent voluntary association; they felt they simply could not jeopardize the independence of the group by seeking federal funds or status. In addition the directors maintained that the very nature of the individualized work of the NRA, which dealt with the intimate recreation life of the people, ought to be free from the spirit of bureaucracy. Furthermore, they argued, a private NRA, unlike a federal agency, could be apolitical and take the militant attitude frequently called for in leading local campaigns against corruption and for emergency funds for public recreation.[16] Finally, it is doubtful whether Braucher himself, with his years of experience in daily command of the NRA as well as the once-huge War Camp Community Service, could have adjusted to becoming a cog in the federal bureaucracy.

The Association was, of course, hardly alone in its financial predicament; most cities and citizens by 1932 had similar problems. As rolls of jobless workers on relief mounted incessantly, cities trimmed their budgets for recreation and other services. Yet at the same time participation in public recreation programs continued to climb. Increasingly both the NRA and numerous local recreation leaders emphasized municipal recreation not only as a needed service to the unemployed but also as a source of jobs, both in the recreation leadership field and in the construction of facilities. Leaders of the NRA urged city officials not to bow to the financial pinch and eliminate public recreation from municipal budgets. To meet the rising demand for cheap public recreation, the NRA encouraged cities to recruit and train more volunteers and workers on relief. In New York, for instance, the local field worker of the NRA initiated a program to use relief dollars for hiring selected jobless people as playground leaders. The field secretary also provided special in-service training institutes for these several hundred workers.[17]

Meanwhile the directors of the NRA modified their long-standing policy of regarding the city as the only really suitable level of government for extensive, organized recreation. Realistically, the board decided that in the emergency of the depression, the NRA ought to aid state agencies interested in putting jobless men to work in local recreation systems. Welfare officials from New Jersey and Massachusetts were among the first state representatives to use this expert advice from the NRA. In both states pilot programs utilizing citizens on relief as leaders in organized recreation were soon underway. These programs were adaptable to vast expansion in case more funds became available. The most concentrated emergency aid by the NRA to a state, involving numerous specialists and a statewide survey, was to begin shortly in New Hampshire at the request of progressive Governor John G. Winant, a director of the NRA.[18]

With Braucher and the NRA increasingly active in local and state governmental plans to maintain and expand public recreation despite the depression, it was natural for the Association to be approached by men who were considering the use of federal relief in the field of recreation. An obvious place for such action to begin was in the White House, but President Hoover felt that relief, through which recreation might supply both jobs and aid to morale, was primarily a private and local responsibility. Characteristically, he appointed a committee of social workers and other citizens both to advise him and to serve as a clearinghouse for better ideas on relief administration from local authorities. Social worker Fred C. Croxton, assistant director of the committee, came to Braucher in April 1932 seeking suggestions for a statement on how cooperating local groups might provide organized recreation for the unemployed. In response, Braucher had his staff prepare recommendations and also, recalling wartime experiences, assembled representatives of nine national voluntary associations, most of whom had had experience in the Commission on Training Camp Activities, for discussion of the situation. These meetings developed under NRA leadership into the National Education-Recreation Council.[19]

Some people were not satisfied, however, with the results of the private voluntary approach to recreation and relief for the unemployed and brought more radical ideas to the NRA. The Chicago

Recreation Committee, for instance, urged the NRA to support the addition of funds for recreation projects to congressional bills for federal relief appropriations. This was tempting in view of the municipal financial pinch, but Braucher, Lee, and the directors, ever wary of federal control which they feared might harm local and individual freedom in recreation, opposed the suggestion.[20]

By November 1932 local relief efforts had largely broken down and Hoover's oft-promised prosperity had yet to return. In this crisis American voters rejected Hoover; they elected Governor Franklin D. Roosevelt of New York as president and gave him a sweeping majority in Congress. Roosevelt, who was to expand many federal functions at the expense of local governmental and private action, had long been interested in the NRA, having raised money for the Association and participated in the work of War Camp Community Service.[21] Doubtless the new president's knowledge of the NRA helped convince him of the significance of public recreation and perhaps even made him amenable to spending federal funds for recreation, especially when the funds were part of the much more overriding concern for relief.

As the New Deal arrived with its alphabetical array of experimental emergency agencies, Braucher recognized a tremendous opportunity to strengthen public recreation by using it as a source of jobs, both in construction and in leadership, for people on relief. Yet this realization was balanced in his mind by the very real possibility that if the government began to emphasize leadership and guidance in leisure beyond the mere provision of facilities, the result might mean nationally centralized control of individuals' recreation and overpowering competition for the weakened NRA, to which he had devoted his energies for twenty-four years. Furthermore, while he realized the need for expanding federal powers in national emergencies such as World War I and the depression, emergency agencies frequently had a disturbing tendency toward self-interested perpetuation after the crisis had ended, as had been the case with the Council of National Defense.

Cooperative action by private associations was a possible alternative to federal provision of recreation. As early as March 1933 several national voluntary organizations were working through Braucher and his National Social Work Council on plans to supply educational and recreational opportunities for young men in the camps of the Civilian Conservation Corps, one of the first New Deal agencies. Although the plans apparently did not mature into programs, the agency evolved another scheme for voluntary recreation and educational activities in enrollees' spare time. The greatest contribution of the Corps to public recreation in general was, however, not this internal activity but the construction of thousands of recreation facilities, such as campsites and cabins, in local, national, and, especially, state parks.[22]

In the meantime President Roosevelt moved to reproduce on a national scale the large relief and public works programs which he had initiated in New York state under the direction of social worker Harry L. Hopkins. Braucher apparently did not have much influence with Hopkins, although the latter had recently asked the NRA to secure estimates of needs for public recreation facilities and personnel in New York state.[23] In May 1933 Hopkins went to Washington to head the Federal Emergency Relief Administration. This agency was soon financing construction of recreation facilities, such as parks and swimming pools, and also hiring recreation leaders from relief rolls. That fall Hopkins received command of a new, entirely federal operation, the Civil Works Administration, and had to find jobs for four million people in thirty days. This expensive, hastily contrived agency, among other accomplishments, built or improved three thousand five hundred playgrounds and athletic fields in a few months. Although the NRA prepared a manual for the Federal Emergency Relief Administration and supplied advice in some states through field secretaries, neither CWA nor FERA utilized the assistance of the NRA to any great extent. In fact, there was not even a special authorization from Hopkins for recreation projects, which apparently developed haphazardly.[24]

As these emergency agencies poured unprecedented resources into local public recreation, the leaders of the NRA as well as other private citizens became increasingly concerned with the lack of coordination in the federal programs by professionals experienced in recreation. It was obvious to any discerning person that many of the unemployed people given jobs as recreation leaders were not qualified for such positions. With these matters in mind, Braucher himself went to Washington in December for a conference with Hopkins and his staff. Braucher suggested that Hopkins appoint an experienced recreation professional, presumably from the NRA, to his staff to serve as advisor and also help raise standards of the overall emergency recreation program, which varied considerably from area to area. Hopkins vetoed the idea, however, and showed little interest in other efforts by Braucher to utilize national voluntary groups in administering the emergency operation.[25]

By January 1934 Braucher heard a rumor that there were 65 different proposals for federal aid to recreation before the administration. In a fruitless effort, he volunteered to donate a man to Hopkins's staff and then, through John H. Finley, vice-president of the NRA, tried to persuade President Roosevelt to appoint Fosdick as chief federal consultant on leisure. Braucher possibly intended to have Fosdick create an official organization in which the NRA might play a leading role while yet retaining the advantages of independence. Rebuffed, the directors of the NRA decided not to oppose a federal emergency recreation project, although they believed a national program could be run better by a private organization free from the New Deal bureaucracy. Despite his hostility to federalization, Braucher soon found it expedient to send a representative to the nation's capital to provide consultative service to federal agencies.[26]

In spite of new federal action, the depression dragged on, and Roosevelt in January 1935 proposed to Congress a huge public works operation to give employment rather than relief to several million people. By this time Braucher was convinced that the creation of thousands of jobs in recreation would be sufficiently beneficial to offset the probable lowering of performance standards. Accordingly he had staff members Arthur Williams and George Butler prepare a careful estimate, keyed to the president's message, of nationwide needs for personnel and facilities in public recreation. They reported that in recreation leadership alone eighty-two thousand people over and above current personnel were needed to meet standards of adequacy. To ascertain the validity of the data and broaden support for it, Braucher shrewdly asked several local recreation executives as well as the directors of the NRA for their comments.[27] On April 3 Governor Winant of New Hampshire, by now a confirmed New Dealer, presented the estimate to Hopkins. The NRA also offered again to loan an expert to help set up a federal recreation program, but Hopkins, wary of competition and friction among specialists from different fields and organizations, did not accept.[28] Undoubtedly he preferred to have a man loyal to himself rather than to Braucher administer the project; nevertheless, he did use the NRA's estimate in developing his new agency.

In May President Roosevelt appointed Hopkins head of the just-created Works Progress Administration, or WPA, the work relief agency which in four active years was to do more for public recreation than any other agency of the New Deal. The WPA was to spend over $1 billion on local recreation leadership and facilities. These projects, with 40,000 recreation leaders, were to span the entire nation and to include building or improving 12,700 play-

In the 1930s several groups and individuals rose to prominence more or less independent of the NRA. The WPA by 1936 counted nearly six thousand recreation construction projects underway. Several New Deal agencies sponsored a variety of recreation activities. Chicago recreation executive V. K. Brown was the first president of the Society of Recreation Workers in America.

grounds, 8,500 gymnasiums or recreation buildings, 750 swimming pools, 1,000 ice skating rinks, and 64 ski jumps.[29]

To direct this operation, Hopkins chose Eduard C. Lindeman, a liberal sociologist and lecturer who had long been interested in community organization and recreation. He had served briefly in War Camp Community Service, had written several books on the subject, and taught at the New York School of Social Work. Like Braucher, Lindeman believed in municipal responsibility for public recreation, a wide definition of recreation, and the importance of the wise use of leisure time. In addition, however, as he later argued, democracy did not necessarily depend solely on local power; national planning and federal action were required, he maintained, to deal with problems which were national in scope.[30]

Lindeman found, despite his insistence on federal action, that the recreation projects fostered by the WPA were ultimately dependent upon local acceptance for success. Accordingly he borrowed several techniques long used by the NRA in building grass-roots support for public recreation. He established citizens' advisory committees at local and state as well as national levels and required an invitation from local citizens before entering a town with his recreation enterprise, at first aptly named Community Organization for Leisure. Most of the numerous state committees were apparently ineffective insofar as they did not lay foundations for strong, permanent recreation agencies in state governments. A notable exception was the group in North Carolina guided by sociologist Harold D. Meyer of the state university at Chapel Hill, a member of Lindeman's national staff.

Recreation under WPA auspices was, however, immensely popular at the local level. In the first year operations similar to normal community recreation functioned not only in many of the 1,159 cities with permanent public recreation programs but in 1,045 additional towns where the WPA provided the only organized recreation.[31] Nevertheless it remained to be seen whether cities would accept responsibility for the new projects on their own merits after the passing of the all-important incentive of WPA funds and jobs.

The recreation division of the WPA, with its massive influx of leaders and facilities for public recreation in thousands of communities, surely had a significant and probably positive effect on organized recreation; but it also labored with some serious problems. Three years after initiating the program, Lindeman's health began to fail, and university athletic director G. Ott Romney replaced him. Romney had just completed direction of a WPA national survey which criticized the planning and construction of nearly 25 percent of the thousands of WPA-built recreation facilities.[32] After his survey, both the NRA and the WPA placed far more emphasis than before on extensive pre-planning of facilities for recreation. The NRA even added a long-needed planning specialist to its staff.

Romney had also found that the WPA was continually changing policies, rules, and quotas of employees. The resultant confusion intensified the greatest problem, a lack of well-trained leaders in local recreation activities. The primary task of the agency was to provide jobs for the unemployed; thus 90 to 95 percent of recreation leaders were hired merely because they were eligible to receive relief. Contrary to the emphasis given to training and professionalism by the NRA for decades, the factor most important to the WPA was, understandably enough, the number of man-days of relief afforded rather than the quality of leadership. Lindeman was interested in training WPA recreation workers from the start but left final responsibility to the state committees, which responded with a haphazard variety of in-service training programs varying from one-half to ten hours weekly. The education, based chiefly on conferences and institutes which clearly imitated those held earlier by the NRA, eventually touched 174,000 people. Nevertheless, the WPA was to be in business almost five years and past its peak before adequate provisions for training became possible.[33]

Inadequately prepared leaders were one of several key issues in the relations between the WPA and the NRA. At the time the WPA entered the field of recreation with its huge program, the NRA still comprised by far the greatest single store of recreation expertise in the nation. Despite these assets, the leaders of recreation in the WPA left Braucher for the most part on the sidelines, largely ignoring his effective role in organizing recreation during the crisis of World War I. One desirable action might have been periodic, high-level coordination and systematic joint planning for public recreation looking, for instance, to permanence for local recreation projects begun by the WPA, admittedly a temporary agency. Such regular cooperation never developed, perhaps because of instability in WPA operations and philosophic differences between Braucher and the New Dealers.

Relations between the two organizations, which had been cool at first, gradually improved, however, from the top level down through field workers of both groups. Realizing that neither the NRA nor the WPA alone could adequately serve the recreation needs of all Americans, Braucher, Lindeman, and Romney increas-

ingly cooperated on several matters, including the training problem. Many WPA workers received valuable instruction at institutes
held for them across the nation by specialists from the NRA alone
or in conjunction with the WPA. The regular services of the NRA,
such as publications, information, and assistance with personnel
matters, were available as a matter of course to the WPA.[34]

Braucher and the NRA had considerably more direct influence
on the work of the National Youth Administration than on that
of the WPA. The director of this new agency was social worker
Aubrey Williams, who had spent two years working with Community Service in Cincinnati following World War I. Obviously familiar with the NRA, Williams asked Braucher to loan him a staff
expert on recreation, and Braucher sent Arthur Williams, one of
his key aides, to serve as consultant. The two men worked out a
plan whereby the federal agency, which provided part-time employment for young people of high school and college age, included
in its activities construction of recreation facilities, such as school
playgrounds, and the hiring of youths as recreation leaders. Since
the recreation program of the National Youth Administration did
not require the many highly trained personnel which the WPA
might have used and was also much smaller and simpler than recreation in the WPA, Braucher seems to have considered the agency,
unlike the WPA, as neither a threat to professional standards nor
a potential rival to the NRA.[35]

Besides the WPA and the National Youth Administration, other
federal agencies, both regular departments and creations of the
New Deal, increasingly moved into the field of public recreation
and dealt in varying degrees with the NRA. For instance, federal
authorities charged with constructing public housing turned to
the NRA for assistance. The NRA responded with field service,
advice, recommendation of a consultant on recreation later hired
by the housing agency, and a committee of experts which produced
*Play Space in New Neighborhoods; A Report on Standards of Out-
door Recreation in Housing Developments.*[36] Other federal agencies served by the NRA included the Resettlement Administration,
Tennessee Valley Authority, Children's Bureau, Office of Education,
National Resources Board, Extension Service, and Forest Service.
Some of these offices actively provided facilities and limited leadership for recreation; others were concerned only with planning
or publication.[37] The NRA, hard pressed financially, did not believe recreation operations of any of these agencies were significant
enough to warrant assigning staff members as full-time consultants
in the 1930s.

Certain leaders of the National Park Service (NPS), a federal agency more directly concerned with the active promotion of recreation on a large scale, established close relations with the NRA in the mid-1930s. Chief among these men was Conrad Wirth, son of the developer of the famous park system at Minneapolis and friend of NRA field man Lebert Weir. Some leaders of the NPS still felt that its major function was protection of exquisite scenery. Wirth, in contrast, emphasized outdoor recreation as well as conservation as a primary purpose of the parks.[38] He headed the branch of the NPS charged with overseeing the work of the Civilian Conservation Corps in building recreation facilities for state and national parks.

In general "recreation" to the NPS meant facilities for outdoor recreation activities, such as hiking and camping, in large tracts away from crowded cities. For instance, the NPS developed forty-six large pieces of submarginal farmland into outdoor recreation demonstration areas. Workers on federal relief supplied labor to improve the sites, most of which later were to become state parks. This contrasted with the broader emphasis of the NRA, which counted as recreation both indoor and outdoor as well as urban and rural activities. The NPS also contrasted with the ideas of the WPA, which concentrated on the major area of interest of the NRA, namely, urban public recreation. Even before the formation of the WPA, Thomas Rivers of the NRA had noticed that the NPS tended to stress facilities, whereas Hopkins and his aides with their social welfare orientation thought more in terms of people.[39]

The NPS, unlike the WPA, offered little potential competition to the major work of Braucher and the NRA. When Wirth became much interested in the NRA and asked for the loan of a staff member to aid in planning and research by the NPS on outdoor recreation, the relationship was bound to grow. Braucher assigned James B. Williams, a veteran of twenty years with the NRA, to assist Wirth. Williams remained with the NPS for nearly seven years, with his salary paid at various times by the NRA, the NPS, and a foundation since Wirth had difficulty convincing his superiors to put Williams on the NPS payroll.[40]

As these federal agencies, especially the WPA, moved increasingly into the provision of local recreation with little strategic planning, a perennial problem shared with the NRA, Braucher pondered what the Association might do to raise the quality of leadership in the many new recreation programs across America. While the National Recreation School was facing more difficulty each year in placing its highly trained graduates, hordes of new recreation leaders in the WPA lacked adequate training at the rudimentary level. For these two reasons the NRA suspended operation of the graduate school and replaced the whole program with a series of intensive one-month institutes held in various cities.

These institutes, designed to produce competent staff workers rather than professional executives, emphasized instruction by specialists from the NRA in specific areas of recreation such as administration, music, arts and crafts, and dramatics. The first institutes, intended to upgrade the ill-trained employees of the WPA as well as workers on municipal payrolls, were held in Cleveland and in Pittsburgh, where one hundred emergency recreation workers as well as sixty regularly employed people enrolled in September 1935. By June 1936 nearly three thousand eight hundred students in sixteen eastern and midwestern cities had benefited from such institutes. As training in both city departments and in the WPA improved, the NRA held fewer such institutes. In five years institutes were to train some ten thousand people in forty cities, ten of which hosted more than one institute.[41]

With the graduate school closed, those seeking professionalism in public recreation, including both the leaders of the NRA and others such as a scattering of university professors and a few enlightened leaders in larger municipal recreation departments, sought substitutes for the comprehensive training which the graduate program had provided. Braucher's solution, begun in 1937, was to make an annual award of apprentice fellowships to a few carefully chosen college graduates. The individuals selected would spend an internship year at various tasks on the staffs of the best municipal recreation systems in the country to gain experience in preparation for careers as top-level administrators. While Braucher hoped to have eight to twelve fellows in the program, which was to last for a decade, he apparently found funds for only three awards in the first year.[42]

Although the National Recreation School had closed partly as a result of lack of positions for its graduates, some optimistic leaders of the WPA, particularly Harold Meyer as well as Eduard Lindeman, who made exaggerated predictions of future needs for recreation executives, were eager to develop college programs for professional training in recreation. Over one hundred schools listed isolated courses applicable to recreation, but only a handful of institutions, such as the University of Minnesota, offered organized four-year programs of study. In the middle of 1937 Lindeman asked Braucher if the NRA would join the WPA and the university in sponsoring a conference in Minneapolis to foster improved college curricula for training professionals in recreation. Braucher replied that while the NRA had assisted numerous colleges in establishing scattered courses in recreation and leisure, the NRA would not be justified to encourage training of still more recreation executives when so many such men were currently unemployed. Nonetheless Lindeman and Meyer went ahead late in the year without the official support of the NRA and held the conference, which turned out to be the first of several such meetings.[43]

The Minnesota conference was but one example of an increasing interest outside the NRA in recreation professionalism. Although the Association had served for years as both the one indispensable source of recreation expertise and also as a substitute for a professional association, several competent individuals and other organizations, which one day might compete with the NRA, were gradually advancing toward positions of national prominence in recreation. Municipal administrators of recreation such as V. K. Brown of Chicago and George Hjelte of Los Angeles acquired nationwide reputations. Other important persons, such as Lindeman, Meyer, and to a lesser extent Romney of the WPA, came from backgrounds lacking much connection with either the NRA or municipal recreation.

Some recreation experts became well known in related fields. Such was the case with Jay B. Nash.[44] Because the NRA provided neither overall coordination nor a professional organization for the broadened interests of public recreation in the 1930s, it was only natural for others to attempt to fill the vacuum. Nash, for instance, was influential in one such professional organization, the American Association of Leisure Time Educators, the membership of which included municipal recreation leaders as well as employees of the WPA and YMCA.[45] Other interested people planned a National Leisure Time Committee to coordinate all of the different groups dealing with leisure, presumably including the NRA, and to secure a federal recreation commission. This scheme, in which Nash was also an instigator, apparently aborted in the mid-1930s.[46]

The National Education Association posed a potential threat to the NRA and all other societies wanting recreation to be an independent profession when the Educational Policies Commission of the NEA suggested that leadership in municipal recreation eventually might become part of the public school system.[47] In addition, the American Physical Education Association, the professional association in physical education, formally became a department of the NEA in mid-1937 and announced that recreation would be one of its three main emphases. A year later the department was to assume a new name, American Association for Health, Physical Education, and Recreation. Some leaders of the new organization obviously hoped that through it recreation would become a subdivision of education in America. In practice, however, the membership of the group was to be chiefly teachers of physical education with few professional recreation leaders.[48]

Braucher recognized the potential competition which these new organizations, as well as government agencies such as the WPA, offered to valid continuation of the role of the weakened NRA as spokesman for all of recreation in America.[49] To his credit he saw the need for some national coordination among these various interests if recreation was to function as an effective unit and avoid still further fragmentation. Toward this end he might have initiated joint establishment of a new coordinating group in which the NRA realistically might be one among equals. He favored instead expansion of existing organizations before creating new ones and attempted without great success to revitalize and expand the National Education-Recreation Council which he had originated early in the decade to deal with the problem of recreation for the unemployed. The council, made up of representatives of about twenty national youth-serving, educational, and welfare associations, functioned as a clearinghouse for ideas on recreation. Hoping that the council might also become an effective coordinating body, Braucher supplied staff members of the NRA to serve as secretaries for the council. Near the end of the decade, the council, pragmatically recognizing the expanded role of the national government in recreation, invited federal agencies active in recreation to become members. One session, held in Washington, D.C., drew spokesmen from over a dozen such agencies, but the council, while a useful organization, did not halt the rise of new groups aiming to coordinate certain aspects of recreation on a national scale.[50]

In the meantime municipal administrators of recreation increasingly felt that they, perhaps with the NRA, ought to have their own professional association rather than join groups proposed by leaders in the WPA or NEA. By the mid-1930s municipal executives had already formed several local and state organizations of recreation administrators, such as the Public Recreation Association of New Jersey which had grown in four years from a group begun in a single county. There were also such groups as a regional Eastern Association of Recreation Workers and a national alumni group of the National Recreation School.[51] Despite a growing desire for nationwide organization of recreation workers, Braucher was slow to exert any real initiative.

Finally a report from New Jersey recreation executive F. S. Mathewson to field worker John W. Faust of the NRA virtually forced Braucher to take action. Mathewson, acutely disturbed because several leading local administrators had talked of founding a national professional group by themselves, urged the NRA to act and thus preserve its position of influential leadership. At the next directors' meeting Braucher secured authorization for a Department of Recreation Workers within the NRA.[52] Several months later he wrote to all local executives suggesting that some sort of professional group be formed and asked their opinions. The results of this poll, which Braucher shrewdly arranged to have tabulated by a local leader rather than by the NRA office, showed a majority favoring such a society within, rather than independent of, the NRA.[53] Accordingly, the NRA laid plans for the meeting of executives at the next congress to consider the issue. Meanwhile Braucher and the directors reversed themselves and decided that the proposed group ought to be formally independent although closely related to the NRA. Such an arrangement would give local leaders, some of whom resented what they felt to be paternalism by Braucher, more freedom and also prevent the future possibility of executives trying to replace from within the control of the NRA by Braucher and lay directors.[54]

The recreation executives met in May 1937 at the annual congress and provisionally organized their new society. They elected V. K. Brown of Chicago as chairman of a national committee of sixteen of their peers charged with developing plans for permanent organization at the next congress. Braucher gave full support to the committee, and the founding of the professional group took place at the congress the following year. The group, which was named the Society of Recreation Workers of America but was later to be the American Recreation Society (ARS), was officially independent of, but still connected with, the NRA as Braucher wished. Although Braucher and the ARS cooperated cordially for a period of years, two problems, which were not to be satisfactorily resolved in his lifetime, arose almost immediately. The first was the matter of which persons in various occupations related to recreation were qualified for membership in the ARS; the second, the relationship between the ARS and the NRA.[55]

One issue which later was to cause severe friction between the NRA and dominant elements in the ARS, and on which key lay leaders of the NRA formed strong opinions, was the relation of the federal government to municipal recreation. As local resources for such social services as public education, welfare, and recreation had collapsed in the depression, the federal government had moved to fill the void. In various fields, including recreation, such funding prompted both a desire for permanent federal programs to aid local institutions and a fear of centralized control which might weaken local and individual freedom. Although the NRA was officially neutral on the matter of the federal government in recreation and Braucher at times pointedly silenced staff criticism of federal operations, wariness of federal agencies gradually rose among top leaders of the NRA. Several influential directors of the NRA, among them Susan Lee, daughter of former president Lee, shared their suspicions with Braucher, who was concerned over a potential loss of individual freedom in recreation and also over the very real possibility that some bureaucratic federal agency might supersede the ailing NRA to which he had devoted his life.[56]

Braucher's fears became more urgent as federal agencies, especially the NPS and the WPA, maneuvered for position in the ill-defined area of departmental jurisdiction over recreation after a fashion to be expected whenever governmental agencies expand into new, uncharted functions. Proponents of various schemes for federal action, some of which would obviously duplicate services of the NRA, presented ever more frequent plans.

The National Park Service, already on good terms with the NRA, probably had a better statutory claim to preeminence in recreation than any other federal agency and had moved to solidify its position shortly after the creation of a potential rival, the WPA. In a study of nationwide outdoor recreation resources made for President Roosevelt's new National Resources Board, the NPS, among other suggestions, had made a number of recommendations to expand its own role in recreation, sometimes at the expense of other agencies which had not been given a chance to see the final proposals before publication. Out of the report had come the Park, Parkway, and Recreational Area Study Act of 1936, which had included authorization for the NPS to make a more comprehensive study in conjunction with state and local authorities. This second report, after recognizing a need for coordination among the several federal agencies dealing with recreation, blandly asserted that the NPS was the logical agency to oversee any such coordinating.[57]

To facilitate such aims and build a recreation image for his agency, Wirth of the NPS continued to cultivate his growing cooperation with the NRA. Braucher readily responded since the chief recreation emphases of the two organizations did not over-lap. Realizing the likelihood that some more formal arrangement of federal interests was likely to come, he saw the benefits of mu-tual friendship with the NPS and quietly aided Wirth's ambitious hope to pull major permanent recreation functions of the govern-ment into the NPS.[58]

Meanwhile Lindeman of the WPA had recognized the futility of dealing with interagency rivalry by unilateral recommendations of the sort made by the NPS and had attempted to set up an inter-agency committee on recreation.[59] More importantly, he had been named chairman of the interagency Technical Committee on Rec-reation, a subcommittee of the Interdepartmental Committee to Coordinate Health and Welfare Activities. The Technical Commit-tee reported in 1937 that some thirty-five units of twelve federal departments were engaged in sixty to seventy different programs affecting recreation and leisure with resultant waste, confusion, and duplication caused in part by lack of adequate coordination. To solve the problem the Technical Committee recommended at the very least the immediate creation of a permanent, advisory, interdepartmental committee on recreation and preferably a sep-arate bureau of recreation.

This comprehensive proposal for an independent bureau went far beyond any previous ideas for coordination and suggested an organization remarkably similar to the NRA but with greater pow-ers and resources. The bureau was to provide not only a clearing-house for information on recreation, a research library, and the advice of experts through field service or loan of staff members to federal, state, and local agencies but also was to disburse grants to states and communities and coordinate all federal recreation programs. Despite these attractively grandiose ideas, Lindeman was unable to secure a consensus among the agencies involved in support of the ambitious scheme, which consequently failed. Con-cerned with their own roles in recreation, the National Park Ser-vice and Office of Education in the Department of the Interior and the Extension Service of the Department of Agriculture refused to endorse this major recommendation of the Technical Commit-tee.[60]

While Braucher and the NRA remained officially neutral on the proposals of Lindeman's Technical Committee, the very idea of a scheme for a federal bureau which would duplicate and in all probability replace numerous key services of the NRA was sympto-matic of the institutional weakening the NRA had suffered as it watched the rise of many competing groups during the late 1930s.

No longer was the NRA the prime spokesman for public recreation in America. By the end of the decade Braucher estimated that the NRA would need to better than double its still-dwindling annual contributions to keep pace with the general rise of public recreation.

Organized recreation, to say nothing of the much broader aspects of leisure in general, was attracting so much attention that numerous private associations as well as several federal agencies were moving strongly into the field. Not only voluntary associations such as the NRA but also countless individuals as well as state and local governments had to cope in one way or another, just as they had in World War I, with encroachment by the federal government in the crisis of the Great Depression. As private and public interests vied among themselves and with each other for national influence in recreation, it was evident that municipal recreation was an idea which had outgrown the basic stimulus of its primary sponsor, the NRA.[61] At the same time, however, organized recreation fell considerably short of those minimum standards of adequacy suggested by the NRA. A solution was needed to the problem of meeting local and individual needs with a combination of philanthropic, local, state, and federal resources as well as attaining a harmonious national policy to coordinate public and private interests involved with recreation on a nationwide scale. Yet as foreign affairs and the specter of another global war rose to dominate the American scene, the achievement of this obvious requirement necessarily was postponed.

Although the role of the NRA in World War II was substantially less dramatic that in World War I, the U. S. Navy presented Braucher with a certificate of achievement. New Dealer Mark McCloskey headed the FSA Recreation Division, a federal wartime agency performing many of the tasks once done by the WCCS. Sociologist Harold D. Meyer, twice president of the American Recreation Society, was a key proponent of a permanent federal recreation bureau.

7
The Centralizing Thrust of War

By 1940, while the United States in general was well on the way to solid recovery from the Great Depression, the NRA was at a low ebb in both top-level leadership as well as finances. For several years past, annual contributions, which had reached a total of $386,000 in 1929, had never gone above $144,000. Nevertheless, Braucher rather unimaginatively refused to reevaluate the decision made by Lee nearly two decades earlier against joining community chests. Fearful of compromising the NRA, Braucher was to hesitate another four years before approaching a second promising source of philanthropic dollars—large corporations.[1] Nor did he seek the counsel of professional fund raisers. Top leadership was also a problem; aged John H. Finley, who had succeeded Lee as president of the NRA, died in March 1940. A nephew of Lee declined the position, as did First Vice-President John G. Winant, who was soon to become America's ambassador to Great Britain. Finally, after a year of fruitless search for another lay president, the directors persuaded professional secretary Braucher to become the first salaried president of the Association. This turn away from lay control was, however, more apparent than actual since Braucher had in fact been running the organization more or less singlehandedly for several years.[2]

Meanwhile, weakened by lack of funds and faltering leadership, the National Recreation Association lay vulnerable to encroachments by an assortment of groups, both public and private, which not only duplicated many ongoing functions of the Association but also preempted several entirely new activities which appeared to be logical extensions of its traditional role. The NRA, partly because of its refusal to update conceptions and policies systematically, was in the unenviable position of having fostered a social reform to the point where numerous competing interests emerged with the same basic goals while there was yet neither effective coordination of these groups nor an adequate national acceptance of the desired reforms.

At this crucial time in the history of the NRA, Braucher, like most of his contemporaries, watched with mounting dismay as the rush of events drew the nation into the war which had already engulfed Europe. If millions of citizens were to become soldiers, the NRA might again, as in World War I, play a key role in furnishing recreation for troops in training. The situation was, however, somewhat different from the earlier conflict. Both Raymond Fosdick, chairman of the Commission on Training Camp Activities, and various investigating military authorities had emphatically denounced the confusion and competition among private organizations, such as the YMCA, in charge of in-camp and overseas recreation in World War I. As a remedy the critics had recommended that the military provide its own recreation program. Accordingly Secretary of War Baker had set up a Morale Division in the Adjutant General's Office, and the Army General Staff had incorporated the idea in its planning.

By 1940, then, the responsible authorities had already decided that the military itself rather than private organizations would operate on-post welfare and recreation programs in the event of mobilization. Representatives of both the army and navy had consulted the NRA about their plans. When war came, the military adhered to these decisions for the most part, although the American Red Cross was given responsibility for recreation in military hospitals.[3] The government had not, however, announced a policy for recreation outside military camps, which had been the domain of War Camp Community Service during World War I; consequently, both the NRA and the organizations which had, in effect, been ousted from on-post recreation recognized a potential opportunity in the off-post vacuum.

In this situation Braucher, ever mindful that voluntary organizations frequently can initiate new activities faster than governmental bureaucracies, recognized that mobilization might bring an even greater influx of recruits and war workers into unprepared towns than in World War I. To meet the problem, he envisioned local committees, thoroughly representative of all interested community segments and groups, which would pattern their operations after WCCS. He wanted to avoid the bickering of the sectarian groups which had occurred in World War I but admitted that he and the NRA alone could not and did not intend to administer a new WCCS or similar operation. Instead he hoped for an overall office, perhaps financed with emergency federal funds, which would be run cooperatively by several national social work organizations to fill the role once occupied by national WCCS. This new group, he believed, also ought to utilize resources of federal agencies such as the WPA.[4]

To implement his proposals, for which he apparently had neglected to make detailed blueprints, Braucher moved in several directions at once, groping for tactical means by which to bring his conception to fruition. Acknowledging the significant expansion of federal powers in both World War I and the New Deal and mindful of the repeated failures of the NRA in efforts to secure congressional action, Braucher reasoned that the White House was the best place to obtain authoritative support for his idea. In May he had lunch there with Eleanor Roosevelt, who was interested in recreation, and told her about the experiences of the CTCA and his plan to avoid repetition of the inter-organizational conflicts of World War I. This contact produced, however, no clear results. Shortly after the fall of France in June 1940, Braucher personally and through his friend Raymond Fosdick made the first of several direct attempts to secure presidential endorsement of the scheme or at least a decision of some sort on the issue. Although Congress authorized the mobilization of the National Guard and was moving rapidly toward peacetime conscription by September, which created an immediate need for planning recreation requirements, President Roosevelt found no time to meet Braucher's request.[5]

Since the federal government did not act, Braucher went ahead on his own and sent field workers to help inaugurate WCCS-type programs in key cities, such as Norfolk, Virginia, which were already feeling the impact of increased defense efforts.[6] In addition he called together a committee, chaired by John E. Manley, professional head of the YMCA, to look into defense community service. Manley initially agreed with Braucher on the need to avoid the earlier mistake of dividing services among a few competing organizations. Besides Braucher and Manley, the committee included leaders of the National Social Work Council, the Community Chests and Councils of America, and the American Social Hygiene Association.

The Manley committee was limited in size at first for the sake of efficiency; nevertheless it was hardly representative of the many and varied groups interested in defense recreation. Braucher had realized that a large, democratic committee would be at best unwieldy, but in opting for a small group he virtually ensured that some omitted organizations would be unhappy. For instance, inclusion of the YMCA and not the Knights of Columbus, although both had served the CTCA, was certain to antagonize numerous Catholics. Consequently several other similar committees soon emerged, one of which included representatives of the WPA and the leading professional societies interested in recreation. Most important was the so-called breakfast meeting, called in October by leaders of the Jewish Welfare Board which, in spite of its work in World War I, had not been included in the Manley committee. The breakfast meeting also counted Manley's YMCA and the Knights of Columbus as members.

Braucher must have been greatly tempted to accept a proffered invitation to join this group, essentially the religious organizations of World War I, which soon became the National United Welfare Committee. Based on the past experience of joint fund raising which had resulted in the millions of dollars used to supplement the work of the NRA for a decade, participation in this new coalition might be expected to stabilize the finances of the NRA. Confronted with this necessity of choosing between power and principle, Braucher stood firm in his convictions. He politely declined the invitation and continued opposition to what he feared might become merely a repetition of the quarrels experienced two decades earlier. In Braucher's absence the group suggested that it, rather than the local community-wide committees proposed by the NRA, become the new WCCS. When Manley himself opted for this recommendation, the committee bearing his name quietly died, leaving Braucher effectively isolated.[7]

In the meantime President Roosevelt, ever willing to expand federal powers, in November 1940 designated Paul V. McNutt, head of the Federal Security Agency (FSA), as national Coordinator of Health, Welfare, and Related Defense Activities, including public recreation. Braucher immediately saw the possibility of using McNutt's new authority as a means to offset the emerging plans of the National United Welfare Committee. Given the emergency facing the country, Braucher at last persuaded himself that public recreation, citizens in general, and perhaps even the NRA, could benefit from a *temporary* expansion of federal authority over various aspects of defense recreation in local communities.

Acting on this decision, Braucher, aided by Fosdick, persuaded McNutt to establish a Recreation Division in his agency in January 1941. On Braucher's advice, McNutt appointed as its director Mark McCloskey, an able, ambitious social worker and ex-head of National Youth Administration projects in New York City. The new Recreation Division eventually was to become the major operating arm of the Office of Community War Services (OCWS) of the FSA.

When the FSA Recreation Division began functioning, the NRA, through the activity of six experienced field workers, had already aided the organization of local defense recreation committees in some fifty cities.[8] This work, however, hardly met the need for national coordination of the confusing array of new local schemes. McCloskey and McNutt, theoretically empowered to proceed with this coordination, still lacked funds and a clear conception of the function of their hastily established office. Consequently they were at first unable to do more than undertake preliminary studies with a few workers loaned by various federal agencies and the NRA.

Meanwhile the National United Welfare Committee had evolved into the United Service Organizations, known eventually throughout the nation as the USO. This body, created as an independent private organization in hopes of avoiding the squabbles of World War I, proposed to raise private funds for community services modeled after WCCS. In addition, the influential USO asked for federal money to construct recreation buildings for its use. Forced to a decision by the rapid rise of the USO, national coordinator McNutt in February 1941 called a meeting of representatives from interested federal agencies and private groups including the NRA. Although McCloskey of the fledgling FSA Recreation Division, Fosdick, Allen Burns of the Community Chests and Councils of America, and Braucher were all opposed to the USO plan, neither the FSA nor the NRA could offer an adequate substitute for the great potential of the organizations united under the banner of USO.[9]

The conference produced a clarification of the roles of the various interests involved in defense community services. The armed forces continued to be responsible for on-post welfare and recreation. The USO, in essence the groups displaced from the camps by the military, in turn displaced the NRA as well as Braucher's camp community service idea and received some of the duties but not the official authority of the defunct WCCS. Braucher still hoped that the USO might be controlled, but he dutifully cooperated with the group after it obtained the sanction of the government and even suspended temporarily NRA fund raising as an aid to the USO drive. Within four years the USO was to spend $179 million, a sum almost exactly the same as that raised by the joint fund of World War I. The USO money went to programs consisting chiefly of hundreds of servicemen's clubs, some 450 of which were built by the federal government.[10] It was not the USO, however, but McCloskey's FSA Recreation Division that was charged with overall supervision and, if need be, organization of local defense recreation programs.

With the USO nearly ready to begin operation and the armed forces rapidly expanding through conscription, McCloskey realized that prompt action was imperative. Despite the plans of the USO calling for voluntary action, the situation was so urgent that the War Department considered using army officers to organize camp town recreation. In contrast the FSA Recreation Division stressed local civilian responsibility not only for the recreation programs provided but also for the coordination of local committees with national agencies and groups such as the USO. Still lacking federal funds, the FSA turned to the NRA for help. Braucher, anxious to help the FSA curb the excesses which might develop in the USO, responded generously. He obtained a loan with which to pay community organizers and district men, supplied six top NRA field workers, and assigned staff member Thomas E. Rivers to recruit field representatives. Using his many contacts, chiefly in municipal recreation, Rivers directed the nationwide interviewing of more than five hundred individuals, seventy-one of whom were eventually hired for the FSA Recreation Division.[11]

Thanks to the timely assistance of the NRA, the FSA soon had an operating arm with a field staff which was to grow to seventy-eight members during the war. During the following months the agency helped organize local defense recreation committees analogous to the earlier local committees of WCCS in some 1,369 cities. More important in the long run, some 250 cities established permanent municipal recreation programs under the influence of McCloskey's agents, and the number of cities reporting public recreation programs, virtually stagnant in the depression, began an upward climb which was to continue for decades. Meanwhile McCloskey, supported by Braucher, struggled successfully to make his agency the primary group responsible for helping local communities organize recreation for servicemen and war production workers and thus supplant other organizations such as the USO and WPA.[12]

In its central position as coordinator of local war recreation activities, the FSA Recreation Division, through both its ideas and actions, reflected the influence of the NRA, although ambitious McCloskey was determined not to be overshadowed by Braucher or anyone else. Several of Braucher's ablest aides and field men remained on loan to the FSA, reportedly at higher salaries than paid by the NRA, for as long as two years. To Braucher's disappointment, two of these men, Charles K. Brightbill and Sherwood Gates, refused to return to the NRA and later attained positions in the FSA Recreation Division second only to McCloskey himself. These special conditions, coupled with the general prestige and acceptance of the NRA and its ideas in recreation circles, made it only natural for the FSA to copy the successful ideas and tactics of the NRA and WCCS. Accordingly the men of the FSA recognized the primacy of local responsibility and initiative through representative local recreation committees, the need to mobilize all public and private resources of cities, and the importance of outside expert aid. McCloskey wanted local committees to offer varied programs of recreation for soldiers, workers, and the general public as well as to minority groups such as Negroes. To accomplish this he emphasized professionalism as well as municipal responsibility and duplicated such NRA services as training institutes and surveys. To support his general field staff, several times as large as that of the depleted NRA, he followed Braucher's example of hiring specialists; McCloskey's new resident expert in design of facilities was actually trained by his counterpart in the NRA.[13]

As the FSA Recreation Division continued to grow and to duplicate numerous services pioneered by the NRA, the NRA hit a new financial low in 1941. A rift gradually developed between Braucher and McCloskey, although they cooperated outwardly. Braucher initially thought highly of McCloskey, and the two stood together against the USO; but McCloskey's outspoken ambition and volatile personality made it impossible for the two men to sustain close cooperation.[14] McCloskey recognized both the inadequacy of the NRA in its presumed role as the foremost spokesman for national recreation needs and the value of unified command in the defense emergency. The FSA Recreation Division had hardly begun operations when Braucher learned that McCloskey wanted power to coordinate NRA field work. Unlike the situation in World War I, however, the NRA had no formal role in the emergency effort, and Braucher refused to surrender the independence of the Association. After this clash Braucher heard reports that McCloskey was inclined to disparage the NRA. Braucher considered the FSA Recreation Division a temporary wartime expedient, whereas McCloskey came to hope for permanence in the agency and was jealous of the corps of experts still on the staff of the smaller NRA.

Braucher, who in good faith had already given McCloskey his best field workers, could hardly have been expected to stand idly by while McCloskey apparently usurped the functions of his benefactor. Anticipating the possibility of a postwar struggle among the NRA, the FSA, and the USO for the permanent position of the leading national organization in recreation, Braucher critically analyzed the strengths and weaknesses of the three groups in such a dispute. He concluded that the results were not encouraging for the NRA. Gradually becoming suspicious of McCloskey's motives, Braucher was determined not to permit the supersession of his beloved NRA, an independent voluntary association, by a federal bureaucracy. As the FSA Recreation Division matured, moreover, McCloskey's hostile attitude was certainly no secret.[15]

Despite McCloskey's feelings and the lack of official sanction for the NRA as a part of the war effort, the Association made numerous contributions to American defense. Of greatest significance, perhaps, had been its role in spurring a definite federal policy for defense recreation in the establishment of an active FSA Recreation Division. The NRA also provided numerous public and private organizations such as the Office of Civilian Defense, the United Service Organizations, the American Red Cross, and the military services with assistance in technical matters and procurement of competent personnel. The chief music expert of the NRA, for example, spent several months with the United States Department of the Treasury developing music to promote war bond sales. Numerous special publications of the NRA, including reprints of pertinent documents detailing the WCCS experience, special manuals prepared for government agencies, and 12 million pocket pamphlets with recreation ideas for traveling soldiers and sailors, aided wartime recreation efforts.[16]

The war was responsible for a modification of most of the normal services of the NRA. As key staff members dealt increasingly with war-related matters, Braucher was forced to suspend some operations, such as the National Physical Education Service. Other areas, even vital fund raising, received decreased efforts, yet the directors of the NRA resisted the possibility of federal grants for ailing voluntary associations. Field service admittedly was generally inadequate since several key men had joined the FSA and remaining workers emphasized aid to war-impacted cities. Municipal departments also lost many able leaders to war agencies, and the strained NRA moved to fill the gap with expanded recruiting and training of substitutes. Other war-induced variations, such as efforts to promote public recreation as an antidote to a national rise in juvenile delinquency, occurred across the spectrum of NRA activities. In addition, Braucher juggled the limited resources of the NRA in attempts to meet newly prominent needs in the field of recreation.[17]

One such rapidly expanding area of activity was industrial recreation. Renewed interest in the matter came as war orders pushed plants toward round-the-clock production. When the federal government imposed wage ceilings, employers discovered that plant recreation programs could be an enticing fringe benefit in competition for loyal workers. The NRA had been interested in industrial recreation for decades, but a shortage of funds for a proposed staff specialist had restricted its actions in the area to consultation, an occasional study, and sessions at annual congresses. In the crisis of war, organizations such as the FSA and the USO entered the obvious void left by the NRA.

Perhaps more significant in the long run, a third group of men, chiefly directors of company-run recreation programs, arose to challenge Braucher's policy whereby the NRA impartially served both labor and management as well as communities interested in employees' recreation. In late 1941, when Braucher refused to compromise his principles, the group obtained support from big business and independently formed what eventually became the National Industrial Recreation Association. This service organization, which became practically a trade association, consciously catered to management interests of big business and ultimately proved more durable than the special field service to industrial recreation which Braucher initiated in mid-1942.[18]

Another area in which events prompted the NRA to action was a rising interest in recreation as a function of state government. Before the war states had developed counterparts to virtually every municipal activity except recreation. Despite urging by some of his staff, Braucher had not pushed state recreation commissions and departments. He had consistently held that recreation ought to be primarily a local function and that state agencies might become politicized or might duplicate the various services, chiefly field work, of the NRA. However, the NRA field service alone was hardly adequate.

Meanwhile the FSA Recreation Division fostered emergency state recreation committees, which numbered eleven by 1943. Braucher was fully aware of these activities, yet he remained skeptical as to the need for state organizations with recreation as their principal function. In April 1943 he decided to begin special field services to state agencies concerned with recreation, such as parks and agricultural extension services, but he continued to ignore the question of state organizations designed specifically for recreation.[19] This policy of neglect drew criticism from Harold Meyer, former promoter of WPA statewide organization and in 1943 head of the pacesetting North Carolina committee. Men such as Meyer advised the NRA to help the state recreation committees expand into permanent agencies offering cities many of the services which the NRA could not adequately provide.

In the next few years, states were to gradually accept a more definite responsibility for new recreation activities in existing agencies. The NRA increased its staff serving these state agencies rather than risk haphazard development of programs by such groups. Braucher tended to favor lodging state responsibility for recreation in existing state units or interagency committees while other experts such as Meyer and the staff at the FSA, imbued with the philosophy of the New Deal and expanding government, preferred new, independent recreation agencies.[20]

Besides industry and budding state agencies, a number of hospitals paid more attention to recreation during the war. The rise of interest in hospital recreation, including therapeutic activities, was, to a large extent, the result of expanded wartime recreation programs of the American Red Cross in some three hundred military hospitals. Although Veterans Administration hospitals also employed recreation therapists, the NRA lacked both funds and manpower to undertake a campaign for recreation programs in civilian hospitals. Despite significant action by the NRA on the issue a decade later, organized recreation was not widespread in

American hospitals and was virtually nonexistent in burgeoning nursing homes nearly a quarter century after the beginning of the war.[21]

Along with expanded hospital recreation, the war brought renewed attention to the supposed need for some sort of overall coordinating group which might be representative of and speak for all of the various organizations and interests, private and perhaps also public, involved in organized recreation. The NRA, whatever its pretensions, was obviously unable to fill that role alone. In the early 1930s Braucher had established for that purpose the National Education-Recreation Council, a forum with national voluntary associations such as the NRA and YMCA and, more recently, some federal agencies active in recreation as members. Yet the council was not broadly representative of all interests in recreation.

At this point Harold Meyer and the heads of several professional associations concerned with recreation but not on Braucher's council recommended that the council be replaced or enlarged. These actions culminated in early 1943 with a conference attended by representatives of several national welfare and professional organizations dealing with recreation. Despite the conference, which was organized specifically to promote action, the scheme, vague and somewhat unclear to begin with, faded away for lack of broad support. In addition the National Education-Recreation Council moved to adjust its activities to fill needs exposed by the conference.[22] The point was clear to Braucher, however, that the NRA was becoming only one of numerous major forces in recreation, several of which understandably resented his apparent assumption that the NRA was still the sole leader of American recreation.

These various interests represented both personal ambition and different points of view regarding the means to achieve the common goal of providing ample local public recreation for the nation. Undoubtedly the major leaders of organized public recreation in the United States, including virtually all administrators of federal programs, municipal executives, and professionals in universities and private associations, agreed with the vital importance of local responsibility, professionalism, and the broad definition of organized recreation as pioneered by the NRA. There was also more or less general unanimity on the requirement for selling public recreation to the general citizenry and the need to triumph over such factors as the work ethic, rampant individualism, and affluence which seemed to foster a desire to seek recreation privately.

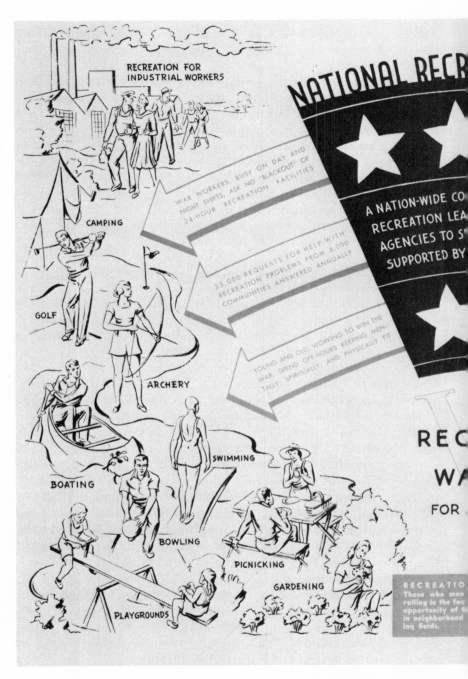

Although the role of the NRA in World War II was diminished from that of

World War I, the Association made a varied contribution to the war effort.

Nevertheless recreation leaders differed on methods to achieve their goals. Braucher, maturing in the Progressive Era when capable individuals had frequently set out to achieve social reform largely through voluntary associations, preferred the approach of the NRA, which continued to operate under these motivating ideas. While the NRA emphasized municipal responsibility, some of the most striking quantitative gains in public recreation had come from federal activities in the depression. Increasingly some leaders, particularly eager men with federal experience such as Meyer and McCloskey, believed a permanent federal recreation agency with plentiful resources could provide more effective national leadership than the weakened NRA. These men were undoubtedly capable and quite ready to carve out positions of influence for themselves in the expanding field of recreation.

McCloskey recognized that his agency, offering many of the services of the NRA, was a logical candidate to obtain primary federal responsibility for recreation. He would have support from followers of recreation in the defunct WPA but could expect to face opposition, as had the WPA, from Braucher as well as the National Park Service, which considered itself the major federal recreation agency. However, supporters of the FSA Recreation Division might be able to consolidate wartime gains and secure permanent status for the agency by overcoming both apathy and outright opposition.

At a long night conference on April 30, 1943, McCloskey and several aides agreed on a general strategy for gaining permanency. They envisioned months of research and a national advisory committee for promotion of a federal bureau to coordinate federal recreation programs and also provide other agencies with technical assistance. The group recognized the crucial importance of congressional legislation for the success of their scheme. Only a few intimates, such as Harold Meyer, were told of the secret session. Just at this juncture, however, McCloskey received additional departmental duties within the FSA and soon became burdened with administrative details which apparently prevented him from carrying out the general procedure agreed upon.[23]

Over a year later, on January 3, 1945, with the end of the war already in sight, leaders in the FSA Recreation Division hastily seized an opportunity to introduce a bill in Congress which would in effect perpetuate their temporary agency more as a duplicate of the NRA than as an overall federal recreation bureau. Obviously such action to establish a federal agency which might render the services of the NRA unnecessary was of immense concern to

Braucher. The bill, which became H.R. 5, was probably drafted in the office of the FSA Recreation Division. It provided for an Office of Community Recreation Services in the Federal Security Agency with an annual appropriation of $450,000, almost exactly the amount currently allotted to the FSA Recreation Division.

The proposed agency was to provide, on request, technical services and advice to states, counties, and cities on all phases of community recreation. A list of suggested functions copied the services of the NRA right down to the concept of strengthening local initiative. The bill, and several others which were to follow in subsequent years, would make the FSA Recreation Division a permanent agency much like the NRA rather than following the broader recommendations of the Technical Committee on Recreation which in 1937 had wanted provision for overall coordination of federal recreation activities.[24]

Although H.R. 5 probably had scant chance for success in a nation moving rapidly toward peace with its predictable rush to demobilize, curtail spending, and end wartime agencies, Braucher was quick to act. He thought the bill would die regardless of NRA action and might easily have ignored the measure entirely. Yet he felt compelled as a matter of principle to take a stand in public against what seemed to him a plan for duplication of the NRA by a hastily contrived bureaucracy dangerous to local autonomy in public recreation.[25] For these reasons he included a statement of opposition to H.R. 5 by leading directors of the NRA when he sent news of the bill to local recreation executives soliciting their opinions. Braucher discovered that few of them had even heard of it.

In early February the professionals on the executive committee of the American Recreation Society disapproved the bill and also asked for local opinion while the directors of the NRA formally reaffirmed their opposition to H.R. 5. Meanwhile field representatives of the NRA and the FSA Recreation Division, obviously acting on orders, stepped up their efforts to obtain grassroots support for opposing views of the issue from local recreation leaders. By April 1945, 203 of 242 local lay and professional leaders had written the NRA opposing H.R. 5, and the bill itself was stalled in a congressional committee with no hearing scheduled.[26]

Meanwhile the continued status of the FSA Recreation Division as well as H.R. 5 came increasingly into question; McCloskey, with his aides Sherwood Gates and Charles K. Brightbill, both of whom had at one time served on the staff of the NRA, moved to broaden the base of popular support for a federal recreation bureau. To do this, McCloskey earlier in the year had vigorously promoted a series of meetings to consider the postwar future of American recreation. In attendance had been representatives from several federal agencies, including the FSA Recreational Division and the Children's Bureau, and private associations, such as the YMCA, USO, and NRA.

On April 11, 1945, twenty-one of these people, with only Thomas Rivers of the NRA voicing strong dissent, decided to form a permanent, independent National Recreation Policies Committee not unlike the Educational Policies Commission of the National Education Association. At first glance the new committee seemed to fill a need, but it also obviously duplicated to a large extent Braucher's existing National Education-Recreation Council. The next month Germany surrendered, and the Appropriations Committee of the House of Representatives promptly voted to terminate the FSA Recreation Division within six weeks. The Senate balked, however, and a compromise extended the agency for another year but slashed its budget in half.[27] Knowing that the end was near, McCloskey resigned his position in June, leaving Gates and Brightbill to dismantle the agency. Nevertheless the desire for a federal bureau of recreation with proven consultative services such as those offered inadequately by the NRA with its limited funds continued to grow. McCloskey, Gates, and Brightbill were to help guide the Policies Committee to endorsement of such an agency within a few months.[28] Unfortunately much of the committee's energy was to be expended in the fight over federal recreation rather than being used for broad, probing analyses of possible recreation policies.

During this time the FSA Recreation Division had been trying to win the support of local recreation leaders for the proposed federal recreation bureau while the NRA was devoting its efforts to drumming up opposition. Both sides recognized that the scheme would have a better chance of congressional approval if the recreation movement was not divided over the issue, although some supporters of the plan naively overestimated the influence of the NRA in Washington. To Braucher and his board of directors the question seemed to involve not only the possible dangers of bureaucracy and centralized control but also the very future of the NRA itself, for which they could envision little or no possibility of major role change. Thus, when some members of the NRA staff did not feel as strongly as Braucher, he reportedly demanded that they, including even longtime field secretary Lebert Weir, either conform or resign.[29] With such crucial personal and institutional gains and losses in various organizations as well as the future of public recreation in America apparently at stake, the conflict soon broadened to become the paramount issue in public recreation in the immediate postwar period which, despite the controversy, was to see great growth at the local level.

In July Gates and Brightbill, heads of the disbanding FSA Recreation Division, moved to regroup and strengthen their forces. Acknowledging the probable failure of H.R. 5, they allied with leaders such as Harold Meyer of North Carolina, an eager promoter of federal recreation. The colleagues recognized the vital importance of considering various alternatives such as backing the establishment of a recreation subdivision in a proposed Department of Health, Education, and Welfare. Of course, no ardent promoter of recreation wanted it to be merely a part of a larger field such as education. Consequently a more desirable route was to modify H.R. 5 into a bill with organized support from the recreation movement in general, perhaps through the emerging policies committee.[30]

At this point professional leaders in the American Recreation Society began to develop a position on the issue of a federal recreation bureau. The society, dating to the late 1930s when it was formed as an independent organization by Braucher and leading municipal recreation executives, was recovering from a wartime membership drain. Although basic unity in the field of recreation was apparently maintained, the federal recreation question was to provide a catalyst for the rising autonomy of the ARS, provoking a sometimes bitter dispute, principally between the ARS and the NRA, which still smoldered more than a decade later.[31]

The opening round came at the ARS convention held in conjunction with the recreation congress in January 1946. One session of the congress developed into a debate on a federal bureau with Harold Meyer, Mark McCloskey, and others closely tied to federal agencies favoring the idea. Two prominent past presidents of the ARS, V. K. Brown and George Hjelte, also backed the proposal, which no local executives of equal stature opposed. Then, at its annual meeting, the ARS, doubtless aware of the inadequate services of the NRA and seeing federal action as a means to fill the gap, formally endorsed a federal bureau to coordinate federal efforts in recreation while simultaneously offering consultative and technical services presumably like those of the NRA. Recreation executive Dana Caulkins, once a member of the NRA staff, cautioned against undue haste and successfully amended the endorsement to provide that the ARS ask the NRA to initiate a joint study on what kind of legislation would be most appropriate.

A high-ranking ARS committee, chaired by F. S. Mathewson of New Jersey, was assigned to promote such a study and met several times during the year with representatives of the NRA. The meetings were, however, unsuccessful. Braucher maintained that the NRA was engaged in its own research on whether a federal bureau was needed at all and could not cooperate on a study with the ARS which, by its action, already assumed that a bureau was necessary and only wanted to examine different structural possibilities. Despite sympathetic urging by some ARS members, Braucher became increasingly suspicious of the actions of some promoters of the federal bureau and refused even to appoint a broad advisory committee which might at least make the NRA study appear more objective. This impasse was to last nearly a year until new officers took over the ARS and discharged the committee with Braucher's study still unfinished.[32]

Braucher's leisurely investigation of federal recreation illustrated some of the problems dividing the NRA and the ARS. While Braucher may well have desired a broad, impartial study, he utilized only his own staff and apparently also used the project as a delaying tactic, as suggested by NRA treasurer Kirby and suspected by opposition leaders, in hopes that wartime organizations as well as the scheme for a federal bureau would fade away. In contrast to earlier research conducted by the NRA staff, the study was still underway with no conclusion in sight and few substantive results some three years later. Meanwhile the NRA might conveniently support the general concept of federal recreation but oppose specific bills for a federal bureau until the fact-finding project was complete. The NRA had made known plans for a wide study including reports on federal recreation agencies, analyses of the extent to which existing organizations met national recreation needs, and opinion-seeking questionnaires as well as interviews by field staff with local and state recreation administrators.

These devices were manifestly not all objective; for example, on one occasion Braucher sent out ballots on a federal bureau with a covering letter strongly opposing the scheme. Nor did the leadership of the ARS appear entirely candid in its actions, notably in the handling of its referenda on the issue and the appointing of Hjelte and Brown to the supposedly impartial Mathewson committee.[33] All of these partisan actions added to the mutual suspicion rising between leading elements of the NRA and the ARS.

While the NRA and ARS could not agree on action, individual proponents of a federal bureau in the FSA Recreation Division, which was scheduled to cease operation in mid-1946, and the Policies Committee drafted a purportedly fresh bill to replace H.R. 5. To attract broader support, the new version, essentially the same as H.R. 5, also provided for a national advisory board of nonfederal public and private authorities on recreation and basically followed recommendations in a memorandum agreed to by all members of the Policies Committee except Thomas Rivers of the NRA. The proposed advisory committee notably omitted potentially competing federal agencies with definite stakes in recreation, such as the National Park Service. Although such exclusions might well have hindered effectiveness of the proposed office, the Federal Security Agency administrator himself endorsed the bill, which appeared in Congress on April 15, 1946, as S. 2070.[34]

The senatorial committee handling the bill quickly arranged hearings for May 13 and, reportedly at the devious suggestion of the FSA Recreation Division, invited a list of witnesses all known to support the proposal. Learning belatedly of this somewhat high-handed tactic, Braucher organized a protest to the committee which resulted in a second hearing on May 27 for opponents of the proposal. Supporters of S. 2070 at the hearings included Federal Security Administrator Watson Miller; Mark McCloskey; Harold Meyer; Roy Sorenson, chairman of the Policies Committee; Ott Romney, former head of recreation in the WPA; and Milo Christiansen, president of the ARS.

Among the opposition were Arthur H. Jones, field secretary of the NRA; Ben Miller, executive secretary of the American Association for Health, Physical Education and Recreation; and Harold W. Lathrop, president of the National Conference on State Parks. Several agencies which might have been interested in the hearings, such as the National Park Service, were still divided between conservationists and recreationists and were not concerned enough to send witnesses.[35] The hearings brought out most of the arguments concerning a federal bureau which had been developed over the past several years.

Arthur Jones of the NRA presented the case against the federal bureau proposed in S. 2070. He claimed that the bill, essentially the same as H.R. 5, had not had sufficient public study and discussion. In addition, NRA polls had found that most leaders of state and local recreation agencies opposed the idea. Jones argued that the recreation services of existing private groups and federal agencies, such as the Extension Service of the Department of Agriculture, ought to be expanded before building a new agency which added nothing to coordination of federal recreation activities. Other arguments used against the federal bureau idea were that it was merely a continuation in peacetime of a wartime agency; it duplicated services already offered by the NRA; and it fostered the dangers of centralization, standardization, and loss of state and local initiative in public recreation.[36] Moreover, the leaders of the NRA and federal agencies such as the National Park Service had obvious reasons based on self-interest for opposing a new federal bureau, and surely some supporters of the scheme had similar motives.

Supporters of the federal bureau based much of their argument on the quantitative inadequacy of local public recreation in general when compared to standards suggested by groups such as the NRA. They also pointed to the lack of resources in public and private organizations fostering organized recreation. A study in the early 1940s had found 94 cities with populations over 100,000 spending an average of only $1.54 per capita on public recreation as compared to a recommended $3.00. The NRA district field service regularly reached only 600 of some 16,000 incorporated places in the nation. Braucher countered that regular field service by any organization to some 13,000 rural communities averaging 703 people each would be both impractical and uneconomical. Proponents of a federal bureau admitted that such an agency might well supersede the NRA in areas such as field services. They maintained, although seldom with concrete suggestions, that the NRA could expand and reshape its functions like private associations in other fields, such as education and welfare, had done when federal legislation encroached upon private philanthropy. They also suggested that the NRA might engage in more research. Another possibility was that NRA might act as the constructive critic and watchdog of federal action.

Although the NRA had published more than two thousand different pamphlets and bulletins by 1946 and had a staff of more than one hundred people, Braucher privately confessed that the small budget of the NRA hampered adequate services and was "the one very real argument" for a federal bureau. While expenditures for local public recreation, as recorded in the yearbooks, ballooned from some $52 million in 1946 to $94 million two years later, the NRA spent only about $370,000 in each of these years. In terms of constant dollars, adjusted for postwar inflation, the expenditures of the NRA were not to surpass the previous peak year of 1929 until fully a decade after the end of the war.[37]

Another weakness of the NRA was the fact that while many of its best staff members and directors were nearing retirement, efforts to attract capable, younger replacements were only partially successful. Not until Braucher himself became physically exhausted and was forced to leave his office for some six months did the NRA, in an obvious case of poor management which recalled Lee's final years and death, begin attempts to find an executive secretary to aid the president. Ironically, some years earlier Braucher had personally designated understudies for each key staff member but had neglected to name a replacement for himself, the most important leader in the Association. Before his illness, however, S. 2070, which probably had little real chance of passage in a generally conservative Congress concerned with postwar economizing, received a favorable committee report. The bill reached the floor of the Senate, where it died when Congress, with elections soon to occur, adjourned on August 2, 1946.[38]

Although the favorable committee report on S. 2070 was to be the height of congressional action on the proposed federal recreation bureau for more than a decade, the controversy continued among the NRA, ARS, and several interested federal agencies. Recognizing that promoters of a federal bureau were not yet likely to give up and that a real need existed for coordination of federal recreation activities, Braucher initiated a simultaneous response to both problems. He proposed that permanent federal agencies establish a Federal Interagency Committee on Recreation as an alternative of sorts to a new bureau and offered the services of an executive secretary paid by the NRA.

While Braucher did not share his proposal with the now nearly defunct FSA Recreation Division, several regular agencies, some concerned with furthering their own influence in recreation, readily accepted his idea. Officials in the Office of Education, for example, wanted recreation recognized as a part of education. In the National Park Service, too, men such as Conrad Wirth probably saw mutual advantages in Braucher's device. Thus leaders of the Extension Service and Forest Service in the Department of Agriculture as well as the National Park Service and Fish and Wildlife Service in the Department of the Interior met confidentially with the Secretary of the Interior on September 6, 1946, to found an Interagency Committee. Six weeks later, with the committee in operation, Braucher revealed its creation to the directors of the NRA, numerous state agencies, and the predictably irritated leaders of the ARS.[39]

The Interagency Committee, which facilitated some coordination and exchange of information, served a useful but limited function. At the same time its very existence provided an argument ment that a new federal agency was unnecessary while leaving its member agencies and the NRA free in their respective domains. With the exception of a stenographer, efforts by the NRA to obtain a federally paid staff for the committee proved fruitless, so Braucher continued to supply an executive secretary. The failure to secure permanent federal funding for even this modest proposal seemed to reveal that promoters of public recreation had not met total success in selling their product to the general public and that certain member agencies of the committee recognized that it was to their advantage to keep the committee innocuous. The committee, aided by the NRA, also fostered several state interagency committees, studied federal recreation activities, and published a few pamphlets. It was to last some sixteen years.[40]

Late in 1946, just after the founding of the interagency committee, sociologist Harold Meyer, critic of the NRA and vocal advocate of professionalism as well as a federal bureau for recreation, became president of the American Recreation Society. The first man in the post who was not a local recreation executive (he would be reelected the next year), he was representative of important figures in recreation outside the influence of the NRA. Soon after his election Meyer announced an ambitious program to double the membership of the ARS, hire an executive secretary, refine professional standards, seek foundation grants for research in recreation, and push the proposed federal bureau.

Although Braucher and his key aides apparently had been suspicious of Meyer since his election, and despite the fact that some other members of the ARS questioned his policies, Meyer made significant contributions to the ARS as an organization. The controversial issue of federal recreation provided a rallying point for his supporters. Under Meyer the ARS nearly doubled its membership, attained greater de facto independence from the NRA, increased its financial resources almost sixfold, opened a permanent office with a paid administrative assistant, and achieved new cooperation with other professional societies concerned with recreation.[41]

The ARS, gradually moving apart from the NRA, had a leading role in postwar cooperation of professional associations dealing with recreation. Much of this activity was financed by the Athletic Institute, a nonprofit organization founded in 1934, which after the war funded several professional conferences and workshops in athletics, recreation, and physical education. In 1946, for instance, the institute sponsored the writing of a joint platform on recreation endorsed by the ARS, the American Association for Health, Physical Education, and Recreation, and the American Association of Group Workers.

More significantly, as the merging of local park and recreation departments increased in the late 1940s and interest in a professional federation arose, the institute financed two joint conferences for the executive committees of the ARS and the American Institute of Park Executives. Although Meyer and other leaders of the ARS originally preferred a broad federation of all interested groups, the participants at the second conference hammered out a plan for the amalgamation of the two societies. Prompted by concern for the fates of their groups, however, both park and recreation men soon had second thoughts about the merger, and the two associations repudiated the scheme. They adopted instead as a long-range objective the unification of professional organizations.[42]

While Meyer moved to strengthen relationships of the ARS with other groups, he also continued the aggressive promotion of a federal bureau. On this issue Braucher, who had been neutral regarding professional merger, actively continued his opposition. Although the NRA and ARS carried on with their normal activities, the long dispute over federal recreation reached what was perhaps its most intense stage during Meyer's presidency.

Much of the controversy centered on the mutual suspicions and actions of outspoken, tenacious disputants such as Meyer, Mc-Closkey, and Brightbill on the ARS side and the reticent, ailing Braucher, usually represented by his capable aides Arthur Williams and Thomas Rivers, for the NRA. While the proposal might have appeared to be a dead issue to numerous observers, the conflict was of crucial importance institutionally and personally to these influential leaders in recreation. Braucher's support tended to come from people in long-standing federal agencies with an interest in recreation, such as the National Park Service, while people of the Federal Security Agency often were more favorable to Meyer's position.[43] Recreation leaders around the country were divided; if most nationally prominent, professional figures endorsed a federal bureau, numerous others, both lay and professional, either followed the NRA or were uninterested.

Congress, too, showed little concern for the issue, but Meyer continued to push the matter. In February 1947 he called a meeting in Washington, D.C., aptly timed the day before a large conference of educators, which drew at least fifty representatives of numerous public and private groups to discuss federal recreation. By then the NRA argued that the Interagency Committee merited a thorough trial before creating a new, untried bureau, while the ARS approved the Interagency Committee but looked on it as merely a beginning. A committee of the ARS soon drafted a new bill, essentially the same as S. 2070, which the society formally endorsed 164–64 at its annual meeting in October, although introduction into Congress did not come until the following March.[44]

Meanwhile Braucher had found another excuse to delay any final NRA decision on overall federal recreation by awaiting an impending report of the prestigious Brookings Institution to a commission on executive reorganization of the federal government headed by former President Herbert Hoover. The key to Braucher's tactic was that he knew and encouraged well in advance the preference for the interagency approach held by the director of the report.[45]

By the time the report, which endorsed the Interagency Committee and did not recommend a separate bureau, became public in early 1949, the single-minded push by the ARS for a federal bureau obviously had begun to wane. The first president of the ARS, V. K. Brown, had succeeded Meyer as head of the society, and relations with the NRA started to improve. Brown, who had worked with the NRA on numerous occasions, had accepted the presidential position in hopes of healing the breach. He conferred with Braucher, and the two men, agreeing that the federal recreation dispute had ballooned disproportionately, decided to form a joint, top-level Committee on Cooperation which would emphasize constructive, united action for the good of the recreation movement on the many matters agreed upon by the ARS and NRA. Neither group altered its views or ended its opposing policy regarding a federal bureau, and the issue of which, if any, private organization or federal agency was to be the preeminent representative of the public recreation movement in the United States remained unresolved. Nonetheless relations between the NRA and ARS definitely seemed to be improving[46]

Meanwhile Braucher's health continued to fail, and the NRA, for all its direction and contributions to American recreation, was obviously in need of new top-level leadership and organizational rejuvenation. The NRA had promoted governmental responsibility, a broad concept of recreation, and professionalism so successfully over the years that expenditures for local public recreation were shooting upward as never before. Yet the ideas promoted by the NRA had obviously outgrown the organization, whose leaders had consistently neglected to periodically reassess its means and ends. For instance, the expenditures of the Association, expressed in constant dollars, still limped along at depression levels despite the general postwar boom, yet cautious Braucher did not venture along several likely avenues of additional financial support. The NRA initiated new programs, such as field service to state agencies, only by curtailing other needed activities, among them special services in music and dramatics. Belated efforts by Braucher and several directors to find a capable, young individual who would serve as executive secretary and devote his life to leading the NRA as Braucher had done were unsuccessful.

Then in early May 1949 Braucher, his health seriously strained, announced that George Dickie, a senior executive of the NRA, would soon become acting manager of the Association. A few weeks later, on May 22, Braucher died, terminating nearly forty years of dedicated, influential leadership in the NRA.[47] With Braucher dead and Meyer no longer head of the ARS, much of the controversy over federal recreation might cool and be replaced by more cooperative ventures. Braucher's death offered the Association an obvious opportunity to reevaluate its entire range of policies and operations, but such a truly searching reassessment required the services of a strongly imaginative leadership just at a time when the NRA was without the one man who had been its primary decision maker for years.

Joseph Prendergast

Joseph Prendergast, a lawyer and social welfare administrator, replaced Braucher as executive head of the NRA. He served from 1950 through the merger of the NRA to form the National Recreation and Park Association.

8
Reorganization: An Expanded Focus

In 1949 the death or retirement of several key leaders in the National Recreation Association signaled the obvious end of an era in the history of the organization. For instance, E. T. Attwell, who had directed the Bureau of Colored Work for nearly three decades, died that year. While out in the field on assignment, Lebert Weir also died, closing a career which had begun forty years earlier when the organization hired him as its first Association-paid field secretary. James E. Rogers, onetime director of the Community Service Training School in Chicago and the National Physical Education Service, retired.

By far the most significant of the losses suffered by the organization was the death of Howard Braucher, which clearly showed that the National Recreation Association had come to a major turning point. As secretary and then president, he, more than any other man, had exercised the ultimate authority over day-to-day decision making within the Association. For years this highly dedicated individual had been personally involved in every major aspect of the work of the NRA. When he died without having chosen, let alone trained, a successor, the directors, long accustomed to following his active leadership, were unable for months on end to secure a replacement.

The board of directors, a somewhat passive body on the whole, did count among its twenty-two members a small number of dedicated laymen who were strongly committed to the continuance of the work of the Association. Board chairman Robert Garrett, a Baltimore financier, had been involved as a volunteer in the recreation movement since 1903. A track and field standout at Princeton and later Olympic champion, Garrett was instrumental in establishing and developing the public recreation and park program in Baltimore.[1] In addition to Garrett, the strength of the board centered around Otto Mallery, a Philadelphia economist; Paul Moore, Jr., an Episcopalian clergyman; Grant Titsworth, a Connecticut industrialist; F. W. H. Adams, a New York attorney; and Susan Lee, daughter of early leader and long-time president Joseph Lee.

Aside from the loss of some key staff members during the time of Howard Braucher's illness and subsequent death, there remained a nucleus of veteran employees who had been carefully recruited by the NRA in the early phases of its work. Among the continuing staff with two decades or more of service under Braucher's leadership were federal and state specialist George Dickie, business manager Rose Swartz, financial authority Arthur Williams, fund raiser and convention manager Thomas Rivers, field service director Charles Reed, consultation specialist George Nesbitt, research director George Butler, and personnel services specialist Willard Sutherland. The academic backgrounds represented among the senior staff ranged from economics to chemical engineering, and the educational institutions attended included universities such as Yale, Drake, and Chicago.[2] While each of these able and dedicated staff members carried much of the same missionary zeal toward the work of the Association as did Braucher, none became active candidates to succeed him. As noted earlier, Braucher did little to prepare key staff members as potential successors to his position.

In addition to a relatively inactive board and aging but dedicated staff, the Association was dependent at the time of Braucher's death upon a limited financial base. The two major sources of funds were receipts from local donors through a sponsor appeal campaign, which in 1950 amounted to approximately $150,000, and an annual grant from the National Recreation School. The school, a separate corporation created by the NRA in 1930, advanced professional training and education for the wise use of leisure with assets derived from surpluses carried over from the War Camp Community Service funds. In 1950 the school appropriated $168,000 to the NRA in return for work carried on in behalf of the school in that year. Earned income from publications, subscriptions, and other services amounted to less than 20 percent of the operating budget.[3]

Prior to Howard Braucher's death and in recognition of his failing health, the board had appointed George Dickie as acting manager and Rose Swartz as acting executive secretary.[4] Both Dickie and Swartz were long-time senior staff members whose loyalty and dependability were unquestioned. Dickie's broad experience had included service as the first superintendent of municipal recreation in Oakland, California, and as first director of the National Recreation School. He was currently serving as executive secretary of the Federal Interagency Committee on Recreation, a coordinating post within the federal government funded by the NRA. Mrs. Swartz's service with the Association dated back to the War Camp Community Service during World War I. Her activities over the years had centered around business affairs including management of the yearly congress exhibits, advertising, and the publications program. Neither Dickie nor Mrs. Swartz was interested in being considered as a candidate for the permanent position of executive director.

The search committee to select a successor to Howard Braucher was chaired by the Reverend Paul Moore. The work of the committee spanned several months and involved an intensive evaluation of a number of candidates. The board was eager to replace Braucher with a man of equal social vision and commitment whose background could extend the influence of the NRA within the broader social structure of community service. Apparently little or no effort was made to recruit from within the ranks of the growing number of municipal recreation executives.[5]

In February 1950 the search committee completed its hunt, and the board unanimously voted the appointment of Joseph Prendergast, a New York lawyer and social worker, as executive director of the Association. Prendergast, a dark horse, was at the time of his appointment an official of the State Charities Aid Association of New York. He had graduated from Princeton University and while there had been a star halfback on the football team and the only student in the history of the university elected president of his class in each of his four undergraduate years. After graduating from Princeton, he had studied law at Oxford and had qualified as a barrister-at-law in England before returning to the United States to be admitted to private practice before the courts of the State of New York and the federal courts, and later to serve in the U.S. Department of Justice.

Prendergast's early years in both private and governmental legal service were interrupted by World War II. He enlisted in the army and rose to the rank of major. During his service, he was wounded and captured but escaped in Germany and ended up in a series of military hospitals. It was during this recuperative period that he decided upon a career in social service. Following the war he received a master of science degree from Columbia University's School of Social Work for graduate coursework in social action and community organization.[6]

Joseph Prendergast, experienced well beyond his few years as a social worker, assumed the post of executive director with relatively little specific knowledge or background in the public recreation field. He was selected to fill the shoes of a forty-year veteran who had given both inspirational and tactical leadership to the development of the public recreation movement virtually from its inception. Unlike Braucher, Prendergast was, since younger, more at home with the New Deal policies which were gaining a stronger place in the American scene. He was faced with the principal task of infusing new leadership and direction into an organization whose staff, board, and financial resources were strongly oriented to the more traditional philosophical and administrative doctrines of his predecessor.

From a governance point of view, the NRA under Braucher's leadership had evolved into a tightly controlled organization with a paid president and a small group of lay directors establishing policy. Yet there was at least one loophole in the official power structure which might have been penetrated by knowing recreation executives. In 1949 the constitution of the NRA provided that each person suggested as a possible director or officer by at least ten persons each contributing five dollars or more during the preceding twelve months was thereby nominated for such position. Election to the board was by vote of the corporate members of the Association who under New York State law were the members of the board of directors. Apparently recreation professionals were either unaware of or largely ignored this nominating provision of NRA's constitution since the board of directors had over the past three decades remained an exclusive lay body. This little-used and unknown part of the constitution was eliminated in 1950, and the NRA board became a totally self-perpetuating body.[7]

Nonetheless anxious to establish a more formal relationship with professional recreation personnel as well as the agencies NRA served, Prendergast implemented a new nonvoting "service membership" arrangement. A five-dollar associate membership was initiated for professionals and volunteers, and a ten-dollar affiliate membership was established for recreation agencies. Both memberships were heavily subsidized through other Association income and provided the member with an extensive range of services including *Recreation* magazine, newsletters and bulletins, and an annual membership directory. The new membership program received the enthusiastic support of recreation and park executives and leaders. By the end of 1951 there were 1,035 individual nonvoting members in 627 communities associated for service and 620 agencies in 529 communities affiliated for service with the NRA.[8] Within a short period of time the NRA had approximately the same number of individual members as did the American Recreation Society whose membership fee was three dollars annually. Presumably there was a high percentage of overlapping memberships between the two organizations. The attractive service package provided by the NRA at modest fees perhaps inadvertently discouraged the ARS from expanding revenue-producing membership services. At any rate, membership fees constituted the main source of revenue for the society for over two decades following its creation.

Despite the conciliatory efforts by ARS president V. K. Brown prior to Braucher's death, there remained areas of suspicion and confusion between the NRA and the ARS. Over the years, for instance, the lack of professional representation on the NRA board had reinforced a view in some quarters of paternalism toward the profession. Aware of such previous differences and sensing some remaining hostility, Prendergast in October 1950 met with all past presidents of the ARS in an effort to resolve any remaining points of contention between the two organizations.

Out of this meeting leaders of both organizations drew up and officially signed a joint membership statement. In that document the NRA was described as follows:

> The NRA is a national, voluntary, civic organization through which professional and lay citizenship participa-

tion can unite to provide the many nationwide services in the recreation field which are essential to the sound growth of recreation throughout the country.[9]

The complementary ARS was defined as:

A national, voluntary, professional fellowship organization concerned with the building of a strong professional group. Its program directed to the profession is designed to improve the quality of professional leadership and thus the quality of recreation services and opportunities.[10]

The joint statement then went on to proclaim:

The NRA and the ARS are glad to subscribe to this joint statement of the primary purpose of both organizations and to join in urging all professional recreation workers to participate in the activities of the Association and the Society as members of both. In this way effective, cooperative action can be developed for the advancement of the recreation movement and the recreation profession.

To the professional recreation workers and to the individual planning to enter the field, membership in the NRA and the ARS is not a case of 'either/or' but of identification with each and support of both.[11]

This statement guided the NRA's relationship not only with the ARS but with all other professional organizations during Prendergast's tenure as executive director.

As another part of Prendergast's general reorganization, the board approved a system of national and district advisory committees composed of leading recreators throughout the country. Professional advisory committees were created in the areas of administration; research; programs and activities; recruitment, training, and placement of personnel; special defense-related services; and international recreation services. District advisory committees were created in each of eight newly formed geographic districts.[12] All appointments to serve on the committees were at the invitation of the executive director, based upon recommenda-

---

Promoting the public recreation movement was a cause to which many NRA staff members devoted their entire professional lives. Pictured on the facing page are some of the senior staff members recruited by Braucher who continued their work under Prendergast's leadership. Each of their careers with the NRA spanned a period of over forty years.

George D. Butler, *Research*

George A. Nesbitt, *Technical Assistance*

Charles E. Reed, *Field Service*

Thomas E. Rivers, *International Recreation*

Willard C. Sutherland, *Personnel Services*

Arthur M. Williams, *Administration*

tions of individual staff members who served as the secretariat to each committee. While this expanded professional involvement strengthened the professionals' ties to the organization, the plan fell short of direct board involvement and representation. To some recreators the approach still smacked of paternalism yet was a welcome move from the more rigid control exercised by Braucher.

One of the more elusive goals of Prendergast's reorganization plan was the systematic organization of the lay leadership of the country interested in recreation. The national and district advisory system provided an effective mechanism for professional participation in the work program of the Association but did not include a decentralized program of citizen involvement. Unlike many other national voluntary organizations such as the YMCA, Boy Scouts of America, Girl Scouts, and others, the NRA operated without local chapters or a local structure. Moreover, the NRA's governance and funding sources were private while its end product—an effective public recreation system—was public and tax-supported. In comparison with similar other national nonprofit organizations, the NRA represented a paradox in terms of the national-local relationship.

Prendergast did, however, instigate a successful Chicago citizens' committee that not only raised funds for the NRA but carried out special projects as well. The committee included influential men and women in the Chicago area who had an interest in promoting the work of the NRA. During the early 1960s the Chicago women's committee organized and conducted a demonstration recreation project for the homebound, and the men's committee undertook a project to preserve open space in the Chicago metropolitan area. Plans to make the Chicago committee the first organized chapter of the Association were interrupted by the merger that occurred in 1965.[13]

Also at the community level citizen boards and commissions affiliated with local public recreation and park agencies provided a major potential source of lay input. For decades the NRA had pioneered and promoted the establishment of this type of citizen group, many times in opposition to such organizations as the International City Managers Association. The diversified pattern of local government throughout the country did not, however, lend itself to a strong, uniform national-local citizen partnership. NRA efforts tended to be in the direction of expanding technical services to boards and commissions while encouraging participation of local board and commission members in district and national conferences. In addition to maintaining informal relationships with recreation boards and commissions, the NRA had periodic contact with thirteen thousand local citizens who supported the Association financially through its sponsor and contributor programs.

Prendergast's initial efforts were placed on expanding and strengthening the national board, a known quantity when compared to the somewhat unclear relationship between the NRA and its typical lay supporter. In 1950 there were twenty-two members on the board of directors with a maximum of forty-eight permitted by the charter. Among guidelines developed by Prendergast and his staff for considering new board members were an interest in the work of the Association, geographical and occupational balance, availability to attend board meetings, and a willingness to raise money. The strategy followed was to recruit a core of active board members yet not exclude those who might contribute in ways other than through regular board attendance. As a result of these efforts an element of revitalization was achieved. However, the problem of poor board attendance remained with an average of only one-third of the board attending scheduled meetings. Like many similar organizations, there was a general apathy among board members toward extensive committee work. Despite impressive efforts to expand and strengthen the board, much of the control of the NRA in actuality remained with Prendergast, who served as secretary and a voting member of the board. During his tenure the office of president remained unfilled, and the office of the chairman of the board became the lay leadership position within the Association.[14]

Various loyal and able men served as chairman under Prendergast. Philadelphia economist Otto Mallery, long-time NRA director, succeeded Robert Garrett as board chairman in 1950 and served until his death in 1956. New York lawyer Francis W. H. Adams served for one year and was followed by industrialist Grant Titsworth in 1958 who continued as chairman until his death in 1960. Titsworth was succeeded by New York banker James H. Evans, who was to play a major role in the eventual merger of NRA with related national recreation and park organizations.[15]

Mallery, however, helped steer the Association through its third venture in stimulating recreation for Americans dislocated by war. The Korean conflict, which broke out in June 1950 with the attack by North Korean Communist forces on South Korea, created the most serious international crisis since World War II. While not of the magnitude of that global conflict, the situation nonetheless demanded a national mobilization effort.

The key role of the NRA in organizing War Camp Community Service during World War I and the supportive role the Association had played in the development of federal and local community service support systems during World War II provided the framework for the NRA's involvement in the Korean War. The focus of the Association's concern in national mobilization efforts was in strengthening those services, specifically recreation, that were essential to the health, welfare, and morale of military personnel and defense-impacted communities.

In the summer of 1950 the NRA participated in a number of conferences organized by the National Social Welfare Assembly which led to the creation of the United Defense Fund (UDF). The function of this new agency, which operated as an unofficial subsidiary of Community Chests and Councils, was to solicit and allocate funds for charitable agencies for national defense services and activities. Other cooperating agencies included the United Service Organizations (USO), United Community Defense Services, American Relief for Korea, American Social Hygiene Association, and the United Seamen's Service. Through its partnership in this federated approach to fund raising, the Association received approximately $410,000 over the five-year existence of the UDF. These funds were used to strengthen the Association's capacity to provide technical services to military and defense-impacted communities across the nation. A fifty-member National Advisory Committee on Defense Related Services was created to advise the NRA in its basic planning in this area.[16]

The NRA's successful experience in the United Defense Fund was instrumental in shifting the fund raising policy of the former away from almost total reliance on the traditional and somewhat expensive local sponsor method. The growth of united funds with their broader support for the inclusion of national agencies after the Korean War prompted the NRA to adopt a policy of seeking support from united funds and chests when it was determined that such action would be mutually advantageous. This change in policy was bolstered by a study of the NRA's fund raising policies and procedures undertaken by John Price Jones and Company in 1955. This study, instigated by Prendergast, represented NRA's first attempt to utilize professional fund raising counsel. The essence of the study's several recommendations was that the NRA should increase its "grass roots" image and develop a stronger decentralized citizen support system to back up its fund raising efforts. The evolution to greater reliance on federated fund raising is supported by the fact that in 1950 the Association received a total of only $801 from three community chests; by 1957 the NRA received $120,574 from forty-four chests and funds; and in 1965 it received $161,310 from ninety-seven chests and funds.[17]

With this apparently broadening base of support, the NRA's traditional services, such as the magazine, annual conference, field service, and consulting work, not only had survived the depression and lean war years but had expanded in magnitude to form the nucleus of the Association's work during the 1950s. In addition Prendergast developed several new initiatives such as the formal International Recreation Service in 1952 and the Consultation Service on Recreation for the Ill and Handicapped in 1953.

The International Recreation Service grew out of increasing contact with foreign nations. Almost from the founding of the NRA there had been an interest in play in other lands. Prior to World War I C. M. Goethe, a member of the board of directors, had made a trip around the world to establish and finance playgrounds in Asia. In 1932 the Association had sponsored the first International Recreation Congress, held in Los Angeles in connection with the Olympic games. Expanding interest in human affairs on an international level after World War II, influenced by the formation of the United Nations, prompted the NRA to establish an International Recreation Service. Long-time staff associate Thomas Rivers headed this new unit, housed in the new Carnegie Endowment International Center located across from the United Nations building in New York City. The International Recreation Service centralized and expanded the NRA's services to recreation leaders and agencies in other countries throughout the world. This organizational unit of NRA was the forerunner of the International Recreation Association which was to be created in 1956.[18]

Another new program of the 1950s was formed to provide recreation services for the ill and handicapped. Over the years the NRA's interest in this area had tended to mirror that shown by society in general. One of the first committees created by the PAA in 1907 had concentrated on play in institutions. Despite the fact that the Association had employed a full-time specialist who provided technical assistance to 158 institutions for children and the aged as early as 1931, it was not until 1953 that the NRA assumed a major role in promoting recreation services for the ill and handicapped. Mrs. Beatrice Hill, a volunteer leader, provided much of the stimulus for this venture and convinced Prendergast of the growing importance of recreation for special groups. The new service provided advice and consultation to individuals and organizations including hospitals, nursing homes, special agencies, and local community groups on developing programs and activities for handicapped and sick people. The unit produced the first film on therapeutic recreation, *Rx Recreation*, and published the results of a national study on recreation in hospitals under the title *Recreation in Hospitals: Report of a Study of Organized Recreation Programs in Hospitals and of Personnel Conducting Them.*[19]

In 1960 the director of this service would be instrumental in creating Comeback, Inc., an autonomous organization devoted exclusively to promoting recreation services for the ill and handicapped. While the new group carried out many of the same type of programs, the NRA nonetheless was to retain its work in the field until the time of the merger in 1965.[20]

Meanwhile the National Recreation Association had marked its fiftieth anniversary in 1956. During its half century of operation, both the Association and the nation it served had survived two world wars and a major depression. Many far-reaching changes affecting recreation had occurred in the American way of life. The population had more than doubled since 1906, and the standard of living had reached an all-time high. During the preceding fifty years, the concept of recreation had broadened to keep pace with changing cultural patterns in the nation. With the growing public acceptance of leisure, nowhere was the influence of the NRA's leadership more apparent than in the area of local public recreation. By 1956 more than three thousand communities had established playgrounds staffed with professional leaders, and over twelve hundred localities had recreation departments headed by full-time recreation executives. City and regional park and recreation agencies owned and operated more than one million acres of park and recreation properties.[21] The concept of public tax-supported recreation had become an accepted tenet of community life, and a new profession had developed around this established public service. The golden anniversary of the NRA not only marked a period of significant accomplishment but represented a new era of opportunity for the Association.

As a part of the anniversary celebration, the NRA purchased and formally dedicated a new permanent headquarters at 8 West Eighth Street in New York City. The series of four-story brownstone buildings, formerly the home of the Whitney Museum of American Art, replaced space the Association had rented since

Left, NRA headquarters building
Center, NRA library
Below, Map of regional offices

NRA purchased the Whitney Museum of American Art in 1956 as the new location for its headquarters. The building housed the NRA library which contained over 5,000 volumes on recreation. In addition to its New York headquarters, the Association maintained field service offices in eight regional areas of the country.

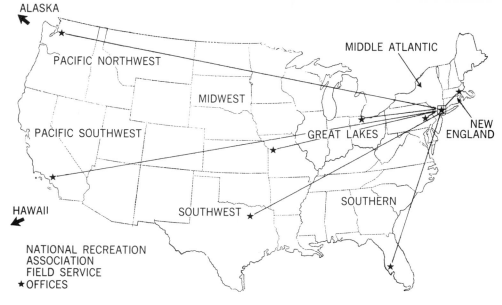

ALASKA

PACIFIC NORTHWEST

MIDDLE ATLANTIC

MIDWEST

PACIFIC SOUTHWEST

GREAT LAKES

NEW ENGLAND

SOUTHERN

HAWAII

SOUTHWEST

NATIONAL RECREATION
ASSOCIATION
FIELD SERVICE
★OFFICES

1922 in the Remington Rand Building at 315 Fourth Avenue. Prior to that time the PRAA had been at 1 Madison Avenue in the Metropolitan Life Building. The Whitney property was purchased at a price of $300,000 with a loan from the National Recreation School. A mortgage was to be amortized at the rate of $3,000 per year. In addition to this annual obligation, Prendergast was to arrange a series of additional payments on the principal over a period of ten years whereby the mortgage would be paid in full by 1965.[22]

The NRA's golden anniversary was also commemorated by the sponsorship of an international recreation congress in Philadelphia. An international meeting had not been held in over twenty years. The event marked the inauguration of the International Recreation Association (IRA), now known as the World Leisure and Recreation Association. This new organization, an outgrowth of the NRA's International Recreation Service, had the full backing not only of the NRA but also of similar organizations and interests in other countries. The directors of the NRA voted to make available without cost the services of associate executive director Thomas Rivers to serve as director general of the new organization for three years, pending the development of independent financial support. The NRA also provided secretarial service and paid the rent for office space in the new Carnegie building for the same period. Three board members from the Association were invited to serve as directors of the new international organization.[23]

The international experiment proved a success, and at the end of the three years, the IRA became totally independent of the NRA. Rivers became the permanent director general of the new body. While relationships between the organizations had been mutually supportive at the outset, some misunderstandings subsequently developed between the two groups. These differences centered on jurisdictional responsibilities and potential competition in fund raising. The NRA board reaffirmed a continuing role for the NRA's International Recreation Service in handling inquiries from foreign countries with reference to American recreation programs received by the NRA. The board also felt it was proper for the NRA to provide exposition and exchange programs so that foreign agencies could be aware of domestic methods and programs, to keep NRA congresses and conferences open to foreign recreation organizations and individuals, and to publish appropriate international news in NRA publications. While the NRA continued to make its services and facilities available to the IRA, Prendergast and the NRA board remained wary of potential service conflicts and possible efforts by IRA to raise funds in a competitive manner from the NRA's traditional sponsors and supporters.[24]

Other new programs started by the Association during the fiftieth anniversary year included the establishment of an internship program and the inauguration of the observance of June as National Recreation Month. The internship program, somewhat similar to a lapsed scheme begun by Braucher in the late 1930s, was a cooperative venture between the NRA, colleges and universities, and selected communities across the country to provide intensive postgraduate experience and study for a select group of graduates from college recreation curricula. National Recreation Month was a nationwide public information and education event designed to give recreation agencies and leaders an opportunity to highlight the importance of recreation in community life. It was tied closely to the opening of summer facilities and services as well as to recognition of community leaders and civic groups who had made outstanding contributions to local recreation movements.[25]

Under Prendergast's direction the NRA not only began new emphases but also achieved greater stability as an organization over the course of more than a decade. Its administrative and financial structure; its constituency and services; and its relationships with other related organizations all had changed at least to some degree from the policies and programs pursued by the preceding administration.

The governing board more than doubled in number since 1950, and while still oriented to the urban Northeast, the geographic composition began to reflect a greater national character. Under Prendergast's leadership, professionals were added to the board beginning in 1960 with the election of George Hjelte, general manager of the Los Angeles Department of Recreation and Parks, and Robert Crawford, commissioner of recreation in Philadelphia. Later the chairmen of the district advisory councils and the chairman of the national advisory council, all professionals, were added to the board.[26]

Yet aside from some new faces, particularly among field staff, few changes were made in staffing patterns of the NRA. Most of the key senior staff members were holdovers from the Braucher era and carried with them the same commitments to the traditional social service mission of the Association. While this provided Prendergast with a strong core of knowledgeable, dedicated, and loyal employees, it did not provide the organization with the vitality of new ideas and directions. Had Prendergast systematically infused the organization with new blood in key staff positions, the focus of its program and influence might have changed more dramatically from that of the past.

There was, however, significant change in sources of financial support. By 1964 approximately 40 percent of the NRA's budget came from earnings including general service fees, sales of publications, and interest on endowments. The remaining 60 percent came from sponsor and individual contributor support (24 percent), united fund and community chest support (19 percent), and recurring grants principally from the National Recreation School (17 percent).[27] Under Prendergast's influence, the NRA had moved markedly toward greater reliance on earned income and upon funds raised through federated fund raising. As a matter of policy, the Association by the 1960s submitted its budget for review to the National Budget and Consultation Committee sponsored by the United Community Funds and Councils of America and the National Social Welfare Assembly. Approval by this body was essential in securing the support of community chests, united funds, and local licensing and endorsement agencies.[28]

The impressive increase in earned income over the previous decade was attributable to the implementation of membership fees, the expanded sale of publications and services, and the growth of the Association's endowment fund. Virtually from its inception, the NRA board had adopted and continuously reaffirmed a policy of placing monies left to the Association by bequest into the endowment fund thereby capitalizing the donor's annual giving; in addition, the board policy required that all monies left to the Association in memory or honor of a particular person be placed in the endowment fund thereby restricting the use of such funds to the income therefrom.[29]

During Prendergast's tenure the NRA continued to receive substantial grants from another key source, the National Recreation School. Prendergast, executive director of both the NRA and the school, was instrumental in restructuring the latter and establishing the National Recreation Foundation.

The school, established in 1926 and incorporated in 1930, had operated for nine years as the building-centered school of the National Recreation Association. From 1935 to 1949 the school had maintained its own staff and conducted training institutes in the name of the Association across the country. Between 1950 and 1956 the school made specific educational grants to the NRA to conduct training programs, and from 1957 to 1965 it made general grants to the Association for broad educational purposes. It also made grants to the International Recreation Association between 1957 and 1960.[30]

In 1964 Prendergast recommended that the National Recreation School be reactivated as the operating educational and research arm of the NRA and that a National Recreation Foundation be established to take over the grant-making functions of the school. An underlying rationale was that the school had a charter which allowed it to undertake certain special activities in the field of education not permitted to noneducational organizations and that such charters had become difficult to obtain. Prendergast envisioned the school as an educational and research department of the Association with two divisions: a National Institute for Recreation Research and a National Institute for Recreation Education. The boards of both the NRA and the NRS approved the proposal which ultimately led to the establishment of the National Recreation Foundation. The creation of a new antonomous foundation also provided the structure for carrying out an earlier trustee goal of making grants not only to the NRA, but also to academic institutions and other organizations for specific research and demonstration projects approved by the foundation board.[31]

Between 1906 and the end of 1965 the Association had raised and expended a total of $45,959,355 for the advancement of the recreation profession and the recreation movement. On December 31, 1965 the Association's endowment fund had a cash value of $1,487,431, an increase of $914,080 over 1950. The principal fund of the newly created foundation had a cash value of $5,647,478, an increase of $3,008,815 over the 1950 assets of the National Recreation School.[32]

The NRA itself as a service organization had developed a constituency of 2,071 affiliated recreation and park agencies and 4,536 individual service associates by 1964. It had about fourteen thousand financial contributors, just short of the large number of individual donors recruited by Howard Braucher. The staff numbered ninety-four, about the same size as in the late Braucher years, of which thirty-four were professional staff including eleven assigned full-time to field service in eight geographic districts.

A summary of the activities carried out by the NRA in 1964 provides an understanding of the program priorities emphasized under Prendergast's leadership. During the course of the year, NRA field staff made 1,211 visits to 620 communities and 100 military installations. They participated in 128 meetings of state recreation societies and seventy-three meetings of other organizations. In addition, they visited fifty colleges and universities, planned and participated in twenty-three meetings of their district advisory committees, and conducted nine district conferences. The field staff held forty-two leadership training institutes which reached more than two thousand people. They also made fifty-six surveys, plans, and special evaluations of recreation areas, facilities and programs.

The NRA personnel service maintained the professional credentials of some thirteen thousand recreation personnel and during the course of the year sent over six hundred notices to those on the active list about some four hundred position vacancies. Formal confidential personnel records of 964 candidates were sent to employers on request. The personnel department in addition administered the national internship program and conducted the annual Institute for Recreation and Park Administration. This office also undertook studies on personnel matters and published pamphlets such as *Personnel Standards in Community Recreation Leadership*.

The NRA program service annually handled over two thousand inquiries on program activities. Each year this department prepared the *Playground Summer Notebook*, and from time to time the agency wrote books and pamphlets on special subjects such as the *Day Camp Program Book*. In the early 1960s the NRA added a consultant on performing arts to its staff to provide leadership for the increasing interest in cultural recreation. A new series of booklets was prepared on the *Performing Arts as Recreation* as was a *Guide to the Organization and Administration of Cultural Recreation Programs*.

The NRA also maintained a correspondence and consultation unit which answered thousands of inquiries each year on various aspects of recreation including during the course of the year 180 requests from forty-three different countries.

The public information and education department organized and coordinated National Recreation Month, edited two different monthly newsletters, administered a citation program honoring laymen for outstanding service to the recreation movement, and handled news releases and overall public relations.

The consulting service on recreation for the ill and handicapped handled over two thousand inquiries annually, developed resource material, conducted training institutes, and participated in demonstration projects.

The research department was responsible for studies, development of planning and operational standards, and preparation of an annual summary of recreation research. One of the principal reports of this department was the *Recreation and Park Yearbook*, published at five-year intervals rather than annually as had been the case in several earlier decades. These major studies furnished a unique record of the growth of recreation leadership, expenditures, and services of public recreation and park agencies throughout the country. Information gathered through the research department provided data for four of the NRA's major books: *Introduction to Community Recreation, Playgrounds—Their Administration and Operation, Recreation Areas—Their Design and Equipment,* and *Community Sports and Athletics.*

An important support element of the research department was the NRA library. Some five thousand bound volumes, two hundred periodicals, and forty-four vertical files were an extensive reference source. A new *Research Newsletter* was inaugurated in 1964 to inform local executives and educators of research trends and developments.

The NRA also maintained a recreation book center which distributed more than seven hundred publications from ninety-eight commercial publishers on various aspects of recreation. A thirty-two page annotated list of the center's books was made available to members to facilitate mail orders.

The national recreation congress, started in 1907, continued to be an important part of the Association's work. Beginning in 1957 the American Recreation Society joined the NRA as a co-sponsor of the congress. Under the joint sponsorship arrangement, the annual conference was managed by a congress policy committee composed of equal representation from the NRA and the ARS. In 1963 2,204 delegates from the fifty states and fifteen foreign countries attended the congress in St. Louis.

Recreation magazine, also dating to 1907, had reached a circulation of 13,400 by 1964. This monthly journal for many years had been accepted as the standard resource on current recreation trends and problems. Its total number of annual pages was 494 and its five sections covered forty-five broad categories of subject matter. Some eighty pages were devoted to advertising.[33]

Essentially all of the NRA's services then had been carried on in some form by the Association virtually from its inception. What had drastically changed was the recreation field itself. While the NRA had modified and expanded its services within the resources available, the diversity and magnitude of the emerging leisure service field, as many advocates came to call recreation, made the NRA increasingly vulnerable to competition from other organizations.

For instance, the Federation of National Professional Organizations for Recreation had been organized in 1953 with the help of the Athletic Institute, a nonprofit organization supported by athletic goods manufacturers. The Athletic Institute became interested in the recreation movement following World War II and sponsored a number of workshops and projects aimed at strengthening the recreation and park field. The new federation was organized to facilitate coordination and cooperation between professional organizations serving the recreation field. Its membership included the American Recreation Society; American Institute of Park Executives; American Association of Group Workers; American Camping Association; National Industrial Recreation Association; Association of College Unions; College Recreation Association; American Association for Health, Physical Education, and Recreation; and the Society of State Directors of Health, Physical Education, and Recreation. Both the NRA and the Athletic Institute, as nonprofessional organizations, served as consultants to the federation. While the NRA's relationships with the member organizations tended to be good, each by its very existence posed a potential threat to the NRA's traditional dominance of the recreation field.[34]

On the social service side, the NRA was a member of the National Social Welfare Assembly, a joint planning and coordinating body of social welfare agencies. Through this group the Association maintained a working relationship with such organizations as Boys Clubs of America, Camp Fire Girls, Boy Scouts of America, and other voluntary recreation-oriented organizations.[35]

Prendergast's earlier legal career in the Justice Department and his knowledge of the federal government enhanced the NRA's influence in Washington during the 1950s and 60s. Indeed, the Association represented the entire field of recreation on such important governmental planning bodies as the Advisory Committee on the Arts of the projected National Cultural Center and the advisory council to the Outdoor Recreation Resources Review Commission. Representatives of the Association appeared before committees of the Senate and the House of Representatives on innumerable bills before Congress relating to recreation and parks. Ultimately a permanently staffed office was opened by the NRA in Washington, D.C.[36]

Despite this increasing range of involvement in the broad recreation field, the NRA, in the eyes of some of its critics, still remained too narrow in its focus. One such critic, Ben Solomon, editor of *Youth Leaders Digest*, went so far as to characterize the

NRA as still mainly a playground association, a charge strongly rebutted by Prendergast in an open letter sent to all service associates and affiliates of NRA.[37]

Nevertheless the Association was increasingly, as had been the case for several decades, only one of many spokesmen for the widening recreation field, spawned in large part by its own actions. During the 1930s, the reader will recall, board member Otto Mallery had stated that the NRA had staked out one of the richest gold mines in the United States, leisure, and had predicted that for years to come others would be mining it.[38] By the opening of the 1960s, this prediction had become a self-fulfilling prophecy. The people of no other country and no other age had anything like the leisure and recreational choices of the American people. *Life* had reported that in 1959 the average American wage earner had about 3,700 free hours, the equivalent of 230 full 16-hour days off a year. The same authority had estimated that the nation was spending $40 billion a year on leisure expenditures, or more than 8 percent of the gross national product.[39] This tremendous growth in leisure and recreation had profound consequences for the National Recreation Association. In measuring the NRA's past performance against its current challenge, long-time park administrator Charles Doell commented that:

> . . . [the NRA] has been the giant in the business. It promoted the introduction of playgrounds into our park systems and play into the park services. It infused into public services the philosophy and therapeutic value of recreation in the fullness of its meaning. It established a school for the education of recreators. It organized a field service to aid administrators in utilizing programs of recreation as well as guiding them as to the kind and number of properties needed for this new service. It did research, suggested standards, made surveys, produced literature. It was represented on practically all important national meetings and studies wherein recreation was related. Truly, NRA has a remarkable record.
>
> However good the past performance of NRA has been, frankly its present day performance is not sufficient for today.[40]

Doell's comments might have been made with equal validity three decades earlier, but not until Prendergast's administration had matured did the Association critically examine the full range of possible courses of action open to it in the circumstances. Faced with the dilemma of insufficient resources to service a rapidly expanding field, the NRA was forced to consider alternatives for the future. One option was to continue its existing goals and current organization with the consequence of facing more competition from related and newly emerging organizations. A second possibility was to abandon its commitment for broad service to the recreation field and concentrate on one or two highly selective areas such as research or public education. Such a choice would have involved encouraging the American Recreation Society and other professional groups to assume the professional service role. A third and seemingly more appealing choice was to merge its resources with other related organizations in order to build a stronger, unified national organization that would be capable of providing strengthened and more effective lay and professional leadership. Prendergast and the board of directors opted for that alternative and embarked on a program of exploring ways in which NRA could coordinate its programs more effectively with related organizations. The results of this course of action are the subject of the next chapter.

James H. Evans

Luther Gulick

Susan M. Lee

Robert W. Crawford

Key leadership for the NRA's involvement in merger negotiations was provided by board chairman James H. Evans and vice-presidents Luther Gulick, Susan M. Lee, and Robert W. Crawford.

9
The Merger of National Recreation and Park Organizations

The decade of the 1960s marked a new era for the NRA, especially in its views regarding the role of the professional recreation leader in the governance of the Association and perhaps more importantly in the relationship the NRA was to develop with professional organizations in the recreation and park field. The election of two prominent practitioners, George Hjelte and Robert W. Crawford, to the board in 1960 marked the increasing recognition by Prendergast and the directors of the growing importance of the professional administrator in the direction of policy in the Association.

By this time the board was undergoing another change in its citizen leadership. With the sudden death of industrialist Grant Titsworth in 1960, the directors elected lawyer-banker James H.

Evans as their new chairman. Evans had become interested in the NRA while serving on the NRA citizens committee in Chicago. He assumed a more active role in the affairs of the Association upon his transfer to New York City as vice-president of the Reuben H. Donnelley Corporation.[1] Evans had been an active member of the executive committee, and his leadership and public relations skills had gained the attention and respect of his fellow directors. It was these same abilities in human relations that would make Evans a central figure in the creation of the National Recreation and Park Association.

An important national development taking place at this time, and one which was to indirectly influence the future of the NRA, was the work of the Outdoor Recreation Resources Review Commission (ORRRC). This bipartisan congressional study panel had been established in 1958 and charged with the responsibility of determining the outdoor recreation needs of the American people for the next forty years. The work of the commission, chaired by wealthy conservationist Laurance S. Rockefeller, was focusing national attention upon the increasing demand for outdoor recreation opportunities by the American public. While the NRA's executive director, Joseph Prendergast, and board member Luther Gulick served on the advisory council to ORRRC, much of the impetus for and direction of the study came not from recreation and park organizations but rather from conservation groups such as the Isaac Walton League.[2]

The ORRRC report pointed out that the overall demand for outdoor recreation would triple by the year 2000 and called for expanded roles by all levels of government in acquiring and protecting needed recreation resources. ORRRC recommendations resulted in the creation of a Bureau of Outdoor Recreation in the Department of the Interior and in the establishment of a major federal grant-in-aid program, the Land and Water Conservation Fund, for acquiring and developing outdoor recreation areas.[3] While the NRA and ARS had vigorously opposed each other over the question of a federal recreation service in the late 1940s, both organizations compliantly supported the creation of the new bureau recommended by ORRRC. However, in its resolution of support, the ARS predictably suggested the deletion of the word "outdoor." By this time the NRA had accepted continuing federal involvement not only as inevitable but also as desirable. Prendergast, however, preferred the establishment of an independent federal recreation commission rather than the creation of a new bureau within the Department of the Interior.[4]

The ORRRC report served as an important stimulant in encouraging the NRA and related organizations to explore ways in which they might cooperate and utilize their resources more effectively. For the NRA it reinforced the fact that the recreation field was growing so rapidly that the Association itself could no longer exercise the leadership it once did. NRA vice-president Luther Gulick, nephew of the founder of the Playground Association of America and a member of the ORRRC advisory council, summed up the changing situation for his fellow directors by stating, "the nation stands on the threshold of tremendous developments in recreation and parks, greater than for two generations; it is important to develop a whole new general strategy, to take a broad look and start anew, concentrating on positive moves."[5] Gulick, who headed the Institute for Public Administration, was becoming an increasingly active and influential member of the NRA board. He along with board chairman Evans and professional administrator Crawford infused a new vitality and leadership into the board.

With the emerging emphasis on outdoor recreation during the late 1950s and early 1960s came new incentives for blending recreation and park philosophies. While the early work of NRA field secretary Lebert Weir had done much to bridge the philosophical gap between the social service-oriented recreation specialist and the natural resource-oriented park administrator, some differences still remained. In 1928 Weir had pointed out the sources of these differences in his highly regarded book on municipal and county parks. He noted that the original concept of parks in the minds of the early park planners was for recreation of a passive, semiactive kind, the dominent ideal being peaceful enjoyment amid beautiful surroundings of a naturalistic kind. Yet he stated that, with the public's expanding ideas of recreation, parks out of necessity had to be planned to accommodate a wider range of activities and park agencies had to be prepared to deal with a series of complex and difficult social problems that were inevitably associated with the urban environment.[6]

The NRA had expanded its interest and involvement in park concerns beyond Weir's early work. For example, NRA staff members George Dickie and Temple Jarrell provided executive staff services to the Federal Interagency Committee on Recreation which brought the NRA into continuous contact with the federal land owning agencies such as the National Park Service, Forest Service and Bureau of Land Management. In the mid-1950s Prendergast had employed William M. Hay, former director of the

Tennessee state parks, and Harold W. Lathrop, erstwhile head of the Minnesota state parks, as district representatives, thus strengthening the Association's capacity to render technical assistance in park management.

By the time of the ORRRC study there was a clear national trend in support of the unified administration of recreation and parks at the local level. As a natural outgrowth of this movement, the National Recreation Association and the American Recreation Society, the recreation-oriented national organizations, became more concerned with park issues, and the American Institute of Park Executives (AIPE), a major advocate for the municipal park movement, became involved to a greater degree with recreation matters. As a result of these overlapping interests, organizational philosophies and goals became somewhat similar, while competition for members and revenue became more intense. Duplicate institutional services, such as national conferences, magazines, and membership promotion, became a matter of consideration not only by members but for exhibitors and advertisers as well. Many professional leaders in the field alluded to the increasing confusion between recreation and park groups and openly spoke out in favor of combining organizations.[7]

The idea of eliminating competition through unification or consolidation of national recreation organizations was not a new one. The suggestion had been made as early as 1909 that the fledgling Playground Association of America merge with the American Physical Education Association. Pioneer Luther Gulick, shortly after he had resigned from leadership of the PAA, had suggested in 1911 the formation of a public recreation federation. His plan at that time had called for changing the Playground and Recreation Association to a "Public Recreation Federation." Under his proposal the general association would have retained control over a majority of the board, the field staff, and common finances. Each special interest organization was to retain its own name, have representation on the overall board, raise the special expenses for its own program subject to approval by a general finance committee, and select its own paid specialized staff.

The basis for his concept of a coordinating recreation corporation had been to eliminate the "considerable duplication between different national organizations having to do with the leisure time among the people of America."[8] In addition to the playground movement, Gulick had proposed including public school athletic leagues, commercial recreation, social centers, boys' clubs, the Boy Scout movement, the Camp Fire Girls (of which Gulick was also founder), and an agency to censor motion pictures. PRAA president Joseph Lee had rejected the proposal on the theory that four of the areas (public school athletics, commercial recreation, playgrounds, and social centers) already were more or less being looked after by the Playground Association. Lee also had felt that the Boy Scouts and the Camp Fire Girls would eventually come into the PRAA structure after leaders of each had "made their own ideas clear and incisive as a separate organization."[9]

Some years later, in 1937, the policy makers of the NRA had declined an opportunity to have the newly formed American Recreation Society become a department within the structure of the NRA. At the time of formation there had been strong sentiment by recreation practitioners to have the new professional organization be a part of the NRA.[10]

In addition to these early efforts at consolidation, a formal attempt had been made in 1948 to amalgamate the American Recreation Society and the American Institute of Park Executives into a new organization to be known as the American Park and Recreation Society. Yet following approval by the executive committees of both organizations, interest in the plan had faded and was not to be rekindled until the merger discussions of the early 1960s.[11]

The formation of the Federation of National Professional Organizations for Recreation in 1953 did, however, establish an organizational vehicle for periodic contact among the ten affiliated organizations. The federation met semiannually; its membership included the executive directors and one appointed official representative from each organization. The joint program was directed at projects of mutual concern and included such matters as the development of an accreditation program for recreation and park curricula and the establishment of common ground for needed federal legislation on recreation. About half of the member groups had recreation and parks as a primary focus, while the remaining agencies, such as the Association of College Unions and the National Association of Social Workers, considered recreation as an important collateral interest.[12]

Whereas unification apparently was never a serious question considered by the federation, some member agencies—especially those whose principal interest was in the recreation and park area —did become independently involved in negotiations for merger in the early 1960s. Key among these were the National Recreation Association, which served as a consultant to the federation, the American Recreation Society, and the American Institute of Park Executives. The National Conference on State Parks, while neither a member of the federation nor active in early discussions, was to become an important part of the deliberations prior to the formal merger. The National Industrial Recreation Association showed an initial interest in these efforts but withdrew as the negotiations became more serious.[13]

Among organizations likely to consolidate, the NRA was by far the largest in terms of financial resources and staff. Its budget for 1963 was $924,000. The NRA staff was made up of approximately one hundred full-time members of which some thirty were professional. The Association had an endowment fund just short of one million dollars and owned a headquarters building in New York City valued at approximately a half-million dollars. Its members and individual contributors numbered eighteen thousand. Most of the NRA's financial support was from philanthropic sources with only 3 percent of its budget coming from membership fees. In addition to its New York headquarters, the Association maintained staff in Washington, D.C. and in eight regional offices throughout the country.[14]

The American Recreation Society, celebrating its twenty-fifth anniversary in 1963, had by that time increased its membership to 4,200 which continued to approximate the number of recreation leaders who belonged to the NRA. The ARS was organized into special interest sections which included armed forces recreation; hospital recreation; public and park recreation; professional education; county, state, and federal recreation; private and voluntary agencies; and religious organizations. An executive director, an administrative assistant, and a secretary made up the ARS staff. The annual operating budget was approximately $50,000, of which 70 percent came from membership dues and the remainder from the sale of advertising and publications. The ARS published its own magazine, *The American Recreation Journal*, and jointly sponsored an annual national convention with the NRA.[15]

The American Institute of Park Executives had been established in 1898 primarily to gather and disseminate information on public parks and recreation areas. By 1963 AIPE's membership included some two thousand park and recreation administrators who constituted the voting membership of the organization. In addition there were about a thousand local park and recreation board members affiliated in a nonvoting capacity. The AIPE's operating budget was just under $190,000, of which approximately 22 percent was derived from membership dues. Much of AIPE's income was generated from a strong commercial exhibit component of their national conference and from an especially successful publication

Joseph Prendergast, NRA

Alfred B. LaGasse, AIPE

Ray R. Butler, ARS

During the unification discussions, executive directors Prendergast, La-Gasse, and Butler served as chief interpreters of their organizations' positions on merger.

program. While AIPE was regarded essentially as a park-oriented organization, it had attracted a sizable group of recreation administrators to the point where its membership was almost evenly divided between park and recreation practitioners. The AIPE headquarters was located at Oglebay Park in Wheeling, West Virginia.[16]

Closely affiliated with the park executives was the American Association of Zoological Parks and Aquariums, an autonomous organization created in 1924 and dedicated to wildlife conservation. Many of the general services of AAZPA were jointly operated for purposes of economy with AIPE out of Oglebay Park. The zoological group was not particularly active in the merger negotiations but merely followed the leadership of the AIPE.

By way of comparison, the total yearly expenditures of both the ARS and the AIPE amounted to just over one-quarter of the existing budget of the NRA. There was the same magnitude of difference in financial resources between the AIPE and ARS. The American Institute of Park Executives had four times the annual budget of the American Recreation Society.

The initiative in the 1960s for improving organizational relationships began with discussions between the NRA and ARS at a combined board meeting arranged by Prendergast and William Frederickson, president of the ARS, in January 1962. This was the first such session to be held in the history of the society. At the conclusion of the meeting conducted by NRA chairman James Evans, the two organizations appointed a joint committee, chaired by public administrator Luther Gulick of the NRA with educator Edith Ball of the ARS as vice chairman, to consider areas of cooperation. As a part of its study procedures the body sent out a questionnaire to the 10,250 members of both organizations seeking their views on organizational relationships. Of the 2,837 who returned the questionnaire, 66 percent were in favor of a complete merger of the two organizations; 24 percent were in favor of some sort of federation; some 6 percent were in support of the existing relationships between the two, and less than 2 percent were in favor of entirely separate and independent organizations.[17] Consequently the directors of both agencies requested that the ARS-NRA joint study committee develop a plan for merger. The committee's proposal included establishment of a professional department and a lay department, each having autonomy in its respective areas of interest. While the committee agreed to a predominantly lay-controlled board, the ARS-NRA scheme did not specify the exact balance between lay and professional representation, the proportion to be dependent upon such factors as fund-raising potential, the presumed impact upon the NRA's tax exemption, and charter status.[18]

Both the NRA and ARS boards received and accepted the recommendations of the joint study committee in principle; however, neither board took action to implement the plan. Each board instead authorized its executive director to broaden the base of merger discussions and to include the American Institute of Park Executives and other interested organizations in the negotiations.[19]

During the course of the early NRA-ARS discussions, the American Institute of Park Executives was independently exploring ways to expand its influence in both the park and recreation areas. The AIPE, under the able direction of executive director Alfred B. LaGasse, had experienced substantial growth during the previous decade. In addition to expanding its membership, the AIPE had increased its budget by 800 percent in ten years. Its program and services were directed primarily to park and recreation administrators. The park organization was governed by a small, closely-knit board that included a president, vice-president, and six directors elected at large. LaGasse, a landscape architect and park administrator by background, had gained extensive training in association management through the American Society of Association Executives, an organization composed largely of trade association managers. His management style with its trade association orientation was at times to conflict with the social work emphasis of Prendergast and with the professional idealism of ARS executive director Ray R. Butler. Butler, relatively new in his position, was a recreation graduate of the University of Minnesota and former recreation director in Shorewood, Wisconsin.

As a part of an organizational self-study, the AIPE polled its membership for opinions on future directions for their group. The response favored moving toward the unification of all professional organizations in the park and recreation field as a first preference. Should this not be possible, there was a concensus among the membership that the AIPE should forge ahead and forcefully assume leadership of the field. The results of the AIPE member survey served as an important element of a long-range planning report prepared by a small committee of senior members and chaired by L. B. Houston, highly respected director of the Dallas park and recreation department. This document, the so-called AIPE Growth Committee Report, strongly supported the concept of unification and recommended that the AIPE executive director, working with his counterparts in other organizations, develop an organizational framework for unification to be submitted to the boards of the respective organizations.[20] With the mandate of his board, LaGasse began a series of intense discussions with Prendergast of the NRA and Butler of the ARS.

One of the early obstacles encountered in the formulation of a plan for merger was the question of how to reconcile the unique differences that existed between the organizations. The ARS and AIPE were both professional membership societies with voting members who elected their officers and board members, who in turn staffed their committees. On the other hand, the National Recreation Association was a national voluntary service organization with no voting members but rather service associates (individuals) and service affiliates (agencies). Committee members were appointed on the recommendations of staff. Professionals who joined the NRA had no voting powers over its board of trustees or its budget. Basic organizational differences were a problem during earlier NRA-ARS discussions, but the issue of professional rights and governing power gained new momentum with the combined support of the AIPE and the ARS.

In seeking to deal with the professional aspects of unification, LaGasse and Butler assumed leadership in devising a draft proposal for unifying the ARS, AIPE, and NRA. The report provided for a professional grouping (AIPE-ARS) under a board of governors, a lay grouping (NRA) under a board of trustees, and a joint board of directors with 50 percent of its members from the governors (professional) and 50 percent from the trustees (laymen). In this report the layman's role was considered to be public relations and fund raising.[21] While this plan, identified as AIPE Executive Director's Report 55, was enthusiastically promoted by both the AIPE and ARS boards, there was little support for the scheme within the NRA board.[22] Vice-president Susan Lee, daughter of former president Joseph Lee and a member of the NRA board's subcommittee on organization relationships, sharply criticized the report in a memorandum to her fellow trustees, stating that the top policy board of a merged agency should have citizen control. She believed that while the number of professionals on the top board should be flexible, they should not approximate 50 percent. Lee's reasoning was that the layman spoke on behalf of the citizen-at-large for whom the service was given, provided a balanced overall view of nationwide needs, and instilled an element of objectivity in the organization which strengthened fund-raising and public relations. She felt that a predominantly lay board provided a stronger liaison with the total community and that such a board was in a better position to act as trustee of contributed and public funds, thus assuring continued tax-exempt status. Susan Lee saw the layman's contribution to be in the areas of interpretation, public education, and finance, while the professional's special place was in the areas of technical expertise and professional skills and services. She viewed the relationship between the layman and the professional not as a "we-they" arrangement but as a mutually supportive venture—one where policy and programs could be discussed and developed harmoniously.[23]

Following its presentation at a joint NRA-AIPE board meeting, the plan recommended by LaGasse and Butler was referred by board chairman Evans to the NRA's special board committee on organizational relationships for study and recommendations. Most of the NRA background work on merger had been carried out by Prendergast and a small committee of the board including Evans, Susan Lee, Robert Crawford, and committee chairman Luther Gulick. The special committee recommended a counterplan for consideration by AIPE and ARS which would have modified the existing NRA board by adding to the board the professional chairmen of all district councils, the professional chairmen or presidents of all special interest sections or organizations and such additional professionals as the board may determine. The NRA counterplan re-stated the principal of a preponderantly lay board yet provided for an executive committee with equal lay and professional representation. AIPE and ARS rejected the NRA suggestion that there should be a majority of lay leaders on the top board.[24]

Gulick had emphasized to his fellow directors that the Association was trying to do something through its efforts for cooperative action that no other field in the United States had done successfully—to keep together the lay and professional leaders in a specialized field. He expressed the view that to accomplish it, the Association would have to lean over backwards without sacrificing conditions of lay participation.[25]

In its counterproposal, the NRA agreed with the principle that the professional organizations in any merger should remain free and independent to act on matters of exclusive professional concern such as professional registration and certification, professional curriculum accreditation, ethical practices, and personnel standards. The board acknowledged that logically these activities would be handled by a professional division within a unified structure. On the lay side the NRA supported the expansion of local citizen committees such as the NRA Chicago committee, the development of a program for friends of recreation and parks, and the establishment of a national center for the advancement of recreation to be headed by a nationwide citizens' committee. Prendergast and the lay leaders of NRA negotiated for an organizational structure much broader than either a professional or a lay society; an organization that would serve the professional yet endeavor to act in the general public interest. The NRA directors felt that, in order for the group to secure the confidence and support of the public, control of funds received from the public as well as broad policies and general services must be the ultimate responsibility of a predominantly lay board of trustees.[26]

One of the most technical aspects of the lay-professional issue was its perceived relationship to the tax status of any new organization created through the merger. One of the prerequisites for the NRA's involvement in negotiations was preservation of the full tax-exempt status of the Association, the most favored tax status among the organizations discussing merger. The Association was tax-exempt under Section 501(c)(3) of the Internal Revenue Code. The major benefit of this particular tax classification was that contributions to such designated organizations were deductible for federal income, estate, and gift tax purposes. The AIPE and ARS, on the other hand, were both classified for tax purposes as trade or professional associations under a different section of the Internal Revenue Code, which prohibited donors from deducting contributions as tax-deductible gifts. Under federal regulations, the NRA thus was characterized as a charitable, educational, and scientific organization operating exclusively in the public interest while the ARS and AIPE were interpreted to be professional associations operating to promote the specific interests of their own members.[27]

NRA received over 50 percent of its budget through fund-raising made less difficult by virtue of this favorable tax status. Over the years the Association had been built upon the concept of serving the public interest. Thus the NRA board maintained a strong stance that any unified organization must direct its broad programs to the recreation interests of the nation through public education and service to both lay and professional interests, communities throughout the country, and public and private recreation agencies.[28]

On the other hand, AIPE and ARS leaders questioned the continuing need for voluntary charitable support in a merged organization, particularly in view of the growing profession and the increased activity of the federal government.[29] They advocated the importance of the professional recreator becoming more self-

After agreement was finally reached by the various boards of directors of the merging bodies, their elected heads conferred with Laurance S. Rockefeller, who was to become the first president of the National Recreation and Park Association. Left to right: Frank McInnis, American Association of Zoological Parks and Aquariums; Frank Vaydik, American Institute of Park Executives; Stuart G. Case, American Recreation Society; Laurance S. Rockefeller; James H. Evans, National Recreation Association; Conrad L. Wirth, National Conference on State Parks.

sufficient and having at least an equal share in policy determination. The value of the franchise and the individual professional member's right to representation was emphasized. The professional groups maintained that a top policy board equally balanced between laymen and practitioners would not in itself jeopardize the ability to gain tax-exempt status. This question of equal representation became an issue of paramount importance to the professional groups and eventually led to an apparent impasse in negotiations with the NRA, sparking an initiative between AIPE and ARS for a merger of these two organizations. A plan was developed by a joint AIPE-ARS committee and subsequently submitted to their memberships recommending the creation of an Institute for Recreation and Parks.[30]

Aware of the possibility that the NRA would be left in a weakened position should AIPE and ARS merge independently, NRA trustees authorized the development of plans to provide selected vital services to strengthen the Association. Included would be establishment of an office in Washington, D.C., to give special attention to federal and state legislation; reactivation of the National Recreation School as the education and research division of the NRA with an Institute for Recreation Research and an Institute for Recreation Education; and creation of a national center for the advancement of recreation to be headed by a nationwide citizens' committee. The directors further envisioned construction of a new headquarters building in New York City, which would serve as a national showcase for recreation and house an academy honoring past, present, and future professional and lay leaders in the field of recreation and parks. From among these ambitious programs, the Association moved immediately on the proposal for a Washington office and by January 1965 had acquired office space at 1750 Pennsylvania Avenue, just one block from the White House and two blocks from the Department of the Interior.[31]

In addition the NRA for the past few years had made substantial progress in strengthening relationships with its constituents and increasing the role of professionals in its work. Beginning with the election of two recreators to the NRA board in 1960, Prendergast had gradually expanded his philosophy of progressively bringing in more practitioners at the policy-making level. By 1963 there were six professionals among the directors of the NRA—three prominent recreation executives and three nationally recognized park executives. In 1964, faced with an apparent deadlock in merger negotiations, the chairmen of the NRA's eight district advisory committees, all professionals, were added to the board, and the group approved the principle of electing to membership as well the presidents of selected related organizations.

Thus with a seeming stalemate in the negotiations between AIPE and ARS on the one hand and NRA on the other, the potential for organizational conflict and competition grew stronger.[32] Out of this environment of confusion and concern emerged the unsolicited counsel of some elder statesmen in the park and recreation field. One important suggestion came from Conrad Wirth, president of the National Conference on State Parks, past president of the AIPE, and board member of the NRA. Wirth suggested the creation of "Park and Recreation Associates." This plan would require no organizational changes or surrender of established responsibilities but would operate through a forum consisting of three representatives from each member organization. The groups would undertake cooperative projects that were of mutual advantage and would endeavor to present a united front to the public.[33] Through this proposal the National Conference on State Parks (NCSP) became an active participant in merger discussions. The NCSP had been formed in 1921 by Stephen Mather and other leading conservationists for the purpose of encouraging the states to acquire and preserve scenic areas of importance. Its membership included professional resource managers and citizens concerned with the development of state parks.

Wirth was instrumental in having Laurance Rockefeller, a prominent conservationist, invite representatives of the three negotiating organizations and the National Conference on State Parks to meet in New York City to discuss the new idea. While the American Recreation Society chose not to be represented at this meeting, delegates from the other bodies unanimously agreed to submit the concept to their respective boards. Although there was favorable reaction to the Wirth proposal on the part of the NRA, NCSP, and AIPE, the ARS and AIPE continued to work on a new constitution and bylaws that would merge their professional societies.[34]

Another option to end the deadlock in negotiations came from Charles K. Brightbill, head of the Department of Recreation and Park Administration at the University of Illinois. Brightbill, a former NRA staff member and a past president of the American Recreation Society, had not been involved in formal negotiations up to this point. He earlier had advocated total organizational unification, fearing that a merger of only two of the groups would create further dissension in the recreation and park field.

In August 1964 while in Europe, Brightbill wrote to the presidents and executive directors of each of the negotiating organizations offering a plan for resolving the impasse on the composition of the policy board. His plan recommended a predominantly lay board chosen as follows:

> *Policy Establishing Group*: The top, governing board shall consist of laymen and professionals on the basis of 2 to 1, respectively. One third (⅓) of the board, designated here as Item "A", shall be appointed from among laymen now serving on the NRA Board. These appointees shall serve until their successors are appointed, and shall have the power to appoint their successors, ad infinitum. One third (⅓) of the board, designated here as Item "B", shall be chosen by the profes-

sionals for *definite* terms of office, and in a manner to be determined by the professionals. The last one third (⅓) of the board shall be *laymen* nominated by the professionals, submitting a list of three (3) laymen for each one (1) layman needed. From these nominations, the previously selected two thirds (⅔) of the board, namely, Items "A" and "B" shall elect individuals to bring the board to full membership.[35]

While Brightbill's proposal received enthusiastic support from NRA, the reaction of the professional groups was not as positive. Although supporting the concept of total consolidation, both the ARS and AIPE maintained their positions regarding equal professional balance on the policy board.

In their effort to secure a union of at least the professional groups, the AIPE and ARS submitted proposed constitutional amendments to their members recommending the establishment of an Institute for Recreation and Parks (IRP) and an American Park and Recreation Society (APRS). The IRP was to be the umbrella professional association under which special interest branches would be organized. The APRS was to be the first branch to be organized, representing practitioners from the public recreation and park area. The membership of the AIPE and ARS voted overwhelmingly in favor of the merger of these two groups. Despite this approval of the plan to create the Institute for Recreation and Parks, both boards supported the continuation of efforts to reach an agreement with the NRA on overall unification.[36]

While major differences of opinion existed between the NRA and the professional organizations, an environment of mutual respect had developed among the elected leaders of the negotiating groups. NRA board chairman Evans had been particularly effective in winning the admiration and respect of AIPE president Frank Vaydik and ARS president Stuart Case as had Luther Gulick. Both NRA leaders had earlier hosted a meeting of the top officers of ARS and AIPE in New York City to discuss areas of agreement and disagreement. Although this private meeting did not produce results, it did provide a forum for board level discussions.[37] Through such earlier contact, there appeared to be a sincere desire on the part of the top leadership of each body to find a solution that would make possible total merger. The suggestion was made again that perhaps the executive directors were too close to the negotiations to find a way out of the existing impasse.

As a result of the adversary positions between the NRA's Prendergast and LaGasse and Butler of the AIPE and ARS respectively, tension at the executive directors' level had increased. For example, during some of the more heated stages of negotiations, the NRA had been characterized as largely a staff-directed institution with a somewhat inactive lay board, an organization that in reality depended heavily upon the professional both in terms of staffing its committees and consuming its services. Some of the major NRA services were viewed as being competitive with those of the professional societies. AIPE chief LaGasse had suggested that the major difference between the NRA and the other organizations was in their hierarchical structures with the professional groups operating through the franchise and NRA operating through a patronage system. He further hypothesized that, should a breach between the NRA and the professional organizations occur, the fight would be to get professional rather than lay support.[38] This somewhat one-sided analysis failed to recognize the broader public service environment in which the NRA operated and did not take cognizance of the pioneering work that the NRA had done in establishing each of the service areas.

LaGasse's harsh assessment however drew attention to the apparent dominance of the NRA's policy-making by Joseph Prendergast and prompted some to question the validity of a staff-controlled network of national and district advisory committees established by the Association in the 1950s. Many of the NRA's services, including its conferences, magazine, and other publications, were indeed directed to but not controlled by the recreation and park professional. Yet the executive directors of the AIPE and ARS failed to recognize that the NRA as a national voluntary service organization operated in much the same manner as many other similar agencies, that is, with a lay-controlled board and a dominant staff structure. During the negotiations, the NRA thus found itself in the difficult position of soliciting the political support of the recreation and park professional in merger negotiations while deemphasizing his policy-making role compared to that of the layman.[39]

Despite the move by the AIPE and ARS to proceed with their merger each organization, including the NRA, had passed a resolution favoring another joint meeting by the officers of the various boards of directors for the purpose of developing a statement of philosophy, principles, and policies related to merger, federation, and/or other relationships. The presidents of the AIPE and ARS took the initiative to call a meeting to which the NRA and NCSP agreed to attend.[40] Key officers from each group, excluding the executive directors, were invited to participate. Board chairman James Evans and vice-president Robert Crawford represented

NRA. The affair, held in Chicago on December 5, 1964, was hosted and chaired upon mutual consent by Robert W. Ruhe, a respected and well-informed recreation and park administrator in Skokie, Illinois, who had not been active in previous merger negotiations. The meeting, during a major midwestern snowstorm, produced a proposal for merger that was unanimously endorsed by all of the board representatives in attendance. The principles agreed to constituted the basis for the formation of the National Recreation and Park Association.

The proposal for merger which was to change the future destiny of the NRA expressed these beliefs and conditions:

PROPOSAL FOR MERGER

It is the expressed belief of the officers of the American Institute of Park Executives, American Recreation Society, National Conference on State Parks, and National Recreation Association that each organization reaffirm its strong conviction that the ever-increasing needs and demands for recreation and park facilities and services can best be served through the collective and unified strengths of lay and professional persons.

It is further recognized and reiterated that a unified and concerted effort on the part of all aforementioned organizations shall result in more effective services. To this end, it is believed that these organizations should collectively utilize their respective talents and resources by joining into one service and professional association dedicated to the task of unification of effort in the recreation and park field.

The implementation of such beliefs can best be accomplished by a merger of all lay and professional societies and organizations dedicated to this common purpose in the following manner:

1. The establishment of an association by amending the present charter of the National Recreation Association so as to include the principles and objectives of the new organization, while at the same time preserving the benefits derived from the existing charter which has been tested and proven over the last half century.

2. The name of the new organization shall be National Recreation and Park Association.

3. There shall be established a policy-making body called the Board of Trustees to govern the National Recreation and Park Association consisting of 60 members, twenty of whom shall be laymen, twenty professional persons and twenty laymen nominated by the professional group.

4. There shall be established an Administrative Board consisting of twenty members from the Board of Trustees, ten of whom shall be professionals and ten of whom shall be laymen. These members shall be chosen by the Board of Trustees. This Administrative Board shall be responsible for supervising the carrying out of the directions and policies of the Board of Trustees and employ the staff as authorized by the Board of Trustees.
5. There shall be established a professional division of the National Recreation and Park Association governed by a Board of Governors and representing the various professional interests and sections. The professional groups shall initiate their own form of organization and determine the best methods of organization, geographic representation, and selection on the Board of Governors.
6. There shall be established a lay division of the National Recreation and Park Association governed by a Board of Directors and representing the various lay and civic interests in the recreation and park field. This lay group shall initiate their own form of organization and determine the best methods of organization, geographic representation and selection on the Board of Directors.[41]

The proposal set in motion an intensive effort to bring about the necessary constitutional and other legal changes necessary to unify the organizations. While the executive directors welcomed the settlement, they nonetheless continued to negotiate hard for their own interpretations of the proposal. Ruhe, upon request of the leadership of the joint boards, continued to serve as a moderator until all of the constitutional and legal changes had been made.[42]

Apparently the success in reaching an agreement was in large part a result of the able and determined elected leadership of the negotiating organizations. NRA representatives Evans and Crawford were effective in helping to achieve a consensus on the issue of a predominantly lay board. The board structure agreed upon was similar to the formula suggested earlier by former ARS president Charles Brightbill.

Once the proposal for merger was agreed upon, Evans, along with Luther Gulick and Conrad Wirth, persuaded Laurance S. Rockefeller, who had headed the Outdoor Recreation Resources Review Commission, to accept the role of president of the new organization.[43]

Using the merger formula, refinements were made and agreements reached for initial appointments to the new board of trustees. The National Recreation Association board of trustees became the board of directors of the lay division of NRPA and nominated twenty-one lay trustees to the top board, selecting the most active laymen from the existing NRA board. Under the prearranged procedures, the NRA was not permitted to nominate professionals from its existing board. The American Institute of Park Executives and the American Recreation Society restructured their proposed Institute for Recreation and Parks to become the professional division of NRPA. By mutual agreement between the professional organizations, the American Institute of Park Executives nominated ten lay trustees and eleven professional trustees and the American Recreation Society nominated eleven lay trustees and ten professional trustees, thus providing an overall balance of two-thirds laymen and one-third professionals. The AIPE selected its senior statesmen, past presidents of the group, as its professional representatives on the new board while the ARS chose only its most recent past presidents as well as current board and committee members to fill its authorized professional vacancies. In this process, the ARS neglected to place many of its prior top leaders such as Harold Meyer, Milo Christiansen, and Charles Brightbill on the new board.[44]

One organizational task that did not flow smoothly was the problem of selecting an executive director for the newly created NRPA. Many members of the NRA board had assumed that Joseph Prendergast would be the logical choice for the top salaried position, principally because of his legal background and his broad expertise. However, AIPE executive director Alfred B. LaGasse had himself decided to become a candidate for the chief executive's position. Prendergast and LaGasse, both capable administrators, had assumed and maintained strong organizational stances during the merger negotiations—many times in opposition to each other. With the structure of the new board, there was no clear-cut line of support for either candidate. The task of resolving the executive issue was placed in the hands of a small committee consisting of Evans of the NRA and the presidents of each of the merging associations. After several conferences, some of which included Prendergast and LaGasse, a compromise solution was reached in which Prendergast was appointed executive vice-president and secretary, and LaGasse was made executive director and general manager. Under this arrangement, Prendergast became the chief executive officer of NRPA responsible for external affairs such as fund-raising and public relations, and LaGasse became the principal administrative officer with responsibility for the internal

affairs of NRPA including the overall management and administration of the operations of the Association. According to the compromise arrangement, Prendergast was the senior staff officer.
Both he and LaGasse were authorized to attend all board meetings
in an ex-officio capacity. ARS executive director Ray Butler subsequently was appointed an associate executive director in charge
of the professional division.[45]

With the management decision out of the way, a major obstacle
had been cleared in making NRPA a reality. Audits and property
transfers were made in December 1965. In accepting the presidency
of the newly-formed Association, Laurance S. Rockefeller stated:
"We have entered a new era in this country . . . an era where parks,
recreation and the quality of the environment have become a major item of public concern. With these developments come heavy
responsibilities. So it is timely, fitting and important that we
strengthen our ties of organization and mutual cooperation. Our
combined strength will be far greater than the sum of the individual components. The stakes are great for our organizations,
for our professions and for the public good."[46]

For the National Recreation Association January 1966 indeed
marked the dawn of a new era, albeit an age which had been
arising within the field of parks and recreation for at least a generation. How the ideas, people, and services of the Association;
its followers; its colleagues; and its related organizations were to
fare after the rendezvous is another tale.

For sixty years *Recreation* magazine promoted the fundamental philosophy of NRA and interpreted new developments and trends in recreation.

10
A Trial Balance

When the NRA was founded in the early twentieth century, there had been little systematic development of any programs or facilities for public recreation in the United States. In 1900 federal interest in recreation had been confined to a few isolated national parks, and states had paid almost no attention to the subject. Only one county, Essex County, New Jersey, had created a park system before 1900. Several hundred cities had made a beginning toward provision of public parks, but these parks, often inaccessible to many residents, had been predominantly landscape parks whose administrators had frowned on the idea of active games and sports. A small number of supervised playgrounds, generally restricted to summer use, had begun to take shape in some fourteen cities by 1900, but no city had yet established a recreation department or commission. Most playgrounds had been initiated and maintained by private charity, with only a few cities contributing public resources to this purpose. The concept of recreation leadership as a profession had been unknown, and the literature on playgrounds had consisted almost entirely of occasional articles in a small number of periodicals.

PUBLIC RECREATION TAKES HOLD

By 1965, in contrast, public recreation as espoused for decades primarily by the NRA had become an established part of American culture and an accepted responsibility of all levels of government. Outdoor recreation was available in national, state, and local park systems. Expenditures for public recreation by local governments, emphasized for nearly half a century by the NRA and its predecessors, exceeded by several times the combined state and federal outlay. In 1965 the yearbook of the NRA reported that a record $905 million had been spent on local parks and recreation. Over 120,000 paid leaders, nearly 20,000 of them professionals employed on a year-round basis, staffed these programs of varied recreation for all citizens. Several professional associations served municipal recreation leaders.

City recreation administrators and other interested persons might benefit from the many informational, educational, and technical services of the NRA. In 1965 the Association had a budget of approximately one million dollars, more than in any previous year. These funds enabled the Association to provide an extensive range of services to the individuals and citizens it served. To carry out its program the NRA could rely upon an experienced staff and draw upon a heritage of leadership in fostering public recreation since the beginning of the century. By the 1960s, despite its past successes, the Association had reached a plateau where it was unable to keep pace with the many areas encompassed by the rapidly expanding field of recreation.

The development of municipal recreation in the United States in the early twentieth century was but one of a number of inter-related social reforms originated in response to industrialization and urbanization. As such, public recreation was closely related to the broader thrust for social justice which had similar origins and became a major element of the progressive movement. Municipal recreation, evolving from children's playgrounds, was intimately associated with attempted corrections of inadequacies in parks, housing, education, and health as well as other ills arising in the congested industrial cities of the nation. All of these reforms were intellectually united by an increasing emphasis in public and private circles on the important effect of environment on individuals. Many urban social reformers rejected Darwinian determinism and set out confidently to improve society by upgrading the environment of the city. Numerous progressives came to believe that one such improvement, supervised playgrounds and recreation, could foster constructive citizenship and simultaneously provide creative, worthy outlets for leisure energy which might otherwise be spent in crime or misguided ways. As is frequently the case with social innovations, the general public had to be educated systematically to recognize the full value of such reforms.

In various local situations, such as finding resources and legal authority to replace a block of tenements with a playground and small park, reformers found that both organized groups of citizens and the power of government were necessary ingredients for effective, peaceful change. For this purpose, existing groups such as churchgoers motivated by the social gospel, public school teachers, women's organizations, social workers, and civic associations frequently provided proponents of public recreation. By 1905, when notable progress in municipal recreation had been made more or less independently in several American cities, including Boston, Chicago, and New York, varied urban problems and potential solutions turned out to be much the same everywhere. Progressive citizens moved increasingly from the local to the national level to launch reform groups dedicated to voluntary action for nationwide improvement of specific social ailments.

Given these conditions the originators of the Association, progressive educators Luther Gulick and Henry S. Curtis, had little trouble persuading leading playground advocates from several cities to band together in 1906 as a promotional association. Since another national organization had already claimed the field but was relatively inactive, Gulick's individualism, typical of his day, seemed to compel him to form his own group. With other early leaders he recognized that public recreation had three great needs to meet if it was to become widely accepted: adequate, permanent financing by municipal tax dollars; efficient, professional leaders to administer organized recreation; and a broad, popular concept of recreation and creative leisure to include varied year-round activities for all citizens. This last item was to have far-reaching implications, since the shrinking American workweek had already resulted in ten additional hours of weekly leisure between 1850 and 1900 and was to bring twenty more hours of free time by the early 1960s.

To promote their three goals for quality public recreation, Gulick and Curtis initially depended on their own experiences, such as Gulick's creation and financing of the Public School Athletic League in New York and elsewhere, to provide for the new organization. Although Curtis copied several devices from Germany, which had supplied the impetus for the first American playground three decades earlier, the Association was a typical response to a need by well-meaning urban reformers of the progressive era. The principal leaders—Gulick, Lee, and Braucher—were all strongly committed to the ideal of maximizing individual freedom within the framework of political democracy and regarded municipal recreation as a vital element in the fulfillment of this aspect of American life.

Practical promotion of such ideas required, above all else, financial backing. The founders might have been able to persuade the federal Office of Education to undertake a costly program of spreading their message to a large number of cities across the nation, but the commitment of the leaders of the Association to local responsibility and individual freedom precluded this alternative. Instead, they opted for private support and relied on part-time volunteers and meager resources for a year until they landed support from the Russell Sage Foundation. This new stability enabled the Association to undertake systematic fund raising, to recruit a paid, professional staff, and to pioneer more effective methods of operation, such as field service, which were to become permanent.

While the spread of American public recreation accelerated significantly in the first years of the Association, the institution itself soon developed serious organizational problems. Its ambitious leaders quarreled over issues and personalities; Gulick appeared unsuited for effective administration; and the tight control of funds by the foundation, itself a substantial organization which might well have absorbed its offspring, provoked dissension among the independent-minded directors of the Association.

These internal problems, coupled with the withdrawal of foundation backing and the resignation of both Gulick and Curtis, greatly endangered the future of the Association. In the face of this dire situation, new leaders Braucher and Lee took command of the organization in 1910 and by supplying vigorous, united, executive leadership molded the Association into a stable institution. This second administrative team, which brought experience in so-

Today most communities provide their citizens with comprehensive recreation programs and facilities that include opportunities for all ages.

New federal and state grant-in-aid programs undertaken in the 1960s greatly accelerated the development of public recreation facilities.

cial work as well as needed skill in management and fund raising, proved an effective combination. Within a few years the capable pair perfected the basic institutional forms of the Association and built it into a $100,000-a-year operation.

Like many other progressives, the two leaders had great confidence in expertise and fully expected the Association to use that quality in guiding the development of municipal recreation across the nation. They recognized that the most effective way to achieve this aim was to provide outside, short-term, expert assistance to individual cities and to this end rejuvenated and expanded the field service of the Association. The field workers, billed as "efficiency experts," suggested systematic yet custom-tailored solutions to the recreation problems encountered in local communities. Specialization in recreation as in other fields included, of course, the risk of a lessening awareness of the broad perspective characteristic of some earlier urban reformers, whose interests had embraced a whole spectrum of social concerns. Given the increasing complexity of society, however, specialization was no doubt inevitable if the Association was to deal effectively with the problems it attacked.

In 1917 mobilization for World War I unexpectedly presented Lee and Braucher with a temporary opportunity to greatly expand their organization both conceptually and physically. They transformed it into an institution to coordinate off-post social services, of which public recreation was only a part, for millions of troops stationed in training camps throughout the nation. In entering this field they joined the mainstream of the so-called "community movement" then in vogue among social workers. This enlarged function, which was launched under the institutional banner of the War Camp Community Service, logically was built upon the proven ideas and techniques perfected earlier by the Association; it succeeded primarily because of the fervent patriotism and civic cooperation of wartime.

When peace arrived unexpectedly, Braucher and Lee, along with many other social workers, grossly overestimated the permanence of this cooperative spirit. Flushed with the success of WCCS, the two leaders discounted warnings of the inevitable postwar letdown and attempted to found a national movement for peacetime community service and social cooperation which would center on the creative use of leisure. Although this ill-planned operation quickly folded in the unfavorable postwar atmosphere, Lee and Braucher returned to the narrower work of the Association with an awareness of the necessity for expanding federal powers in national emergencies as well as several million dollars in unspent WCCS funds to supplement their work.

The postwar decade was a time of marked growth for nearly all types of public and private leisure activities as well as a period of substantial expansion for municipal recreation. The Association, garnering record contributions in these prosperous years, increased its normal programs while at the same time embarking, somewhat haphazardly, on several new ventures to broaden its services. These included highly successful special services to promote physical education in the public schools, programs to train thousands of volunteer leaders for rural organized recreation, the founding of the first school for systematic preparation of professional recreation executives, and several projects for scholarly research and publication in the field of recreation.

Although the Association could point to many solid achievements, there is little evidence to suggest that its leaders developed the practice of making regular, critical analyses of their operations, goals, and policies in the early decades. Had they done so, the institution might have attained a more balanced record. Such periodic reassessments, either by the staff members themselves or by impartial outsiders, might well have enabled the Association to increase the effectiveness of its actions in dealing with the inevitable changes which any institution or society must face as time passes. Despite the fourfold budgetary expansion, which in 1929 reached a record that was unsurpassed for decades, contributions to the Association in the years 1919–1929 lagged behind the rising expenditures by American municipalities for local public recreation. In addition, the position of the Association as the leading national organization in the field of recreation was seriously challenged by various individuals and groups seeking to establish independent positions of leadership in several phases of recreation where the Association had previously assumed it enjoyed unquestioned primacy.

During the 1930s the continued multiplication of professional groups interested in various aspects of recreation and the entry of the federal government into the field on a substantial scale impaired the credibility of the NRA as the primary source of recreation expertise and influence in the nation. As the depression wore on, declining contributions forced the Association to curtail its program, and aging leadership lacked the resilience to cope with such a challenge. In these circumstances it was scarcely surprising when several of the newly organized competing organizations achieved national prominence in recreation. Since recreation in both theory and practice could readily be considered as a part of other related fields, such as education and social work, certain professional groups, for instance the National Education Association, naturally wished to encompass recreation leaders. This rising concern with professionalism, aped by the hundreds of local executives in the several functional subspecialties of recreation, forced Braucher somewhat belatedly in 1937 to seize the initiative in forming the American Recreation Society.

As most interested professionals wanted the new society to be an integral part of the NRA, Braucher faced the dilemma of choosing between power and principle. It seemed to him that once the professionals in the operating echelons all around the country became members within the NRA, they would soon demand a share in the formulation of policy. Confronted with this probability, he chose to retain personal control of the Association by encouraging the creation of an independent American Recreation Society and continuing with docile lay membership on the board of directors of the National Recreation Association, which seldom challenged his leadership. With his power thus secured, however, he used it with almost universal restraint in actions which he sincerely believed would be most beneficial to recreation as a whole. In opting for a separate professional group, Braucher also lost the potential opportunity of formally adding a new function to the NRA. By making the Association the official professional society for recreation in the nation, he almost certainly would have provided greater institutional stability, especially if other organizations jeopardized the existence of the Association by invading its primary area of operation, which is to say, field work. However, there were few, if any organizational models for Braucher to follow. Then, as now, most social welfare organizations tended to be dominated either by laymen or by professionals rather than a combination of the two.

Governmental as well as private interests increasingly sought to carve out areas of responsibility in public recreation. Encroachments from this quarter posed a dual threat to the NRA; governmental, especially federal, agencies could count upon much more extensive funding, and by virtue of budgetary measures they could impose centralized control. But centralized control was precisely what the leaders of the NRA did not want. The very premise of the National Recreation Association was that recreation should be primarily a local responsibility. And this basic philosophy seemed threatened by New Deal agencies which offered to provide funding for organized recreation directly to towns and cities across the nation. Nevertheless Braucher, recognizing the need for tem-

In an evermore complex and technological society recreation and park agencies increasingly must provide opportunities for personal fulfillment and well-being.

porary federal relief in the depression, did what he could to improve the quality of federal recreation efforts while preserving municipal freedom and initiative as well as the private voluntary nature of the NRA. In spite of his action, the Works Progress Administration, the federal agency primarily involved, launched its program without paying much attention to the fears of the NRA concerning centralized control. The services of the NRA were, however, welcome at the National Park Service, an agency which was competing with the WPA for principal federal jurisdiction in recreation but did not impinge upon the NRA in its major operations. If the NRA perceived an advantage in splitting potential competition, certain leaders in the National Park Service saw that it was in their interest to gain recognition by the NRA as the primary federal recreation agency.

Following the depression, events on the home front during World War II revealed the inevitable centralizing tendencies of a nation at war, which further weakened the validity of the NRA's claim to be a single private organization representing the entire movement for public recreation. First the powerful factions forming the United Service Organizations (USO) defeated Braucher's plan for loose local coalitions to fill recreation requirements of visiting servicemen. Then the Federal Security Administration Recreation Division, which Braucher had initially fostered as a governmental counterbalance to offset supposed flaws in the private USO scheme, developed centralizing ambitions of its own to duplicate the inadequate services of the NRA and to become the foremost permanent federal agency in recreation. This maneuver revived the conflict among various elements of the federal government seeking primacy in recreation and also led to a serious struggle between the recreation professionals in the American Recreation Society and its parent organization, the National Recreation Association. After the demise of the wartime FSA Recreation Division and following several years of dispute over a central federal recreation bureau, leaders on both sides of the issue admitted the futility of further acrimony, although the basic question remained unsettled. Shortly after the beginning of this move for reconciliation, Braucher died, and the NRA arrived at a major crossroads in its existence.

The appointment of lawyer-social worker Joseph Prendergast as Braucher's successor resulted in the development of new organizational strategies. For instance, the establishment of nonvoting service memberships and the creation of a system of national and district professional advisory committees brought about increased opportunities for involvement in the affairs of the NRA by professional practitioners. Prendergast was successful in expanding and stabilizing sources of revenue for the NRA, both through federated fund raising and by increasing earned income with the sale of publications and other services. During the decade of the 1950s the NRA strengthened its organizational image by acquiring a headquarters building in New York City and by establishing regional offices in each of its eight geographical districts.

Despite these efforts to enlarge and strengthen its services the NRA was still unable to keep pace with the rapidly growing field of recreation. Among the management alternatives open to it in these circumstances was the possibility of merging the resources of the NRA with related organizations. By the early 1960s a new federal bureaucracy, the Bureau of Outdoor Recreation, had arisen and professional groups in recreation and related fields were discussing potential union. In addition, members of such groups including NRA, in several polls seemed to favor combination of efforts by national nongovernmental recreation agencies.

In this climate, Prendergast and the directors of the NRA selected a course of action leading to merger as the one offering the greatest potential for the agency. The Association participated in an intensive three-year period of negotiations with the American Recreation Society, the American Institute of Park Executives, and the National Conference on State Parks which culminated in the formation of the National Recreation and Park Association. Central to the merger agreement for the NRA was the preservation of its favorable tax status and the continuation of a top policy board composed preponderantly of laymen.

Over the years, the NRA was clearly more successful in promoting its major ideas than in selling itself. While it would be nearly impossible to measure with any accuracy the ideological impact of the Association on millions of Americans, it was evident that by 1965 numerous groups and individuals were successfully peddling many of the same basic ideas as the NRA. Supporters of public recreation believed in the importance of specialized training and professionalism among leaders of organized recreation. The concept of governmental responsibility at all levels, with emphasis on local government, was also widely accepted in recreation circles. Recreation experts in both governmental and private organizations recognized the need to provide opportunities for all citizens to enjoy creative leisure through a variety of activities.

By 1965 the advocates of organized recreation, at the NRA and elsewhere, had reason for both optimism and concern. Municipal recreation, as recorded in the year-books of the NRA, reached record highs that year and might well capitalize further on the general prosperity of an affluent society. The perceptive observer might also note, however, that the overall need for additional public recreation, when measured with standards suggested by the NRA, was still great.

During this whole period, certain basic tendencies in American society posed a continual potential threat to the spread of public recreation. Even though abundance could generate tax dollars for additional support of municipal recreation, increased wealth frequently meant that many citizens merely bought more televisions and personal recreation equipment while simply ignoring public recreation. This tendency in a sense suggested that municipal organized recreation in an affluent America might become more a social service to the poor, the old, and the very young than an institution enjoyed by all. The individualist streak in the American character seemed to find expression in people who provided their own recreation or purchased commercial recreation rather than joining group activities at municipal recreation centers. Nor was the centuries-old work ethic dead. Businessmen frequently played golf for health, not for fun; even the phrase "constructive leisure" implied that free time had to be profitably used rather than "wasted." In short, despite all their talk of education for leisure, the professional leaders in public recreation, including the NRA, had not fully bridged the communications gap between themselves and the general citizenry.

In addition, many professionals had not critically examined some of their most basic assumptions. If recreation was such an individual phenomenon, did recreation leaders have a right to assume a common identity of tastes by expecting people to react favorably to selected lists of "good" activities? Surely the "need" for recreation varied immensely from person to person, making determination of standards of adequacy far more complex than merely taking a survey of opinion or somewhat arbitrarily deciding what people ought to have. At least some critics were inclined to ask if participating in a community recreation program was really any more desirable a use of leisure than staying home with a beer and a televised baseball game.

Thus during nearly sixty years the National Recreation Association and its predecessors provided significant leadership in fostering the expansion of organized municipal recreation in the United States. The Association rendered important services, such as field assistance to local proponents of public recreation, a central clearinghouse for information, and training programs as well as the formulation of standards to further the establishment of a new profession on a solid footing.

Despite these substantial achievements, the National Recreation Association was increasingly frustrated in its hope to be the primary representative and guide of public recreation in the United States. With the expansion of federal bureaucracies and the increasing activity of other organizations in the leisure service field, this unresolved problem may be no easier for a new generation of leaders than it was for its founders. But the administrators of tomorrow will at least have the benefit of some insights regarding the experience of their predecessors, as summarized in this study, as well as the experience gained to date by a single, united lay-professional service organization, the National Recreation and Park Association.

Notes

NOTES TO CHAPTER 1

1. Dan Golenpaul (ed.), *Information Please Almanac* (32nd ed., New York, 1977), p. 65. "Leisure: Where No Recession Is in Sight," *U.S. News & World Report*, LXXXVI (January 15, 1979), 41. See Sebastian De Grazia, *Of Time, Work, and Leisure* (New York, 1962), pp. 453–55 for tables of rising consumer expenses for recreation from 1909 to 1959.

2. U. S. Bureau of the Census, *Statistical Abstract of the United States: 1977* (98th ed., Washington, D. C., 1977), pp. 231, 236, 843. "Leisure," p. 44. The latter statistics are for people of 12 years and over participating in a given activity five or more times a year.

3. "Leisure," p. 41; Golenpaul, *Almanac*, p. 395.

4. Edwin M. Fitch and John F. Shanklin, *The Bureau of Outdoor Recreation* (New York, 1970), pp. 107–10; "Federal Legislation for Land Acquisition," *Recreation*, LVIII (January 1965), 22–23.

5. Martin H. Neumeyer and Esther S. Neumeyer, *Leisure and Recreation: A Study of Leisure and Recreation in their Sociological Aspects* (3rd ed., New York, 1958), pp. 371–72.

6. U. S. Bureau of the Census, *Abstract:* (91st ed., 1970) pp. 200, 423; (99th ed., 1978) p. 310. There are a number of introductions to the subject of recreation. For examples, see George D. Butler, *Introduction to Community Recreation* (5th ed.; New York, 1976); Reynold E. Carlson *et. al.*, *Recreation and Leisure: The Changing Scene* (3rd ed.; Belmont, Cal., 1978); H. Douglas Sessoms, Harold D. Meyer, and Charles K. Brightbill, *Leisure Services: The Organized Recreation and Park System* (5th ed.; Englewood Cliffs, N. J., 1975); Allen V. Sapora and Elmer D. Mitchell, *The Theory of Play and Recreation* (3rd ed.; New York, 1961); and Richard G. Kraus, *Recreation and Leisure in Modern Society* (2nd ed.; Santa Monica, Cal., 1978). Compare Arnold W. Green, *Recreation, Leisure, and Politics* (New York, 1964), a questioning, provocative survey of recreation in America.

7. Butler, *Introduction* (4th ed.; New York, 1967), pp. 10–11. The terms "recreation," "play," and "leisure" are closely related and are used with varying degrees of refinement by authorities. See the references in the above note.

8. Clarence E. Rainwater, *The Play Movement in the United States* (Chicago, 1922), pp. 8–10. Foster R. Dulles, *A History of Recreation: America Learns to Play* (2nd ed.; New York, 1965), provides a general survey of popular tastes and activities in recreation from colonial times to the 1960s. He shows that many important trends in recreation, such as the rise of athletics, sports, and commercial amusements were well underway by the mid-nineteenth century.

9. Dulles, *History*, pp. 182 ff., 347; Frederick W. Cozens and Florence Stumpf, *Sports in American Life* (Chicago, 1953), p. 112. Like Cozens and Stumpf, John A. Krout, *Annals of American Sport* (New Haven, 1929), relates sports to other factors and trends in American society. As early as 1917 Frederick L. Paxson, "The Rise of Sport," *Mississippi Valley Historical Review*, IV (September 1917), 143–68, recognized the importance of sports. See also John R. Betts, "The Technical Revolution and the Rise of Sports, 1850–1900," *Mississippi Valley Historical Review*, XL (September 1953), 231–56.

10. As late as 1909 recreation accounted for only 3 percent of total consumer spending. De Grazia, *Of Time*, p. 446. Recall that the figure had risen to over 6 percent by 1970. See also Dulles, *History*, pp. 214–19, 288–91.

11. Cozens and Stumpf, *Sports*, pp. 35–37; Roland L. Warren, *The Community in America* (Chicago, 1963), p. 161; Harold U. Faulkner, *The Quest for Social Justice, 1898–1914*, A History of American Life (New York, 1931), pp. 283–84. Often on cheap land at the end of the line, the mechanical rides and dance halls of the trolley lines could be an important source of fares.

12. Blake McKelvey, *The Urbanization of America, 1860–1915* (New Brunswick, N.J., 1963), pp. 160–64, 196; Delos F. Wilcox, *The American City* (New York, 1904), pp. 150–53.

13. Simon Patten, *Product and Climax* (New York, 1909). See also Robert A. Woods, ed., *The City Wilderness* (Boston, 1898), pp. 176–201, for a social worker's view of amusements in a slum.

14. By 1960 this same figure was down to 38.5 hours. De Grazia, *Of Time*, however, on pp. 63–90 and 441–43 cites additional data to prove that these "average" statistics may be misleading and low. He maintains that such factors as increased travel time to and from work help to show the fallacy of equating declining work weeks with great increases in free time. At any rate, authorities disagree on the amount, not the fact, of increased free hours since the mid-nineteenth century. See Leo Wolman and Gustav Peck, "Labor Groups in the Social Structure," in *Recent Social Trends in the United States* (New York, 1934), pp. 828–29, and George B. Cutten, *The Threat of Leisure* (New Haven, 1926), p. 31.

15. Horace Greeley, *Recollections of a Busy Life* (New York, 1873), p. 118, cited in Dulles, *History*, p. 209. The idea of leisure goes back at least to Aristotle; see De Grazia, *Of Time*, pp. 3–61, for historical perspectives on leisure.

16. Dulles, *History*, p. 209; Cutten, *Threat*, pp. 150–63; Florence Kelley, "Right to Leisure," *Charities*, XIV (September 2, 1905), 1055; M. E. McDowell, "Right to Leisure," *Recreation*, IV (January 1911), 328.

17. Pp. 121–22; see also pp. 156–59, 168.

18. (Modern Library edition; New York, 1934), pp. vi, xiv, 1–7, 271–75. The book, Veblen's first, was reprinted four times in its initial decade and was his only successful book in terms of sales.
19. Quoted by Harold L. Ickes in "Space for Play," *Recreation*, XL (July 1946), 180. See also Clark W. Hetherington, "Development of Recreational Philosophy," *Recreation*, XXV (May 1931), 89, 111; and Cutten, *Threat*, pp. 15–16. Indeed, Cutten's view of leisure as a "threat" and the emphasis decades later by prominent experts in recreation of a need for "creative" or "constructive" use of leisure may indicate that work-oriented values had considerable impact on America for most of the twentieth century. Another persistent bias was the discouragement of recreation on Sundays. Dulles, *History*, pp. 4–21, 203–09. Not until 1928 did Massachusetts legalize Sunday afternoon baseball. *Recreation*, XXII (January 1929), 546.
20. The following information on theories of play comes mainly from Sapora and Mitchell, *Theory*, pp. 77–112.
21. Adna F. Weber, *The Growth of Cities in the Nineteenth Century: A Study in Statistics* (New York, 1899), pp. 21–22, 40. Weber's definition of "urban" included all towns with populations of over 8,000. For an introduction to the development of American cities, see McKelvey, *Urbanization*, and his sequel, *The Emergence of Metropolitan America, 1915–1966* (New Brunswick, N.J., 1968). Arthur M. Schlesinger, *The Rise of the City, 1878–1896*, A History of American Life (New York, 1933), is still useful.
22. Rainwater, *Play*, p. 10.
23. Clifford W. Patton, *The Battle for Municipal Reform: Mobilization and Attack, 1875–1900* (Washington, D.C., 1940), pp. 7, 14–15.
24. Schlesinger, *Rise*, pp. 83, 110. Reformer Jacob A. Riis provided graphic contemporary accounts of the slums of New York in the 1890s in *The Children of the Poor* (New York, 1892), *How the Other Half Lives* (New York, 1890), and *A Ten Years' War* (Boston and New York, 1900). See also Robert W. DeForest and Lawrence Veiller (eds.), *The Tenement House Problem* (2 vols.; New York, 1903).
25. Riis, *Children*, pp. 15, 17; James Ford, *Slums and Housing* (2 vols.; Cambridge, 1936), I, 187–88.
26. DeForest and Veiller, *Tenement*, I, xiv–xviii, 3, 8, 243.
27. Riis, *Other Half*, pp. 61, 167, 170–71, 183.
28. Riis, *Other Half*, pp. 61, 181, 216–19; Seymour J. Mandelbaum, *Boss Tweed's New York*, New Dimensions in History—Historical Cities (New York, 1965), pp. 52–53.
29. Riis, *Children*, pp. 92–106; *New York Tribune*, May 27, 1889, p. 7.
30. Jacob A. Riis, "Playgrounds for City Schools," *The Century Magazine*, XLVIII (September 1894), 657–60; Joseph Lee, *Constructive and Preventive Philanthropy* (New York, 1902), pp. 144, 145.
31. Riis, *Ten Years' War*, pp. 207–08, 211; *New York Tribune*, January 1, 1891, p. 2, and December 31, 1893, p. 13. For examples of park board problems, see the *Tribune*: January 1, 1887, p. 5; January 6, 1887, p. 8; February 27, 1889, pp. 4, 6; March 6, 1889, p. 6; April 26, 1890, p. 4; August 1, 1890, p. 6; February 22, 1891, p. 6; June 10, 1892, p. 11.
32. *New York Times*, April 22, 1886, p. 4; Henry H. Reed and Sophia Duckworth, *Central Park: A History and a Guide* (New York, 1967), pp. 24, 46.

33. *New York Times*, October 8, 1891, p. 9; Lee, *Philanthropy*, p. 143.

34. DeForest and Veiller, *Tenement*, II, 5–9.

35. Henry Steele Commager, *The American Mind* (New Haven, 1950), pp. 41–54.

36. Accounts of these years may be found in books such as Samuel P. Hays, *The Response to Industrialism*, The Chicago History of American Civilization Series (Chicago, 1957); Harold U. Faulkner, *Politics, Reform, and Expansion, 1890–1900*, The New American Nation Series (New York, 1959); Carl N. Degler, *The Age of the Economic Revolution, 1876–1900*, Scott, Foresman, American History Series (Glenview, Ill., 1967); Robert H. Wiebe, *The Search for Order, 1877–1920*, The Making of America (New York, 1967); George E. Mowry, *The Era of Theodore Roosevelt, 1900–1912*, The New American Nation Series (New York, 1958); and Gabriel Kolko, *The Triumph of Conservatism: A Re-interpretation of American History, 1900–1916* (New York, 1963).

37. Mowry, *Roosevelt*, pp. 16–37, provides a brief introduction to the flow of ideas in the period. More detailed studies include: Commager, *Mind;* Ralph Gabriel, *The Course of American Democratic Thought* (2nd ed.; New York, 1956); Sidney Fine, *Laissez Faire and the General Welfare State* (Ann Arbor, 1956); Richard Hofstadter, *Social Darwinism in American Thought* (Philadelphia, 1944); and Morton G. White, *Social Thought in America; The Revolt against Formalism* (New York, 1949).

38. See material on Luther Gulick, Joseph Lee, and Howard Braucher in the following chapters.

39. Much of this sketch of the progressive reformers' characteristics comes from Mowry, *Roosevelt*, pp. 85–105. Other insights into both reform and reformers include: Daniel Aaron, *Men of Good Hope* (New York, 1951); David Chalmers, *The Social and Political Ideas of the Muckrakers* (New York, 1964); Eric Goldman, *Rendezvous with Destiny* (New York, 1952); Richard Hofstadter, *The Age of Reform* (New York, 1955); Daniel Levine, *Varieties of Reform Thought* (Madison, 1964); and David W. Noble, *The Paradox of Progressive Thought* (Minneapolis, 1958).

40. Frank Mann Stewart, *A Half Century of Municipal Reform: The National Municipal League* (Berkeley, 1950), p. 12; Patton, *Battle*, p. 55.

41. See William A. Tolman, *Municipal Reform Movements in the United States* (New York, 1895); Albert Shaw, "Our Civic Renaissance," *Review of Reviews*, XI (April 1898), 415–27; Wilcox, *City;* Lee, *Philanthropy;* and Charles Zueblin, *A Decade of Civic Development* (Chicago, 1905), and *American Municipal Progress* (New York, 1920). Also Richard F. Knapp, "Parks and Politics: The Rise of Municipal Responsibility for Playgrounds in New York City, 1887–1905" (unpublished M.A. thesis, Duke University, 1968).

42. Lawrence A. Cremin, *The Transformation of the School* (New York, 1961), pp. 3, 5, 20. General histories of American education include Edgar W. Knight, *Education in the United States* (3rd ed.; New York, 1951), and R. Freeman Butts and Lawrence A. Cremin, *A History of Education in American Culture* (New York, 1953). See also Theodore R. Sizer's more detailed *Secondary Schools at the Turn of the Century* (New Haven, 1964).

43. Ellwood P. Cubberly, *Public Education in the United States* (Boston, 1919), pp. 393–94; Ernest R. Bayles and Bruce L. Hood, *Growth of American Educational Thought and Practice* (New York, 1966), pp. 177–79. The use of

public health as a justification for certain educational and recreational programs may be a promising area for further research. On public health, see
Mazyck P. Ravenal, ed., *A Half Century of Public Health.* . .(New York, 1921),
and Wilson G. Smillie, *Public Health.* . *.1607–1914* (New York, 1955).

44. Knight, *Education*, pp. 526–27; Willis Rudy, *Schools in an Age of Mass
Culture* (Englewood Cliffs, 1965), pp. 20, 34–38. Other social and educational
theories of American educators are revealed in Merle E. Curti, *The Social
Ideas of American Educators* (2nd ed.; Paterson, N.J., 1959), and Vivian T.
Thayer, *Formative Ideas in American Education.* . .(New York, 1965).

45. Rudy, *Schools*, pp. 73, 76–79; Knight, *Education*, pp. 544–45.

46. Curti, *Ideas*, pp. 218–53. Edgar B. Wesley, *NEA: The First Hundred
Years* (New York, 1957), is incomplete.

47. Cremin, *School*, is a standard work on progressive education. See Sol
Cohen, *Progressives and Urban School Reform* (New York, 1964), for the impact of the movement in New York.

48. Quoted in Cremin, *School*, pp. 99–100. See also Curti's essay, in *Ideas*,
on Dewey, pp. 499–541.

49. (Chicago, 1899), pp. 12–13, 15, 53, 81.

50. See George E. Johnson, "Educational Value of Play," *Pedagogical Seminary*, III (1894), 97, and "Child-Study on the Playground," National Education
Association *Proceedings* (1908), pp. 917–24. Also Aaron Gove, "Public School-
houses and their Use as Centers of Instruction and Recreation for the Community," *Education*, XVII (March 1897), 407–11, and E. A. Kirkpatrick, "Play
as a Factor in Social and Educational Reforms," *Review of Reviews*, XX
(August 1899), 192–96.

51. Arthur Weston, *The Making of American Physical Education* (New
York, 1962), pp. 32–41, 50–53. See also Charles W. Hackensmith, *History of
Physical Education* (New York, 1966); Emmett A. Rice, John L. Hutchinson,
and Mabel Lee, *A Brief History of Physical Education* (4th ed.; New York,
1958); and Norma Schwendener, *A History of Physical Education in the
United States* (New York, 1942).

52. "The Park Movement in the United States," *Garden and Forest*, VI
(May 24, 1893), 221; Reed and Duckworth, *Central Park*. Charles E. Doell and
Gerald B. Fitzgerald, *A Brief History of Parks and Recreation in the United
States* (Chicago, 1954), is sketchy but very broad.

53. *Public Parks* (Brookline, Mass., 1902), pp. 47–50, 107–08, 112. See Charles
S. Sargent's editorials in *Garden and Forest* (1888–97) for similar views.

54. "Playgrounds and Parks," *Garden and Forest*, VII (June 6, 1894), 221–22;
"Municipal Playgrounds," *Garden and Forest*, IX (December 16, 1896), 501;
and "City Playgrounds," *Garden and Forest*, X (December 8, 1897), 480. The
concept of the landscape park as an escape from the city was, in a sense, a
rural-oriented reaction rather than a positive response to the unnatural city.
Similar comments could be made about state and national parks and forests.
For related ideas, see Arthur A. Ekirch, *Man and Nature in America* (New
York, 1963); Leo Marx, *The Machine in the Garden* (New York, 1964); Rod-
erick Nash, *Wilderness and the American Mind* (New Haven, 1967); Hans
Huth, *Nature and the American* (Berkeley, 1957); and Henry Nash Smith,
Virgin Land (Cambridge, Mass., 1950). The conservation movement, too, is
involved in the relationship of man and nature but also, like the national

forests, deals with the wise use of resources. See Samuel P. Hays, *Conservation and the Gospel of Efficiency* (Cambridge, Mass., 1959).

55. Mel Scott, *American City Planning Since 1890* (Berkeley, 1969), pp. 1–109; Cozens and Stumpf, *Sports*, p. 183. See also John W. Reps, *The Making of Urban America* (Princeton, 1965), and Roy Lubove, *The Urban Community* (Englewood Cliffs, 1967).

56. For details on the changing image of charity and the rise of modern social work, see Frank J. Bruno, *Trends in Social Work. . .*(New York, 1948); Roy Lubove, *The Professional Altruist* (Cambridge, Mass., 1965); Frank D. Watson, *The Charity Organization Movement in the United States* (New York, 1922); Harold L. Wilensky and Charles N. Lebeaux, *Industrial Society and Social Welfare* (New York, 1958); and Kathleen Woodroofe, *From Charity to Social Work in England and the United States* (London and Toronto, 1962). Lee, *Philanthropy;* Anthony M. Platt, *The Child Savers* (Chicago, 1969); and Walter L. Stone, *Development of Boys' Work in the United States* (Nashville, 1935), offer examples of the breadth of social work.

57. McKelvey, *Urbanization*, pp. 154–55; Lubove, *Altruist*, pp. 1, 18, 21, 35–36, 119, 159.

58. See Allen F. Davis, *Spearheads for Freedom* (New York, 1967), on settlements about 1890–1914.

59. *Ibid.*, p. 27. See Aaron I. Abell, *The Urban Impact on American Protestantism, 1865–1900* (Cambridge, Mass., 1943), and also his *American Catholicism and Social Action* (Garden City, 1960). Also Charles H. Hopkins, *The Rise of the Social Gospel in American Protestantism, 1865–1915* (New Haven, 1940); and Henry F. May, *Protestant Churches and Industrial America* (New York, 1949).

60. Quoted in Hopkins, *Rise*, p. 120. See also pp. 54, 319.

61. Charles H. Hopkins, *History of the YMCA in North America* (New York, 1951), pp. 141, 392–402.

62. *Ibid.*, pp. 161–75, 179–95, 483–85, 605. Nationally-organized youth work was still in its initial stages in the early 1900s. Some groups, such as Earnest Thompson Seton's Woodcraft Indians and Daniel Carter Beard's Sons of Daniel Boone, were in operation and foreshadowed the ultimately larger Boy Scouts of America, Camp Fire Girls, and Girl Scouts, all started before 1917.

63. On fund raising, Scott M. Cutlip, *Fund Raising in the United States* (New Brunswick, 1965), is a standard work. The more plentiful writings on philanthropy and foundations include Edward C. Jenkins, *Philanthropy in America* (New York, 1950); Robert H. Bremner, *American Philanthropy*, The Chicago History of American Civilization Series (Chicago, 1960); and a special bibliography in Russell Sage Foundation, *Report* of the Princeton Conference on the History of Philanthropy in the United States (New York, 1956).

64. Ann D. Walton and Marianna O. Lewis, eds., *The Foundation Directory* (2nd ed.; New York, 1964), p. 19.

65. Cutlip, *Fund Raising*, pp. xii, 7, 39–47.

66. *Ibid.*, pp. 206–07; Jenkins, *Philanthropy*, pp. 105–07.

67. Sidney Dillick, *Community Organization for Neighborhood Development* (New York, 1953), pp. 43–44.

NOTES TO CHAPTER 2

1. Rainwater, *Play*, pp. 13–22. While early American playgrounds and gymnastics followed German models, the settlement idea and municipal socialism came from Britain. See Arthur Mann, "British Social Thought and American Reformers of the Progressive Era," *Mississippi Valley Historical Review*, XLII (March 1956), 672–92. A comparative study of the development of public recreation in different nations, stressing cultural backgrounds, could be of significant value.

2. Rainwater, *Play*, pp. 23–36; Lee, *Philanthropy*, pp. 163–64.

3. Rainwater, *Play*, pp. 36–43, 50–51. See also Everett B. Mero, ed., *American Playgrounds* (Boston, 1908), p. 249. The beginning of the playground movement in most of these cities has yet to be recorded in a scholarly manner.

4. The only biography of Lee is Allen V. Sapora's lengthy "The Contribution of Joseph Lee to the Modern Recreation Movement and Related Social Movements in the United States" (unpublished Ph.D. dissertation, University of Michigan, 1952); see pp. 17, 39–70.

5. *Ibid.*, pp. 72–109, 373–76; Edward T. Hartman, "Joseph Lee, Creative Philanthropist," *Recreation*, XXXI (December 1937), 546–47, 583.

6. Massachusetts Civic League, *Annual Report* (Cambridge, 1900), p. 3, cited in Sapora, "Lee," p. 112. See also pp. 88–111.

7. Sapora, "Lee," pp. 112–15, 146–47. When Lee died in 1937, the statutes of Massachusetts still carried 100 league-sponsored laws. *Boston Transcript*, January 4, 1936. The reference is in the papers of the now-defunct National Recreation Association (NRA). The records are held, some independently and some interfiled, in the files of the successor organization, the National Recreation and Park Association (NRPA), in Arlington, Virginia, and are referred to as "NRA." The professional papers of Howard S. Braucher, executive secretary and later president of the NRA, are in the same place and are cited as "HSB." Joseph Lee is cited in subsequent notes as "Lee," and Howard Braucher as "Braucher." Minutes of meetings of the board of directors of the NRA are cited as "NRA Board, date." Minutes of the executive committee are referred to as "NRA Ex Com." "NRA-M" denotes other records of the NRA in the Social Welfare History Archives, University of Minnesota Libraries, Minneapolis, Minnesota.

8. Lee, *Philanthropy*, p. 4. Also Lee, "Robert A. Woods," *Recreation*, XIX (June 1925), 166; Sapora, "Lee," pp. 139–43; and George D. Burrage, "With the Class of 1883 at Harvard," *Recreation*, XXXI (December 1937), 532.

9. Sapora, "Lee," pp. 127–34, 144–45; George D. Butler, *Pioneers in Public Recreation* (Minneapolis, 1965), p. 9; *Recreation*, XXXVI (February 1943), 639; Lee to Braucher, February 26, 1930, NRA.

10. Sapora, "Lee," pp. 147–99; Henry W. Holmes, "Prophet in Education," *Recreation*, XXXI (December 1937), 527–29.

11. Lee, quoted in Theodate Geoffrey, "Joseph Lee, Philosopher," *Recreation*, XXXI (December 1937), 571.

12. Lee, *Philanthropy*, p. 213, and quoted in *Recreation*, IV (October 1910), 239.

13. *Recreation*, XIX (March 1926), 661; NRA Board, September 22, 1932.

14. Lee, *Philanthropy*, p. 7.
15. Lee, "The Community: Maker of Men," *Recreation*, XVI (January 1923), 467.
16. Lee, "The Permanents," *Recreation*, XVI (December 1922), 403–08. Lee to Braucher: August 13, 1925; November 6, 1925; and January 12, 1931; NRA. See too Butler, *Pioneers*, pp. 4–5.
17. Lee, "Play and Democracy," *Recreation*, XVII (November 1923), 438; "At the National Recreation Congress," *Recreation*, XXXI (December 1937), 567; Braucher, quoted in *Recreation*, XV (September 1921), 355.
18. Braucher, "Walking with Joseph Lee," *Recreation*, XXXI (December 1937), inside rear cover; in the same issue, see p. 541 and Geoffrey, "Lee," p. 569. Lee, quoted in *Recreation*, XV (July 1921), 241.
19. Lee to Braucher, February 26, 1930, quoted in *Recreation*, XXXI (December 1937), 575.
20. Lee, "Charity Workers," *Recreation*, XIV (January 1921), 587; "An Interview with Joseph Lee," *Recreation*, XXX (February 1937), 521; Sapora, "Lee," pp. 204–06.
21. Lee, *Philanthropy*, pp. 170–81; Butler, *Pioneers*, p. 2; Sapora, "Lee," pp. 216–28, 249, 256–58. Examples of Lee's standards are in Lee, "A System of Public Playgrounds," *Chautauquan*, XLIII (June 1906), 352–59.
22. These ideas are summarized in *Play in Education* (New York, 1915). Lee was a prolific writer. Sapora, "Lee," p. 340, counted two books, almost two hundred fifty pamphlets or articles in periodicals, and eight hundred items in newspapers. George E. Johnson, *Education by Play and Games* (Boston, 1907) influenced Lee and dealt with much of the same material as Lee's *Play*. In contrast, Henry S. Curtis's *Education Through Play* (New York, 1915), published a few months before Lee's *Play*, was much less theoretical and far broader as a practical manual on the relation of recreation to the school.
23. Lee, "Play as an Antidote to Civilization," *Recreation*, V (July 1911), 110–26; "Whence Cometh My Strength," *Recreation*, XIV (December 1920), 531–32; "Play, the Architect of Man," *Recreation*, XXI (December 1927), 460–63; *Philanthropy*, pp. 218–25. Sapora, "Lee," pp. 263, 267.
24. Lee: "Play and Health," *Recreation*, XIX (September 1925), 338; *Recreation*, XIX (January 1926), 565; "Are We Carrying the Play Idea too Far?," *Recreation*, XXIII (October 1929), 444–46.
25. Riis, Introduction to Lee, *Philanthropy*, pp. vii–x; Butler, *Pioneers*, p. 2; Sapora, "Lee," pp. 211, 221–22, 279, 342.
26. Sapora, "Lee," p. 279; J. W. Buel, ed., *Louisiana and the Fair* (St. Louis, 1904), VI, 2064–67.
27. Doell and Fitzgerald, *Parks*, pp. 48–49; Harlean James to Braucher, October 21, 1937, NRA; *Recreation*, XLII (March 1949), 559; Sapora, "Lee," pp. 280–83. A study of the development of the group, known today as Urban America, would yield insight into trends in the history of parks and city planning.
28. Information below is from Knapp, "Parks and Politics."
29. "Seth Thayer Stewart," *Recreation*, II (August 1908), 12.
30. Butler, *Pioneers*, pp. 27, 30; Curtis, "The Play Movement in Germany," *Chautauquan*, XL (January 1905), 445–48.

31. Ethel J. Dorgan, *Luther Halsey Gulick, 1865–1918* (New York, 1934), pp. 1–7, 22–27; John Collier, "Luther Halsey Gulick," *Recreation*, XII (October 1918), 252–54; Weston, *Physical Education*, pp. 44–45; Hopkins, *YMCA*, pp. 245–68. In 1886 only 17 YMCA secretaries at a conference in Springfield were physical educators; by 1901, there were 313 such men. Also Gulick, "Physical Education—A New Profession," *Physique*, I (July 1891), 112–15.

32. Dorgan, *Gulick*, pp. 35, 52–55, 83–84; Hopkins, *YMCA*, pp. 254–55. Also Gulick, "Psychological, Pedagogical, and Religious Aspects of Group Games," *Pedagogical Seminary*, VI (March 1899), 135–51.

33. Dorgan, *Gulick*, pp. 71–92; "The Public School Athletic League of New York," NRA bound pamphlet no. 37. *New York Times*: December 21, 1904, p. 10; January 1, 1905, p. 9; May 13, 1905, p. 1; June 21, 1905, p. 14.

34. See "Psychology of Play," *Association Outlook*, VIII (February 1899), 112–16. His *A Philosophy of Play* (New York, 1920) summarizes much of his thought. Dorgan has the most complete bibliography of Gulick.

35. Gulick, *Philosophy*, p. 11. Also see pp. 12, 125, 230–31, 266–82. He also recognized such more practical factors as the relation of play to physical and mental health.

36. Gulick, *Philosophy*, p. xiv.

37. Rudy, *Schools*, pp. 343–44. See too Gulick: "Play and Democracy," *Charities and the Commons*, XVIII (August 3, 1907), 481–86; "The Social Function of Play," *Journal of Education*, LXXXI (June 3, 1915), 598–99; and *Recreation*, I (April 1907), 7.

38. Dorgan, *Gulick*, pp. 1–24, 39; J. H. McCurdy, "Luther Halsey Gulick," *Recreation*, XXX (July 1936), 297.

39. McCurdy, "Gulick," pp. 297–99; Dorgan, *Gulick*, pp. 29, 39–40, 60, 116–17, 129, 133–34.

40. Quoted in Butler, *Introduction*, p. 83. See too, pp. 81–85, and Rainwater, *Play*, p. 20.

41. Henry S. Curtis: "How It Began," *Recreation*, XXV (May 1931), 71; statement, annotated by Lee, with a statement by Braucher (1926) in HSB; *Mind and Body*, XXXIII (1926), 200–01.

42. See file of correspondence between ACA leaders and Curtis in HSB.

43. This group, hereinafter referred to as the PAA, was the NRA by its original name. Playground and Recreation Association of America (PRAA) was the name of the organization from 1911 to 1930.

44. Curtis and Weller to Woodruff, March 5, 1906, HSB; Curtis and Braucher, statements, HSB; Weller, "Playground Origins," HSB.

45. Roosevelt viewed playgrounds as a deterrent to delinquency; he had first become interested in them through his friend Jacob Riis, crusader against slums in New York. In Washington as President he supported Weller's efforts. Riis, *Theodore Roosevelt the Citizen* (New York, 1904), pp. 129–54; Roosevelt to Riis, January 3, 1895, in Elting Morison, ed., *The Letters of Theodore Roosevelt* (Cambridge, Massachusetts, 1951), I, 419–20; Roosevelt to Weller, July 6. 1903, and W. Loeb, Jr., to Weller, March 18, 1905, Library of Congress, Roosevelt MSS.

46. Braucher, notes, HSB; "NRA—History: Early Years," pp. 4–5, NRA; Sapora, "Lee," pp. 262–63, 286.

47. *Washington Evening Star*, April 12, 1906, p. 10; NRA Board, April 12, 1906. There are numerous other accounts of these meetings. See a typed copy of PAA, *Prospectus* (1906), in NRA. Both HSB and NRA contain several statements, some copied from others, on the early PAA. *Recreation*, XXV (May 1931), and XLIX (June 1956) are special historical issues.

48. NRA Board, April 12, 1906. This early constitution is also in *Recreation*, I (June 1907), 13–15.

49. *Washington Evening Star*, April 13, 1906, pp. 11, 14; April 14, 1906, pp. 2, 8; April 15, 1906, p. 10; April 16, 1906, p. 7.

50. Pp. 7–10, NRA.

51. NRA Broad, April 13, 1906: *Recreation*, I (May 1907), 5, 12–13. The story of the growth of public recreation in Washington, yet to be told, is a chronicle of local and national agencies, both public and private, all working within one city.

52. NRA Ex Com, local quorum, December 5 and 12, 1907; HSB; "Report of Progress by Secretary," January 16, 1908, HSB; Henry S. Curtis, "Washington Sites Available for Playgrounds," *Recreation*, I (March 1908), 14–20; Butler, *Pioneers*, p. 32.

53. Congress was not always favorable; the chairman of the appropriations committee of the House of Representatives once ridiculed leadership in recreation on the floor of the House: "You might as well undertake to teach a fish to swim as to teach a child to play!" Quoted by James E. West, "What the Recreation Movement Means to America," in NRA, *Proceedings of the 26th National Recreation Congress* (New York, 1941), p. 113. Such works are cited below as "*Proceedings*, year." See also *Recreation*, III (January 1910), 10, and U.S., Congress, House, 61st Cong., 2nd sess., March 8, 1910, *Congressional Record*, XLV, 2918–31.

54. NRA Ex Com, local quorum, June 2, 1906; NRA Board, June 20, 1907; Secretary's report, June, 1907, NRA. PAA members are listed in *Recreation*, I (November 1907), 13–15.

55. Dorgan, *Gulick*, p. 99; Henry S. Curtis, *The Play Movement and its Significance* (New York, 1917), pp. 15–16.

56. NRA Ex Com, local quorum, June 2, 1906; Seth Stewart to Clinton Woodruff, June 4, 1906, HSB.

57. The papers were all printed in *Charities and the Commons*, XVII (August 3, 1907), 471–565.

58. John M. Glenn, Lilian Brandt, and F. Emerson Andrews, *Russell Sage Foundation, 1907–1946* (2 vols.; New York, 1947), I, xvii, 13, 18, 32–33. In 1907 the widow of New York financier Sage established the foundation, which actually had made a $3,000 grant for use in an exhibit at the Jamestown Exposition to the PAA before the Chicago congress. Weller later credited Curtis with enlisting the Sage support. Weller, "Playground Origins," HSB. NRA Ex Com, local quorum, May 15, 1907.

59. Glenn, Brandt, and Andrews, *Sage*, I, 33, 59, 70; Butler, *Pioneers*, p. 58; Dorgan, *Gulick*, pp. 99–100. Gulick's then-handsome salary was $7,000, almost twice his starting salary with the New York schools. "Early History of the NRA," HSB. The funds were intended to help the PAA to help itself rather than be a perpetual grant. NRA Ex Com, local quorum, November 15, 1907.

60. NRA Board, October 29, 1908; Glenn, Brandt, and Andrews, *Sage*, I, 71; Rainwater, *Play*, p. 20.

61. "Jamestown Playground Exhibit," *Recreation*, I (October 1907), 3–6; Glenn, Brandt, and Andrews, *Sage*, I, 70–71; Butler, *Pioneers*, p. 66; Lee Hanmer, "Drumming for Playgrounds," *Recreation*, XXV (May 1931), 77–79; NRA Ex Com, local quorum, December 12, 1907.

62. Curtis, *Play Movement*, p. 16; "Report of the Committee on a Normal Course in Play," NRA *Proceedings*, 1908 (New York, 1909), pp. 343–46. The three courses, published in 1910, were *A Normal Course in Play for Professional Directors, A Course in Play for Grade Teachers*, and *An Institute Course in Play*. The course was later replaced by Butler's *Introduction*. Alice O. Bronson, *Clark W. Hetherington, Scientist and Philosopher* (Salt Lake City, 1958), pp. 36, 90–91; Butler, *Pioneers*, pp. 19–21; H.S. Curtis, "The Normal Course in Play," *Recreation*, III (October 1909), 20–22.

63. NRA Ex Com, local quorum; March 12, 1907; January 16, 1908; April 16, 1908. Also *Recreation*, I (March 1908), 13, and II (April 1908), whole number.

64. Curtis, "How It Began," p. 106; NRA, *Proceedings*, 1908, pp. 24–49.

65. Dorgan, *Gulick*, p. 101; Butler, *Pioneers*, pp. 57–58; *Recreation*, I (January 1908), 3; NRA Ex Com, local quorum, December 12, 1907, and September 12, 1908.

66. Glenn, Brandt, and Andrews, *Sage*, I, 75–77; Butler, *Pioneers*, pp. 56–57; Gulick, "Study, Promote, Advertise," *Recreation*, IV (December 1910), 297–301. In varying degrees every president from Theodore Roosevelt to Franklin Roosevelt supported the NRA.

67. NRA, *Proceedings*, 1908, pp. 361–70.

68. NRA Board, September 12, 1908; NRA Ex Com, April 27, 1909; Braucher-Gulick correspondence, 1909, NRA.

69. Braucher finished at Cornell in 1903 and went to Portland in 1905. NRA, *Howard Braucher Memorial Booklet* (New York, 1949), pp. 9, 30–31; Braucher, notes, NRA; *Recreation*, I (September 1907), 15, and (November 1907), 14. The needed biography of Braucher does not exist; the booklet above is the best substitute.

70. Allen T. Burns, "Howard Braucher and his Contribution to the Enrichment of Human Life," in NRA, *Proceedings*, 1949, pp. 22–24; NRA, *Braucher*, pp. 12–14; George Butler, interview, Sarasota, Florida, July 30, 1970.

71. Braucher, "The Reality of Recreation," *Recreation*, XXXII (September 1938), 321. Perhaps a dozen more editorials, mostly in the 1930s, stress similar themes.

72. The other areas were health, education, and work. Braucher: "Play and Worship," *Recreation*, XXXIX (January 1946), 505; "Abundant Living," *Recreation*, XXXII (October 1938), 379; *Recreation*, XVI (September 1922), 290; to George W. Murray, March 26, 1925, NRA; notes, NRA. Mrs. Braucher to author, July 28, 1969.

73. Braucher: "Shall We Chain It Down?," *Recreaton*, XXIV (September 1929), rear cover; "Freedom," *Recreation*, XXVI (November 1932), 457; "Recreation Workers and the Preservation and Development of Democracy," *Recreation*, XXX (September 1936), 281; "Freedom," *Recreation*, XXXV (September 1941), 349; "Planning for Freedom of Living," *Recreation*, XXXIX (February 1946), 561.

74. Butler, *Pioneers*, pp. 96–97; Braucher: notes, 1911, NRA, and "What Next?," *Recreation*, XXX (January 1937), 473; E. Dana Caulkins, interview,

Durham, N.C., January 29, 1970; Arthur E. Todd, interview, Washington, D.C., March 19, 1970.

75. Braucher: "What are the Ultimates," *Recreation*, XXIV (August 1930), 285, 307–08; "Playgrounds: Build for the New Era," *Recreation*, XXVI (April 1932), 1; "Abundant Living," *Recreation*, XXXII (October 1938), 378–79. Braucher wrote no books. Most of his views are expressed in articles and editorials in *Recreation*, many of which are collected in *A Treasury of Living* (New York, 1950).

76. He did not, however, emphasize the term "leisure" much until the 1920s, when "new leisure" became familiar among a number of writers. See "The Machine Revolution," *Recreation*, XXIV (February 1931), 585.

77. Braucher: "Play and Social Progress," *Recreation*, XVI (June 1922), 101–04; "Recreation," *Recreation*, XXIV (January 1931), 529; "Congress Afterthoughts," *Recreation*, XXXI (July 1937), 209.

78. Braucher: to Charles Stillman, September 25, 1929, NRA; "The Spirit of the National Recreation Movement," *Recreation*, XXXII (February 1939), 593; "Thirty-seven Years," *Recreation*, XXXVII (May 1943), 57.

79. Braucher, "Jane Addams," *Recreation*, XXIX (June 1935), 137.

80. Sapora, "Lee," pp. 269–75, 286–89. E. B. Mero: "Massachusetts Adopts Playground Law," *Recreation*, II (January 1909), 17–21; "A Report of the Massachusetts Playground Campaign of December 1908," December 16, 1908, NRA.

81. Braucher, statement on the early PAA, October, 1926, HSB. NRA Ex Com. local quorum: February 20, 1908; April 30, 1908; November 5, 1908. Butler, *Pioneers*, pp. 29–30.

82. NRA Board, May 14, 1909, verbatim debate of the PAA council.

83. NRA Board, June 19, 1909.

84. Dorgan, *Gulick*, pp. 98, 100–01; Braucher, notes of meeting with Dorgan, December 19, 1932, NRA.

85. *Recreation*, II (March 1909), 15–16; *Recreation*, III (January 1910), 10–12.

86. Braucher, notes, c. 1911, NRA. The two organizations eventually divided the field and Hanmer, Braucher's friend since college days, cooperated with the PAA numerous times. Hanmer pushed such things as city planning for recreation and the wider use of schools. When Hanmer retired in 1937, the foundation ended its work in recreation, saying that the NRA by then provided adequate services. Glenn, Brandt, and Andrews, *Sage*, II, 511–12; Hanmer, "Confidential Memorandum," August 25, 1936, HSB; Butler, *Pioneers*, pp. 68–74.

87. NRA Board: May 14 and June 19, 1909; Butler, *Pioneers*, pp. 57–58.

NOTES TO CHAPTER 3

1. Braucher, notes of conference with Mrs. Ogden L. Mills, April 26, 1947, NRA; *Recreation*, XXXI (December 1937), 515.

2. Sapora, "Lee," pp. 293–95, 336–38, 341, 377; Schwendener, *History*, pp. 133–34.

3. Sapora, "Lee," pp. 259–60, 291–92, 296–97; "Joseph Lee and the NRA," *Recreation*, XXXI (December 1937), 539–41; Braucher, "Joseph Lee," *Recreation*, XXIX (July 1935), 185.

4. Sapora, "Lee," pp. 259–60, 291–92, 296–97; Lee, "The American Play Tradition and Our Relation to It," *Recreation*, VII (July 1913), 158.
5. Sapora, "Lee," pp. 297–98.
6. *Ibid.*, pp. 292–94.
7. Williams, "Comments on MSS of Allen V. Sapora," NRA.
8. Braucher to Mrs. Lee, August 5, 1937, NRA.
9. See NRA Ex Com, December 8, 1922; and Lee to Braucher, December 12, 1929, and July 18, 1930, both in NRA. Also Hugh McK. Landon's tribute to Braucher in NRA, *Proceedings*, 1941, pp. 99–100.
10. George Butler to author, March 5, 1970; Caulkins, interview, January 29, 1970. Unfortunately the official minutes of the board rarely indicate much discussion or argument. A large percentage of actions are recorded as "unanimous."
11. NRA Board: June 19, 1909, January 23, 1911.
12. NRA Board, April 27, 1927.
13. NRA Board, February 27, 1918; Braucher to Mrs. Lee, May 20, 1941, NRA; Braucher, notes of meeting with Otto Mallery, May 22, 1946, NRA; Butler, *Pioneers*, p. 107.
14. NRA, Brancher, pp. 38–42; Butler, interview; Joseph Prendergast, interview, Washington, D.C., April 21, 1970.
15. Braucher wrote frequently about democracy, yet there was little democracy within the NRA staff. This seeming paradox is partially explained by Braucher's confidence in himself as a benevolent, superior leader, a trait found in a significant number of progressives in the era of Theodore Roosevelt.
16. Both colleagues and other associates readily admit to Braucher's great power and influence within the NRA. Butler, interview; Caulkins, interviews; Sidney Lutzin, interview, Washington, D.C., May 28, 1970; Harold D. Meyer, interview, Chapel Hill, N.C., March 2, 1970; Willard Sutherland to author, May 26, 1970. It would be an error, however, to aassume that Braucher's staff was a weak, submissive lot; a number of them, and some who left the NRA, made significant contributions of their own to the development of recreation.
17. Sutherland to author, May 26, 1970; Prendergast, interview; Reynold E. Carlson to author, June 23, 1970; George Hjelte to author, June 1, 1970; V. K. Brown to author, April 23, 1970; Mark McCloskey, interview, cited in Dorothy M. Lancaster, "The Impact of the Works Progress Administration upon Public Recreation in the United States" (unpublished Re.D. dissertation, Indiana University, 1967), p. 196.
18. Other similar agencies were not all as lucky as the PRAA in securing such long-term, devoted leaders. See Foster R. Dulles, *The American Red Cross: A History* (New York, 1950). But, as the NRA was to learn later, longevity in high positions has its risks too, such as the frequent inflexibility of old men faced with new situations and the vacuum created when aged executives without chosen successors become incapacitated.
19. Rainwater, *Play*, pp. 20–21; Gulick to Braucher, memorandum, c. January 1910, NRA; "The Playground Situation," April 7, 1910, NRA; Lee, "The Playground Movement in America," c. 1912, HSB.
20. NRA Board: May 10, 1911; June 5, 1912.
21. See *Recreation*, I (June 1907), 13–15, for the first constitution. NRA Board: September 10, 1908; April 22, 1910; June 7, 1910. The *Report* of Veil-

ler's committee (April 1910) and the new constitution (June 1910) are in NRA.

22. NRA Ex Com, local quorum, April 30 and May 21, 1908; "Report of the Committee on Incorporation for 1908–09," April 1910, NRA; NRA Board: April 1, 1909; January 23, 1911. National incorporation would permit annual meetings to be held across the nation rather than only in New York state.

23. See Braucher's proposed bills, 1914 and 1915, in NRA. The real bills were H. R. 7622 and H. R. 12105, both 64th Cong., 1st sess., 1916. T. S. Settle, "Work with Congress. . . ." August 1–3, 1916, HSB.

24. The remainder of this chapter discusses, mainly in topical arrangement, the major tactics used and ideas promoted by the PRAA. Although these techniques and concepts continued in later decades, following chapters will not deal systematically with all of these matters again but shall focus on several major issues and significant changes facing the PRAA after 1916.

25. See lists of directors in Recreation, for example, I (May 1907), 16; XVIII (April 1919), inside rear cover. The preponderance of businessmen was a valuable aid to financing the PRAA but was to hinder relations in later years with the growing ranks of professionals in recreation who by then had little, if any, representation on the board. In addition, the influence of Braucher and Lee no doubt increased as the board became filled with men lacking daily contact with public recreation.

26. See Recreation, XLIX (June 1956), 263, 265. Most of the early staff were social workers.

27. PRAA leaflet 17, "Needs of the Recreation Movement in America," December 12, 1911, NRA; Carlson to author; F. S. Mathewson to author, June 10, 1970.

28. NRA Board: January 23 and March 9, 1911; January 3 and March 28, 1914. Caulkins, interview.

29. Braucher: to Kirby, April 22, 1913, NRA; "A Problem," c. 1913, NRA; to Lee, April 4, 1914, NRA; notes, c. early 1915, NRA. Braucher may even have considered resignation. C. M. Goethe to Braucher, March 10, 1914, NRA. Lee recognized the serious nature of the situation and wrote Dwight F. Davis: "Mr. Braucher is at present being killed by this work (fund raising) and if he is killed, we simply can't go on." June 15, 1914, NRA.

30. Athur S. Link, Woodrow Wilson and the Progressive Era, 1910–1917, The New American Nation Series (New York, 1954), p. 75; NRA Board, May 22, 1914; Lee, "The Work of the PRAA and the Immediate Need," October 1914, NRA.

31. Braucher, "Why It Is Hard to Secure Money for the PRAA," confidential memorandum, October 1, 1915, NRA.

32. NRA Board: April 22, 1910; March 28 and May 22, 1914. I found no data in the NRA MSS verifying the exact effect of the talks with Kent on PRAA income.

33. Braucher, "Play for America," Recreation, X (March 1917), 480–85; Braucher to E. Dana Caulkins, November 29, 1916, University of Rochester, Caulkins MSS.

34. NRA Board: May 10, 1911, March 9, 1912; January 12, 1916. NRA Ex Com: July 7, 1916; March 21, 1917. Butler, Pioneers, p. 96. James E. West, "Historical Statement. . .Boy Scouts of America," HSB; William D. Murray, The History of the Boy Scouts of America (New York, 1937), pp. 24–30, 39–40; NRA Board, June 11 and November 5, 1910. The Scouts soon became well-

established on their own. The PRAA did, however, help administer the less-dynamic Federated Boys' Clubs, *Recreation*, VIII (November 1914), 288.

35. This was in 1909. Charles E. Hartsoe, "The Contributions of Charles K. Brightbill to the Recreation Movement" (unpublished Ph.D. dissertation, University of Illinois, 1970), p. 82 note. Despite some interest in 1916, recreation administrators themselves did not form a professional association until 1937. Charles English, MSS "Autobiography," p. 33, loaned by E. Dana Caulkins; American Recreation Society (ARS), *The American Recreation Society: Its Early Years (1937–1952)* (Washington, D.C., 1953), p. 1.

36. Braucher, "A Year's Work of the PRAA," *Recreation*, IX (February 1916), 370–73; "Activities and Needs of the PRAA," *Recreation*, V (July 1911), 141–42; Lee, "The American Play Tradition and Our Relation to It," *Recreation*, VII (July 1913), 155–56.

37. "Activities and Needs," p. 141. By March 24, 1914, the PRAA listed forty different committees. List, NRA.

38. "Report of the Committee on Badges," *Recreation*, V (December 1911), 320; "The Athletic Badge Test for Boys," *Recreation*, VII (April 1913), 33–37; Braucher, "Play for America," p. 474.

39. Apparently by 1915 at least 1,250 people had subscriptions. *Recreation*, IX (February 1916), 381.

40. The compilers included only those cities returning data in the listings for a given year. Thus cities which were known to have public recreation were sometimes omitted from the tables if their answers did not reach the PRAA. The yearbooks, however, comprise almost the only records on the growth of public recreation on a national basis and may be assumed to give a fair indication of the increasing importance of organized recreation in American life. For a simple yearbook, see *Recreation*, V (January 1912), 326–50.

41. Books by PRAA authors included Lee's *Play* (1915) and Weir's *Vocational Recreational in Indiana, 1916* (Bloomington 1917). The NRA MSS contain seven volumes, with over three hundred items, of early pamphlets and other publications.

42. NRA Ex Com, February 13, 1915; Sapora, "Lee," p. 197.

43. Although Hanmer had held the first institutes, the program was accelerated late in 1910. Pendleton Dudley, "The New England Playground Institute," *Recreation*, IV (February 1911), 387–92; Butler, *Pioneers*, pp. 67–68.

44. Abbie Condit, "Tenth Anniversary of the PRAA," *Recreation*, X (November 1916), 274–76; Otto T. Mallery, "The Grand Rapids Play Congress," *Recreation*, X (January 1917), 354–55; Braucher, "Play for America," pp. 478–80.

45. NRA, *Braucher*, p. 11; *Recreation*, IV (December 1910), 313–14. After a fruitless appeal to the Russell Sage Foundation, the PRAA raised funds by itself to supply field service. NRA Board, April 22, 1910. Braucher wanted only the best men, leaders dedicated to hard work and service to others, as field secretaries. Braucher: notes, March 28, 1916, NRA; to George Knox, March 12, 1910, NRA.

46. "The Awakening of Neighborhood Life in America," *Recreation*, IX (October 1915), 234–43; NRA Board, January 25, 1913.

47. Francis R. North, "News from the Front," *Recreation*, VII (July 1913), 170–73. NRA Board: January 13, 1914; May 24, 1916. Braucher, notes, Decem-

ber, 1916, NRA. The Caulkins MSS provide examples of a field secretary's daily reports and initial and return work in several towns. Braucher's formal procedures for field work are in: "Field Work of the PRAA," April 30, 1920; "Policy of Field Work," October, 1916, revised September, 1920; and "The Work of Securing Field Appointments," all in NRA.

48. Braucher, "Play for America," p. 475; map of field work, NRA.

49. "Making a Recreation Survey," *Recreation*, VII (April 1913), 19–25.

50. Haynes, "Recreation Survey, Milwaukee, Wisconsin," *Recreation*, VI (May 1912), 38–66; Thomas S. Yukie, "The Community Recreation Survey, 1908–1952," *Journal* of the American Association for Health, Physical Education, and Recreation, XXV (May 1954), 27–28, 58. PRAA agents dominated the making of surveys for decades.

51. Braucher: "Year's Work," p. 381; "Play for America," pp. 487–91. This predominance continued throughout the life of the PRAA, with a peak of $250,000, about five-sevenths of the total budget, used in the field in 1924. After that year, both the amount and percentage of the budget earmarked for municipal field work declined. The item was, however, almost twice as large as any other important, long-run budgetary category and, before the death of Braucher, about one-half of total yearly expenditures. *Recreation*, e.g., XVIII (April 1925), 52–53, often carried the annual financial statements of the PRAA, which since 1929 are available at the NRPA.

52. The following pages will isolate components of these three major ideas and discuss each topically rather than attempt a simultaneous development. At some points the ideas tend to overlap; my division thus has been somewhat arbitrary. Lack of space precludes any discussion in depth of the ideas or, in many cases, specific declarations by the leaders of the PRAA on the relation of the PRAA to the parts of the general concepts. It is reasonable to assume, however, that the recurrence of articles in *Recreation* on a particular topic indicates interest by the PRAA. Therefore much of the following writing is based on a content analysis of *Recreation*.

53. Mrs. J. J. Storrow, "Folk Dancing," *Recreation*, V (August 1911), 16–19; "Community Music," *Recreation*, VIII (July 1914), 139–42; "Pageants to be Given During the Summer of 1911," *Recreation*, V (June 1911), 105–07; Mrs. Braucher, "Problems of Dramatic Play," *Recreation*, VI (December 1912), 324–28. The PRAA did not try to sell a specific list of new activities but simply provided the opportunity for local groups to see the wide spectrum and choose all or part of it.

54. Lee, "What Are the Best Games for Boys in Crowded Cities?," *Recreation*, VI (January 1913), 373–75; Henry S. Curtis, "New Games for the People," *Recreation*, VII (May 1913), 66–73; "Closing Days on the Summer Playgrounds," *Recreation*, VIII (January 1915), 357–59.

55. Lee, "Play for Home," *Recreation*, VI (August 1912), 146–58; John H. Chase, "Home Playgrounds in the Basement," *Recreation*, IX (September 1915), 220–22.

56. See T. S. Settle, "Recreation for Negroes in Memphis," *Recreation*, IX (March 1916), 441–45, for a rare early article dealing with Negro recreation.

57. Alexander Johnson, "Report of the Committee on Play in Institutions," *Recreation*, V (May 1911), 38–49. The PRAA, and many others interested in recreation, did not generally emphasize recreation in hospitals until the

American Red Cross had demonstrated the process in two world wars. Another institution with a new interest in recreation was the church. See the special issue of *Recreation* for March 1910; Allen Hoben, *The Minister and the Boy* (Chicago, 1912); Henry A. Atkinson, *The Church and the People's Play* (Boston, 1915); and Richard A. Swanson, "American Protestantism and Play: 1865–1915" (unpublished Ph.D. dissertation, Ohio State University, 1967).

58. David Blaustein, "The Schoolhouse Recreation Center as an Attempt to Aid Immigrants in Adjusting Themselves to American Conditions," *Recreation*, VI (December 1912), 329–34; Braucher, "What a Neighborhood Play Center Ought to Be," *Recreation*, IX (January 1916), 338–40.

59. Doell and Fitzgerald, *Parks*, pp. 65–66; Dillick, *Community*, pp. 59–61, 63. Many articles in *Recreation*, such as the entire October 1913 issue dealt with social centers.

60. Myron T. Scudder, "The Rural School as a Social Center," *Recreation*, V (September 1911), 200–04.

61. Garland A. Bricker, "Solving the Rural Recreation Problem," *Recreation*, VI (November 1912), 269–75; Henry S. Curtis, "The Organizer of Rural Recreation," *Recreation*, VI (November 1912), 282–85; Silas A. Persons, "Rural Recreation Through the Church," *Recreation*, VI (March 1913), 456–65.

62. C. M. Mayne, "What a Corporation Can and Does Do for the Recreation of Its Employees," *Recreation*, VII (February 1914), 448–51. Industrial recreation, then a part of "welfare work," was still a new development in 1900; only a few plants had such things as club rooms and lounges. By 1899 the YMCA, however, had 30 years' experience in Y's for railroad employees, the elite of labor. Jackson M. Anderson, *Industrial Recreation* (New York, 1955), pp. 40–52; Hopkins, *YMCA*, pp. 233–37. See also William H. Tolman, *Social Engineering* (New York, 1909), p. 298–324, and Ida M. Tarbell, *New Ideals in Business* (New York, 1916). The PRAA, however, lacked funds for much work in the field until the 1940s.

63. NRA Board, June 19, 1909; Weir, *Vocational Recreation*; "By Way of History," HSB.

64. See Richard H. Edwards, *Popular Amusements* (New York, 1915); Jane Addams, *The Spirit of Youth and the City Streets* (New York, 1909); and Michael M. Davis, *The Exploitation of Pleasure* (New York, 1911). Bruno, *Social Work*, pp. 406–17, has some critical comments on the subject.

65. Julia Schoenfeld, "Commercial Recreation Legislation," *Recreation*, VII (March 1914), 461–81; Belle L. Israels, "Recreation for Money," *Recreation*, VI (April 1912), 28–30.

66. Butler: *Pioneers*, p. 98; interview. Since these early years, however, much commercial recreation, such as bowling alleys and pool rooms, has gained new respectability.

67. NRA Board: May 10, 1911; June 5, 1912; November 22, 1913; March 28, 1914; November 10, 1915. Braucher, note, November 1912, NRA.

68. Dewey, *Democracy and Education* (New York, 1916), p. 327; Croly, *Progressive Democracy* (New York, 1915), p. 429; Hopkins, *Rise*, pp. 316–17.

69. Weir, *Vocational Recreation*, pp. 5, 12; Lee, "Play the Life Saver," *Recreation*, VIII (March 1914), 417–22; John Collier, "Leisure Time, the Last Problem of Civilization," *Recreation*, VI (June 1912), 93–106; John H. Finley, "The Wisdom of Leisure," *Recreation*, IX (January 1916), 335–38.

70. George A. Bellamy, "Evening Recreation," *Recreation*, V (October 1911), 239–44; Abbie Condit, "What Constitutes a Year-Round Recreation System," *Recreation*, XI (July 1917), 198–201.

71. NRA, *Proceedings*, 1908, pp. 290–301; "New Jersey Playground Law," NRA bound pamphlet 60; Butler, *Pioineers*, pp. 22, 120; "Report of the Recreational Inquiry of the State of California," *Recreation*, IX (June 1915), 91–95.

72. Braucher, "A Year's Campaign. . .," 1912–13, NRA bound pamphlet 129.

73. See John Ise, *Our National Park Policy: A Critical History* (Baltimore, 1961), and Robert Shankland, *Steve Mather of the National Parks* (New York, 1951).

74. Braucher, notes, c. 1914, NRA.

75. "A Brief History of the Playground Movement in America," *Recreation*, IX (April 1915), 10.

76. Howard Bradstreet, "The Street as a Playground," *Recreation*, V (March 1912), 417–19; Lee, "Playground Situation in Massachusetts," *Recreation*, VI (April 1912), 2–3; Braucher, "What Is Fundamental to a Neighborhood Center," *Recreation*, X (September 1916), 208–10.

77. Dwight F. Davis, "The Recreation Commission," *Recreation*, VI (September 1912), 206–08; "Arguments Advanced for a Recreation Commission," *Recreation*, V (January 1912), 351–53; "Report of Committee on Organization and Administration of a Playground," *Recreation*, IV (November 1910), 259–69.

78. Congress leaflet, HSB.

79. Julia C. Lathrop, "Taking Play Seriously," *Recreation*, X (January 1917), 356–63; John Bradford, "Children's Gardens and Playgrounds in Pensacola, Florida. . .," *Recreation*, IV (May 1910), 53; William H. Stevenson, "The Third Play Congress," *Recreation*, III (August 1909), 5–7.

80. Quoted in *Recreation*, XI (May 1917), 65.

81. F. J. Bruno to Braucher, September 30, 1915, NRA. For more examples of people citing the early effects of the PRAA, see Mero, *Playgrounds*, p. 17; "Awakening of Neighborhood Life," pp. 239–40; Braucher, "Year's Work," pp. 376–78; Elizabeth Burchenal, "The Nature and Function of Folk Dancing," *Recreation*, X (February 1917), 434; Atkinson, *Church*, p. 149.

82. The yearbooks were printed in *Recreation*, so my references below are to the periodical. Years used as examples vary slightly according to available data.

83. "Playground Facts" (1910), *Recreation*, V (April 1911), 23; "Playground Facts (1916), *Recreation*, X (March 1917), 492–93.

84. "Playground Facts" (1911), *Recreation*, V (January 1912), 333; "Playground Facts" (1916), p. 494.

85. "Playground Facts" (1912), *Recreation*, VI (February 1913), 409–10; "Playground Facts" (1916), 494.

86. "Playground Facts" (1910), p. 23; "Playground Facts" (1916), pp. 496–497.

NOTES TO CHAPTER 4

1. "America's Call to the Colors," *Recreation*, VIII (November 1914), 286.

2. Gerald B. Fitzgerald, *Community Organization for Recreation* (New York, 1948), p. 65; Dillick, *Community*, pp. 44, 47. See also Charles H. Cooley,

Social Organization (New York, 1909), and Edward J. Ward, ed., *The Social Center* (New York, 1913). R. Jackson Wilson, *In Quest of Community* (New York, 1968) has essays on several intellectuals' concepts of community c. 1860–1920. Jean B. Quandt, *From the Small Town to the Great Community* (New Brunswick, N.J., 1970) is more pertinent to the Progressive Era.

3. Quoted in Rainwater, *Play*, p. 144. See also Woods' collected papers, *The Neighborhood in Nation-Building* (New York, 1923).

4. Rainwater, *Play*, pp. 117–78; Doell and Fitzgerald, *Parks*, pp. 65–68; "County Unit System of Community Service in North Carolina," *Recreation*, XIV (January 1921), 603–09.

5. Lubove, *Altruist*, pp. 175–77; Arthur E. Wood, *Community Problems* (New York, 1928), pp. 342–43. The social unit scheme, blasted as "socialism" by local officials, was dependent on outside funds and most successful in the relatively noncontroversial realm of health services.

6. Howard Braucher: "What a Neighborhood Play Center Ought to Be," *Recreation*, IX (January 1916), 338–40; "The World at Play," October 1915, HSB.

7. Rainwater, *Play*, pp. 146–53; Wood, *Problems*, pp. 361–63; Doell and Fitzgerald, *Parks*, p. 65.

8. "Three Years' Work of the PRAA: December 1, 1916–November 30, 1919," *Recreation*, XIV (April 1920), 16; NRA Board, January 10, 1917.

9. Braucher to Rudolph Bertheau, October 16, 1926, HSB; Braucher to E. Dana Caulkins, February 6. 1917, Caulkins MSS; Cozens and Stumpf, *Sports*, p. 206; NRA Board, March 28, 1917; "The Recreation Movement in War Times," *Recreation*, XI (June 1917), 137–41.

10. Raymond R. Fosdick, *Chronicle of a Generation* (New York, 1958), pp. 135–41; Frederick Palmer, *Newton D. Baker* (New York, 1931), pp. 296–302. Fosdick, who had turned down a chance to become a field secretary for the PRAA in 1913, considered Braucher an "intimate friend." Rowland Haynes, notes of meeting with Fosdick, January 4, 1913, NRA; Fosdick to Ralph Hayes, June 25, 1919, Record Group 165, series 393, Commission on Training Camp Activities, National Archives. Such a source will be written hereinafter as "RG 165.393, CTCA, NA."

11. Josephus Daniels, secretary of the navy, appointed a Navy CTCA after much persuasion by Baker. Fosdick, *Chronicle*, p. 157; Braucher, notes of meeting with Fosdick, September 25, 1940, HSB; Fosdick to the author, July 26, 1970; Baker to Fosdick, April 18, 1917, HSB, *Recreation*, IX (October 1917), 349, lists members of both CTCAs, which in effect were one organ. Lee and Braucher attended almost every meeting of the CTCA. CTCA Minutes, RG 165.403, CTCA, NA.

12. Fosdick, *Chronicle*, pp. 143, 165. See also Palmer, *Baker*, pp. 307–09.

13. There is no definitive study of the CTCA. Two popular accounts are Edward F. Allen [and Raymond B. Fosdick], *Keeping Our Fighters Fit: For War and After* (New York, 1918), and Joseph H. Odell, *The New Spirit of the New Army* (New York, 1918). Also *War Department CTCA* (Washington, D.C., n. d.), and *The War and Navy Department CTCA's* (Washington, D.C., n. d.), copy in HSB. The volumes by Fosdick and Palmer are also useful, as are U. S., War Department, Annual Reports, *Report of the Chairman on Training Camp Activities* (Washington, D.C., 1918), and "Community War

Recreation Services—Its Meaning—Plan of Work—Accomplishments," *Recreation*, XI (October 1917), 349–54.

14. Davis, *Spearheads*, p. 225.

15. Voted by the CTCA on May 5, 1917, and quoted in *Recreation*, XI (October 1917), cover. Also Sapora, "Lee," p. 303.

16. "War Camp Community Service: A Summary," p. 3, HSB; George A. Nesbitt to E. Dana Caulkins, May 17, 1917, Caulkins MSS.

17. CTCA Minutes, May 19, 1917, RG 165.403, CTCA, NA; NRA Ex Com, December 21, 1917; WCCS Business Committee, July 31, 1917; Cutlip, *Fund Raising*, pp. 189–95; Braucher to John D. Rockefeller, Jr., December 7, 1917, NRA.

18. Correspondence of Braucher with Rockefeller and his aides, NRA, HSB.

19. Fosdick to Braucher, telegram, December 1, 1917, RG 165.393, No. 12339, CTCA, NA; Braucher to WCCS workers, December 8, 1917, RG 165.393, No. 12309, CTCA, NA; NRA Board, September 28, 1918; WCCS Board, November 6, 1918.

20. NRA Board, November 20, 1940; "WCCS: A Summary," p. 3, HSB; Braucher to Louis Kraft, October 25, 1940, NRA.

21. Sapora, "Lee," p. 305; Butler, *Pioneers*, pp. 4, 100; "WCCS: A Summary," pp. 3–5, HSB; NRA Board, December 5, 1917.

22. See the 183-page *Handbook of WCCS: Policies, Fundamental Principles, and Instructions* (New York, 1918), and NRA Board, February 27, 1918.

23. See Robert B. Brown, *WCCS Calls* (New York, 1918); *WCCS: A Retrospect* (New York, 1920); and special issues of *Recreation*, XI (January and March 1918).

24. ". . . Report for Rockefeller Foundation, Florence Samuels," [1919] HSB; *WCCS and the Negro Soldier* (n. p., n. d.), copy in HSB.

25. NRA Board: February 27, 1918; September 28, 1918; November 6, 1918. Lee to Felix Frankfurter, June 9, 1918, RG 165.393, No. 31891, CTCA, NA; "WCCS: A Summary," p. 15; *Retrospect*, pp. 30–31.

26. Braucher to NRA Board, May 14, 1918; WCCS Business Committee July 9, 1918; Cutlip, *Fund Raising*, pp. 139–40, 398; Dulles, *Red Cross*, p. 145; Lee to Fosdick, October 25, 1917, RG 165.393, No. 41918, CTCA, NA: Lee-Braucher correspondence for November, 1918, NRA.

27. NRA Board, January 16, 1918. The other groups in the joint campaign were the YMCA, which reaped $108,000,000; YWCA; National Catholic War Council (Knights of Columbus); Jewish Welfare Board; American Library Association; and Salvation Army. *Report* of the United War Work Campaign (n. p., September 30, 1921), p. 14, copy in HSB; Cutlip, *Fund Raising*, pp. 139–49.

28. Fosdick, *Chronicle*, p. 144; Clarence H. Cramer, *Newton D. Baker* (Cleveland, 1961), p. 104.

29. The transfer took place on September 15, 1919. Fosdick found quarrelling and inefficiency in the programs of the voluntary associations and suggested to Baker that the Army itself in the future handle troops' on-post leisure. Glenn, Brandt, and Andrews, *Sage*, I, 251; Minutes of CTCA, December 20, 1918, RG 165.403, CTCA, NA; Fosdick, *Chronicle*, p. 182; Palmer, *Baker*, p. 206; and a copy of Fosdick's report to Baker in NRA.

30. By December 1919, WCCS had been discontinued in some 600 cities. In 135 cities, most of them towns near permanent or not yet de-activated military bases, WCCS continued on a reduced scale. WCCS Board, December 3, 1919. WCCS Ex Com: November 20 and December 4, 1918; January 23, 1919. Frank A. Fetter, "WCCS Policy during Demobilization," *Recreation*, XIII (May 1919), 66–67; "WCCS: A Summary," pp. 12–15, HSB.

31. Fosdick to the author, July 26, 1970; Braucher to Woods, May 21, 1919, RG 165.393, CTCA, NA; Woods, *Neighborhood*, pp. 220–21; Cozens and Stumpf, *Sports*, pp. 195–96. Rainwater, *Play*, p. 186; Bruno, *Social Work*, p. 388; Butler, *Pioneers*, p. 100; Allen Burns in NRA, *Proceedings*, 1949, p. 25.

32. "Three Years' Work" tells of PRAA activity from 1917 to 1919. "Playground Facts," *Recreation*, XII (April 1918), 3–9; Abbie Condit, "Recreation Facts," *Recreation*, XIII (October 1919), 307–11.

33. Braucher to Rudolph Bertheau, October 16, 1926, HSB; Braucher to Fosdick, May 8, 1919, NRA; Fosdick to Braucher, June 25 and 28, 1919, NRA; Baker to Braucher, June 14, 1919, RG 165.393, No. 51968, CTCA, NA; Braucher to Lee, April 15, 1919, NRA.

34. Braucher to Bertheau, October 16, 1926, HSB; NRA and WCCS Boards, January 19, 1919; CS Board, March 4, 1919; NRA Board, March 12 and May 28, 1919.

35. Clarke A. Chambers, *Seedtime of Reform* (Ann Arbor, 1967), pp. 1–23.

36. Rainwater, *Play*, pp. 45–46. Books of this sort include Mary Follett, *The New State* (New York, 1918); Ida Clarke, *The Little Democracy* (New York, 1918); Hart (New York, 1920); John Daniels, *America via the Neighborhood* (New York, 1920); and Eduard Lindeman, *The Community* (New York, 1921).

37. See William J. Breen, "The Council of National Defense: Industrial and Social Mobilization in the United States, 1916–1920" (unpublished Ph.D. dissertation, Duke University, 1968); Clarke, *Democracy*, pp. 1–3, 8–10; and Dillick, *Community*, pp. 71–73. The American Red Cross is covered in Dulles, *Red Cross*, pp. 164, 214, 221–23; Lindeman, *Community*, p. 156; and Hart, *Organization*, pp. 222–23, who deals briefly with all of these schemes on pp. 218–25.

38. Lee, "Unrest," p. 30, in James E. Rogers, *Community Service: An Interpretation* (New York, n.d.).

39. Quoted in Rogers, *Community Service*, p. 2. Also Lee, "The Community, Home of Lost Talents," *Recreation*, XIII (August 1919), 171–76; *Objectives of CS* (New York, 1921) copy in NRA; L. A. Halbert, "CS as a Builder of Morale for the Institutions of Civil Life," *Recreation*, XIII (August 1919), 190–200; Weaver Pangburn, "The War and the Community Movement," *American Journal of Sociology*, XXVII (July 1920), 82–95; and Charles F. Weller, "Community Organization versus Institutionalism," *Recreation*, XII (November 1918), 362–72. "The Goals of CS" (Bulletin No. 87, January 29, 1920), copy in NRA, is also useful. See CS Board, March 4, 1919, for the broad purpose of CS as stated in its constitution.

40. CS Board, September 24, 1919; Braucher, "CS in America during the Next Few Years," NRA. The Rockefeller memorial actually gave $250,000 to CS from 1919 to 1921. Braucher to CS Board, May 1919; Braucher-Rockefeller correspondence, 1919, NRA; proposal, exhibits A and B, NRA.

41. "CS," September 1, 1919, NRA; *Recreation,* XVI (August 1922), 191–92.

42. Statements of policies and operation of local CS programs include: "CS: What It Is," August 1922, NRA; "The First Year of CS," NRA; "WCCS Bulletin No. 99," HSB; "CS Bulletin No. 69 revised," NRA; "Suggestions regarding. . .Organization in Local Communities," NRA; and Braucher, "CS not an Administrative Body," *Recreation,* XIV (June 1920), 150–51.

43. CS Ex Com: August 19, 1920; March 24, 1921.

44. Lee, "Recreation and Americanization," NRA; Lee to Garland W. Powell, October 29, 1923, NRA. By 1924 WCCS had spent some $800,000 in organizational and community work with the American Legion. The work gradually terminated as WCCS used up its capital. WCCS financial statement, September, 1918–1923; George Dickie to Lemuel Bolles, May 11, 1923; Braucher, notes of meeting with Fosdick, February 5, 1926; all in HSB. Roscoe Baker, *The American Legion and American Foreign Policy* (New York, 1954), pp. 29–49; Richard S. Jones, *A History of the American Legion* (New York, 1946), pp. 225–38.

45. CS Ex Com: December 1 and 17, 1919; September 29, 1920. Statement in HSB.

46. WCCS Board, December 1, 1920; English, "Autobiography," ch. on "WCCS," pp. 16–18; Memoranda to Braucher, December 1919, NRA; CS Board, May 18, 1921; Braucher to NRA Board, September 18, 1922; NRA Board, October 9 and December 6, 1922.

47. Cutlip, *Fund Raising,* pp. 129–33, 207.14.

48. "First Year of CS," pp. 13–17, NRA. CS Board: September 24, 1919; January 19 and May 18, 1921. CS Ex Com: January 21, 1920; March 24, 1921.

49. Dillick, *Community,* pp. 68–78, 102; Wood, *Problems,* pp. 336, 344–45; Lubove, *Altruist,* pp. 172–95; Jesse Steiner, "An Appraisal of the Community Movement," *Social Forces,* VII (March 1929), 333–42, and "Whither the Community Movement," *Survey,* LXII (April 1929), 130–31; Maurice Stein, *The Eclipse of Community* (Princeton, 1960). See also case studies such as Robert S. and Helen M. Lynd, *Middletown* (New York, 1929).

50. WCCS financial data, HSB. CS Ex Com, March 31, 1922; CS Board, May 17, 1922; NRA Board, October 9, 1922.

NOTES TO CHAPTER 5

1. Lee, "Football in the War," *Recreation,* X (December 1916), 320–24. NRA Board: November 10, 1915; November 27, 1916; January 10 and March 28, 1917. Thomas A. Storey, "State Legislation for Physical Training," *Recreation,* XII (November 1918), 346–61.

2. Braucher, notes, November 19, 1931, HSB. NRA Board, September 28, 1918.

3. "National Physical Education Service: A New Emphasis on Physical Education," *Recreation,* XIII (August 1919), 213–16; "Three Years' Work of the National Physical Education Service," *Recreation,* XVI (August 1922), 215–16.

4. Braucher-Lee correspondence, November 1918, NRA; Caulkins, "Report of National Physical Education Service," and Braucher to Caulkins, January 23, 1924, Caulkins MSS.

5. The bills included: H. R. 12652 and S. 3950, both 66th Cong., 2d sess., 1920; H. R. 22 and S. 416, both 67th Cong., 1st sess., 1921; S. 1409, 68th Cong., 1st sess., 1923; and H. R. 4800, H. R. 7450, and S. 2713, all 68th Cong., 1st sess., 1924. Copy of H. R. 22 in Caulkins MSS.
6. Caulkins, interview, January 29, 1970; "Three Years' Work," p. 216; "A National Physical Education Bill," *Recreation*, XIV (January 1921), 629–30; "A Year's Work of the PRAA," *Recreation*, XVI (March 1923), 588–89. Also Caulkins, memoranda, December 1923, Caulkins MSS.
7. "Twentieth Anniversary: National Physical Education Service," *Journal of Health and Physical Education*, IX (September 1938), 424–28, 458; Butler, *Pioneers*, pp. 122–24; Rogers, memorandum, March 1, 1939, HSB. NRA Board: January 14, 1941; April 12, 1944.
8. Butler, *Pioneers*, pp. 160–67; Attwell, "Playgrounds for Colored America," *Recreation*, XV (April 1921), 84–89; "Community Recreation Leadership in 790 Cities," *Recreation*, XXI (April 1927), 6. NRA Board: November 3, 1938; May 28, 1947.
9. Charles S. Johnson, *The Negro In American Civilization* (New York, 1930), p. 308. See also pp. 299–310.
10. NRA Board: October 11, 1913; May 18, 1921; January 24 and December 5, 1923; October 21, 1926. "A Year's Service," *Recreation*, XV (March 1922), 729–30; Braucher, notes, 1914, NRA. District service began in 1921.
11. NRA Board: October 31, 1923; Braucher to Beardsley Ruml, October 28, 1925, NRA; "Brief Report on New York City Work, 1927–1930," HSB.
12. PRAA Financial Statement, *Recreation*, XIX (April 1925), 52–53. Also p. 3, "The Services of the PRAA in 1924."
13. "America at Play, 1923," *Recreation*, XVIII (April 1924), 3; "Summary of Facts," *Recreation*, XIX (April 1925), 18–20.
14. "Report of National Municipal Music Committee," *Recreation*, XIX (January 1926), 554–56. Jesse F. Steiner, *Americans at Play* (New York, 1933), is the best study of trends in recreation in the 1920s. Similar projects could be done for other decades.
15. Lee to John H. Finley, January 6, 1921, NRA; Lee to Braucher, May 24, 1926, NRA; Lee, quoted in *Recreation*, XV (February 1922), 695; NRA Board, October 9, 1922.
16. See Cutten (New York); Pound (New York); and Pound, "The Iron Man," *Recreation*, XVI (January 1923), 445–50. Butler, quoted in PRAA Bulletin No. 1101, copy in NRA. The comprehensive bibliography on leisure in Eric Larrabee and Rolf Meyersohn, eds., *Mass Leisure* (New York, 1958), lists for 1920–1929 about four times as many entries as for 1910–1919 and eight times the amount of 1900–1909.
17. Steiner, *Play*, pp. 31–41. Recreational experts joined the Children's Bureau in 1918 and the Office of Education in 1925. Fitzgerald, *Organization*, p. 156. Robert S. Yard, "The Scenic Resources of the United States," *Recreation*, XVIII (July 1924), 214–15, 265. On state parks, see Beatrice Nelson, *State Recreation* (Washington, D.C., 1928), and Freeman Tilden's similar catalog of sites, *The State Parks* (New York, 1962).
18. *Normal Course* (New York, 1929), pp. 229–34; Butler, *Pioneers*, p. 103; "The National Social Work Council," *Recreation*, XVIII (March 1925), 705–06; "Notes on the Work of the National Social Work Council," HSB. NRA Board: May 22, 1929; January 14, 1941.

19. NRA Board: April 5, 1922; March 14, 1923; May 20, 1925. *Recreation,* XX (March 1927), 640.

20. Braucher to Lee, September 5, 1924, NRA. NRA Ex Com, September 17, 1924. NRA Board: December 3, 1924; February 4, 1925; May 19, 1926.

21. There is no history of the conference; the best short accounts, on which I depend below, are the preliminary checklist to its records in the National Archives and Fitch and Shanklin, *Bureau,* pp. 42–46. See *Recreation,* XVIII (July 1924), 249, for a list of members. The proceedings of the conference were published as Senate Document 151, 68th Cong., 1st sess., 1924, and S. Doc. 117, 69th Cong., 1st sess., 1926. See also U. S. Congress, Senate, *A Report Epitomizing the Results of Major Fact-Finding Surveys and Projects . . . of the National Conference on Outdoor Recreation,* S. Doc. 158, 70th Cong., 1st sess., 1928.

22. NRA Board: December 3, 1924; March 25, 1925; February 3 and May 19, 1926.

23. Braucher, notes, April 30, 1940, HSB; Lee to Braucher, February 18, 1926, NRA; Braucher, notes of meeting with Rudolph Bertheau, November 30, 1927, NRA. Hanmer, "Closer Correlation of the Work of Private Agencies," *Recreation,* XVIII (July 1924), 245–46.

24. See minutes and reports of a committee studying recreation of industrial workers in HSB. Also Butler, *Pioneers,* p. 196.

25. (New York, 1928); "A Nationwide Park Study," *Recreation,* XIX (September 1925), 318; Butler, *Pioneers,* pp. 114–16. Significant data from the study later appeared as U.S. Department of Labor, Bureau of Labor Statistics, *Park Recreation Areas in the United States,* Bulletin No. 462 (Washington, 1928). The bureau financed a new survey, *Park Recreation Areas in the United States, 1930,* Bulletin No. 565 (Washington, 1932). The National Park Service funded later editions, such as *Municipal and County Parks in the United States, 1940* (New York, 1942). On Brown, see Butler, *Pioneers,* pp. 88–94, and Arnold Lewis, "V. K. Brown: Philosophy and Contribution to the Recreation Movement" (unpublished M.A. thesis, University of Illinois, 1955).

26. Butler, *Pioneers,* p. 139; NRA, *Proceedings,* 1937, p. 129; "Index of Numerical Bulletin Lists," NRA; list of handbooks and studies, 1925, NRA.

27. NRA Board: March 6, 1923; December 2, 1925. Braucher and Beardsley Ruml, letter of March 12, 1923, and notes of meetings on September 8 and 16, 1924, NRA. Braucher to Lee, November 20, 1925, and reply, December 1, 1925, NRA. George Butler headed the new department of research and directed studies by the PRAA for many years.

28. Exhibit E, NRA. Studies included [Lebert H. Weir, ed.,] *Camping Out: A Manual on Organized Camping* (New York, 1924); Augustus D. Zanzig, *Music in American Life* (New York, 1932); and Eugene T. Lies, *The New Leisure Challenges the Schools* (New York, 1933). Other publications were technical books such as George Butler, ed., *Play Areas: Their Design and Equipment* (New York, 1928).

29. Richard H. Shryock, *National Tuberculosis Association (1904–1954)* (New York, 1957), pp. 190–91; Bronson, *Hetherington,* pp. 69–76; Butler, *Pioneers,* pp. 24–25. "Budget for Additional Research," "Budget Summary," both in HSB.

30. Stewart, *Reform,* pp. 191–94; proposal, HSB; Shryock, *Tuberculosis,* pp. 214–16.

31. NRA Board, March 19, 1924; "Report of Committee on Code of Ethics" and letter of committee to recreation executives, December, 1928, HSB; "Standards for a Recreation System for a City of 100,000," May 24, 1928, Bulletin M. B. 37, HSB.

32. Butler, *Pioneers*, pp. 4, 121–22; NRA Board, December 5, 1923; "Community Recreation Training Schools," HSB; "The Community Recreation School," *Recreation*, XIX (July 1925), 220. WCCS Board: February 11 and April 7, 1920; May 17, 1922. NRA Board, January 23, 1924.

33. NRA Board: October 31, 1923; March 19, May 21, and September 17, 1924; February 4, 1925.

34. NRA Ex Com, November 4, 1925. NRA Board: October 6 and December 2, 1925.

35. Statement on the school and "National Recreation School" brochure, both in HSB. "Catalogue of Courses," HSB; "A New Training School in Recreation," *Recreation*, XX (July 1926), 231–32; "National Recreation School Presents Graduate Courses in Recreation Leadership," *Recreation*, XXV (July 1931), 237–40. George Dickie served as general director of the school.

36. CS Board, May 18, 1921. NRA Board: December 6, 1922; January 24, 1923; January 23 and December 3, 1924. Arthur Williams, "Memo," October 1, 1929, NRA; "The NRA: Rural Recreation Service," NRA.

37. Bradford's death in 1940 and renewed wartime demands on the PRAA caused the termination of rural work. Butler, *Pioneers*, pp. 181–82; C. B. Smith, "The Government and Rural Life," *Recreation*, XXV (January 1932), 547–49, 588; Charles E. Potter, "The Extension Service," *Recreation*, XXXIV (February 1941), 653–55. Also Bradford to Braucher, April 1940; C. E. Reed, "Rural Recreation Service," July 27, 1945; and reports on rural work, all in HSB.

38. Austin E. Griffiths to Braucher, May 3, 1910, NRA; Andrew G. Truxal, *Outdoor Recreation Legislation and Its Effectiveness* (New York, 1929), pp. 35–39.

39. "The Harmon Foundation," *Recreation*, XVI (April 1922), 19–20; William E. Harmon, "The Value of Parks and Playgrounds in Real Estate Development," *Recreation*, XVII (November 1923), 440–44; "The Harmon Foundation Makes Its Report," *Recreation*, XX (October 1926), 389; "Real Estate Campaign in Progress," *Recreation*, XXI (December 1927), 475–80. NRA Board: January 3, 1914; November 14, 1921; December 5, 1923; February 4, 1927; January 18, 1928. Reports and correspondence, HSB.

40. NRA Board, January 18, 1928. "Report of the Committee on Activities for Girls," *Recreation*, IV (September 1910), 190–202; "The Katherine F. Barker Memorial Field Secretary," *Recreation*, XXII (April 1928), 21; Ethel Bowers, "Giving the Girl a Chance," *Recreation*, XXVI (April 1932), 13–17, 43.

41. NRA Board: December 7, 1927; January 18, 1928; March 28, 1928. "Music Service to Small Towns and Rural Districts," HSB.

42. NRA Board: January 10, 1917; December 6, 1922. J. W. Faust, "Leisure and Living," *Recreation*, XXIV (September 1930), 326; Jay B. Nash, *The Organization and Administration of Playgrounds and Recreation* (New York, 1927), pp. 481–98; Herbert L. May and Dorothy Petgen, *Leisure and Its Use* (New York, 1928), p. 266.

43. "Exhibit E," HSB, is the fullest coverage of problems in financing the PRAA. "Fund Raising Expenses," 1923–1954, NRA.

44. Cutlip, *Fund Raising*, pp. 211–16. NRA Board: January 24, 1923; May 27, 1931. Braucher to Lee, May 5, 1925, NRA; notes of meeting with Lee and D. H. Holbrook, March 29, 1928, HSB. Lee, "Community Chest Finance," 1927, HSB; George Dickie to Mrs. George W. Steele, December 12, 1949, NRA; Harold J. Seymour, *Design for Fund-Raising: Principles, Patterns, Techniques* (New York, 1966), pp. 140–44.

45. "Contributions to the NRA," HSB; Braucher, notes of meeting with Fosdick, December 20, 1926, NRA; NRA Board, October 17, 1929; data submitted to the Rockefeller Foundation, HSB and NRA.

46. "The Services of the PRAA in 1929," *Recreation*, XXIV (May 1930), 60; *This Business of Life: A Report for 1929* (New York, 1930), copy in NRA.

47. "Community Recreation Leadership in 945 Cities," *Recreation*, XXIV (May 1930), 63–73.

48. Statement, 1930, NRA. Memoranda of Roy Smith Wallace to Braucher, January 4, 1928, NRA; November 12, 1929, NRA. "Needs of the Recreation Movement," 1931, HSB; Braucher, notes of meeting with Fosdick, February 5, 1926, HSB.

49. Steiner, *Play*, p. 183.

NOTES TO CHAPTER 6

1. U.S. Department of Commerce, Bureau of the Census, *Historical Statistics of the United States: Colonial Times to 1957* (Washington, D.C., 1960), p. 73. On the depression years, see books such as Harris Gaylord Warren, *Herbert Hoover and the Great Depression* (New York, 1959); Irving Bernstein, *The Lean Years* (Boston, 1960); and William E. Leuchtenberg, *Franklin D. Roosevelt and the New Deal*, The New American Nation Series (New York, 1963).

2. See the discussion on average hours of work in John D. Owen, *The Price of Leisure* (Rotterdam, 1969), pp. 64–68.

3. NRA Ex Com, July 14, 1930; NRA Board, October 19, 1932; Harold D. Meyer, interview, Chapel Hill, N.C., October 14, 1970.

4. NRA Board, October 8, 1930.

5. National Recreation School, "Annual Report 1932," NRA. Jacks: "Leisure Time—A Modern Challenge," *Recreation*, XXIV (December 1930), 475–79; "Today's Unemployment and Tomorrow's Leisure," *Recreation*, XXV (December 1931), 478–82. Jacks, *Education Through Recreation* (New York, 1932), contains the substance of his lectures for the NRA.

6. May and Petgen, *Leisure;* "List of Herbert May Contacts," NRA. NRA Board: October 4, 1928; October 8, 1930; October 19, 1932. "The First World Congress on Recreation," *Recreation*, XXV (November 1931), 447; "First International Recreation Congress Program," *Recreation*, XXVI (July 1932), 188–89; Butler, *Pioneers*, pp. 172, 213–14.

7. Braucher, notes, March 6, 1930, December 3, 1931, HSB. The study, *The Leisure Hours of 5,000 People . . .* (New York, 1934), was summarized in Weaver Pangburn, *Adventures in Recreation* (New York, 1936), pp. 42–45, and in *Recreation*, XXVII (March 1934), 547–50.

8. See "Arts and Crafts for Playgrounds," *Recreation,* XXXII (May 1938), 63–67; "Children's Gardens," *Recreation,* XXXIV (April 1940), 52, 54; and William G. Vinal, *Nature Recreation* (New York, 1940).

9. Mallery to Braucher, September 8, 1933, NRA.

10. Larrabee and Meyersohn, *Mass Leisure,* pp. 397–406; "The White House Conference on Child Health and Protection," *Recreation,* XXIV (January 1931), 551–54. NRA Board: January 17, 1934; June 16, 1935.

11. Fosdick to author, July 26, 1970; Braucher to French Strother, December 10, 1929, HSB; NRA Board, November 8, 1933. The committee's report was published in 1934; a typed final draft is in HSB. Braucher, notes of conference with Fosdick, July 27, 1934, NRA; John H. Finley to Franklin D. Roosevelt, June 23, 1934, Franklin D. Roosevelt Library, Roosevelt MSS.

12. Lies's *The New Leisure Challenges the Schools* was one such cooperative venture. NRA Board: January 15, 1930; October 8, 1930; October 7, 1931; December 14, 1932; March 14, 1934. Lee to Braucher, July 22, 1930, NRA; Braucher to Lee, December 2, 1931, NRA.

13. Butler: interview; *Pioneers.* Arthur Williams, "Institutionalism and the NRA," April 4, 1933, HSB; Lee to Braucher, October 6, 1933, NRA; Thomas Rivers, notes of meeting with Joseph Lee, Jr., January 28, 1935, NRA; Braucher, notes of meeting with Mrs. Joseph Lee, September 22, 1937, NRA.

14. NRA Board: January 15 and October 8, 1930; May 27 and October 7, 1931; February 3, 1932; January 16, 1935; November 3, 1938. Braucher, "Extension Field Work," December 9, 1938, HSB.

15. "National Recreation School, Incorporated: 1931–1956," NRA; list of expenditures, NRA.

16. NRA Board: February 3, 1932; January 20, 1937. Cutlip, *Fund Raising,* p. 213; "Fund Raising Expenses," NRA.

17. John H. Finley, "Recreation in the Unemployment Crisis," *Recreation,* XXV (December 1931), 483–86. NRA Board: October 7 and November 30, 1931; February 3, May 25, and December 14, 1932. "Brief Report on New York City Work . . . ," pp. 11–12, HSB. M. L. Stevens, "Report on Emergency Workers," October 31, 1932, HSB.

18. NRA Board: December 14, 1932, November 23, 1934. William L. Phillips, "The Recreation Movement in Boston and its Place in the National Emergency," *Recreation,* XXVIII (January 1935), 483–86. "New Jersey Produces," *Recreation,* XXVII (November 1933), 365,392; John Colt, "Recreation as a Socially Useful Field of Employment," *Recreation,* XXVIII (November 1934), 370–74; Winant, "Planning for Recreation in New Hampshire," *Recreation,* XXVIII (December 1934), 420-23.

19. The statement was "Recreational Activities for the Unemployed," HSB. NRA Board, May 25, 1932; Braucher, "The National Education-Recreation Council," *Recreation,* XXXIV (February 1941), 639–41.

20. NRA Board, February 3, 1932. See also Braucher, "The Centralized Control of Life," *Recreation,* XXIV (October 1930), 361.

21. NRA Board, December 6, 1922. Braucher, "Franklin D. Roosevelt," *Recreation,* XXXIX (May 1945), 57.

22. NRA Board: March 8 and May 24, 1933; December 14, 1937. John A. Salmond, *The Civilian Conservation Corps, 1933–1942* (Durham, N.C., 1967), pp. 47–53, 139–42, 162–68; Tilden, *State Parks,* pp. 13–16; Fanning Hearon, "The

Recreation Renaissance," *Recreation*, XXIX (September 1935), 289–93, 324–25.

23. Hopkins's MSS at the Franklin D. Roosevelt Library contain only one brief note from Braucher, May 4, 1933. Compare Butler, *Pioneers*, pp. 101, 135.

24. Leuchtenberg, *Roosevelt*, pp. 121–23; NRA Board, January 17, 1934; Jacob Baker, "Nation-Wide Recreation," *Recreation*, XXIX (August 1935), 249–52, 275–76; Searle F. Charles, *Minister of Relief: Harry Hopkins and the Depression* (Syracuse, 1963), pp. 61–64; Lancaster, "Impact," p. 65; "Manual on Recreation Projects under ERA," HSB.

25. Braucher, notes of conference with Hopkins and others, December 4, 1933, NRA.

26. T. E. Rivers, memorandum, December 26, 1933. Braucher: notes of conference with John H. Finley, January 9, 1934; with Gustavus T. Kirky, January 13, 1934; and with Aubrey Williams, January 18 and February 15, 1934, all in NRA. NRA Board: March 14, 1934; January 16, 1935.

27. Braucher to Charles S. Ascher, November 14, 1941, HSB; "Federal Emergency Employment Possibilities in the Field of Public Recreation," HSB; Butler, *Pioneers*, p. 135; NRA Board, March 13, 1935.

28. Rivers, notes of meeting, April 3, 1935; John H. Finley to Hopkins, April 5, 1935; both in HSB. NRA Board: April 17 and May 22, 1935.

29. Leuchtenberg, *Roosevelt*, pp. 124–30; *Recreation*, XXXV (December 1941), 575–76; "The War Recreation Services of Several Federal and National Agencies," *Recreation*, XXXVII (June 1943), 185; Lancaster, "Impact"; James A. Atkins and Austin J. Welch, "Projects Administration Recreation Program," vol. IX of "WPA Program Operation and Accomplishments, 1935–1943," RG 69, WPA, NA.

30. See Gisela Konopka, *Eduard C. Lindeman and Social Work Philosophy* (Minneapolis, 1958); Lancaster, "Impact," p. 166; and Lindeman, *Leisure—A National Issue; Planning for the Leisure of a Democratic People* (New York, 1939).

31. "Emergency Recreation Service in 1935," *Recreation*, XXX (June 1936), 142–49; Lancaster, "Impact," pp. 6, 34, 66, 76–85; 184, 202, 204; Atkins and Welch, "Program," pp. 26, 28, 151, RG 69, WPA, NA. Meyer, interview, October 14, 1970.

32. Lancaster, "Impact," pp. 26, 35, 170; Romney, interview, Washington, D.C., April 23, 1970. Arthur E. Todd, at the author's conference on the history of the NRA, Washington, D.C., April 23, 1970. Participants in the conference, hereinafter cited as "NRA Conference," included Todd, Diana Dunn, Waldo Hainsworth, Sidney Lutzin, Romney, and Wayne Sommer.

33. Dorothy L. Cline, *Training for Recreation under the W.P.A.* (Chicago, 1939), Atkins and Welch, "Program," pp. 100–03, 155–61, RG 69, WPA, NA, is more objective.

34. Romney, interview, April 23, 1970; Lancaster, "Impact," pp. 72–73, 114–15, 159; Atkins and Welch, "Program," pp. 42–44, RG 69, WPA, NA. NRA correspondence with the agency, RG 69.211.6 and RG 69.216, WPA, NA, is trivial.

35. NRA Board: October 2 and December 11, 1935; May 27, 1936. Butler, interview; Meyer, interview; Sommer and Romney, NRA Conference. See also U.S. Federal Security Agency, *Final Report of the National Youth Administration* (Washington, D.C., 1944), pp. 92, 136–37, 226; Betty Lindley and Ernest K. Lindley, *A New Deal for Youth* (New York, 1938); Butler, *Pioneers*, p. 135.

36. (New York, 1939). NRA Board: January 16 and April 17, 1935.

37. Arno B. Cammerer, et al., "National Government Service through Recreation," *Recreation*, XXVIII (January 1935), 465–75, 502–03; Arthur E. Morgan, "Progress in the Art of Living," *Recreation*, XXVIII (December 1934), 415–19, 453. Russell E. Peterson, "A Study of Recent Governmental Participation in Recreation" (unpublished M.Ed. thesis, Springfield College, 1937) is merely a summary.

38. Butler, interview; Ise, *Park Policy*, p. 566.

39. Ise, *Park Policy*, pp. 367–69; "Recreation in the National Park Service," *Recreation*, XL (February 1947), 612; Rivers, notes of conference with John G. Winant, Harry Hopkins, et al., April 3, 1935, HSB.

40. NRA Board: May 23, 1934; January 16, March 13, and May 22, 1935; October 1, 1941; March 3, 1942; and May 24, 1950. Braucher to Wirth: February 8, 1938, and July 9, 1941, RG 79.7 "0–871," NPS, NA. In the same file, see Wirth to Arno Cammerer, memorandum, July 21, 1934, and Wirth to Thomas Rivers, July 30, 1934.

41. National Recreation School, minutes: October 2, 1935; May 27, 1936; January 14, 1941. Weaver Pangburn, "The Institute Comes to Town," *Recreation*, XXX (August 1936), 245–48; list of institutes, HSB.

42. NRA Board: February 5, 1926; October 7, 1937. Braucher, "Apprentice Fellowship Notes," 1937, NRA. "Apprentice Fellowship Report, January 1951," HSB.

43. Atkins and Welch, "Program," p. 37, RG 69, WPA, NA; Fitzgerald, *Organization*, p. 304; Lindeman to Braucher, August 19, 1937, and reply, September 21, 1937, both in RG 69.216, box 529, WPA, NA; NRA Board, March 8, 1938; Butler, interview.

44. Butler, *Pioneers*, pp. 88–94, 187–89, 208–09.

45. Clippings, HSB; Meyer, interview, October 14, 1970.

46. See correspondence and Braucher, confidential memorandum, July 24, 1934, in HSB. Also NRA Board, January 16, 1935.

47. Wesley, *NEA*, pp. 307–08; Braucher, "Where Should the Administration of a Recreation System be Placed?" *Recreation*, XXXIII (August 1939), 257, NRA Board, April 17, 1940; clippings, HSB.

48. Weston, *Physical Education*, p. 81; editorial, *Journal of Health and Physical Education*, VIII (September 1937); Butler, interview; Meyer, interview, October 14, 1970.

49. Braucher, "Individuals and Groups to Be Remembered," NRA; notes of conference with Mrs. John D. Jameson, October 2, 1939, NRA.

50. Braucher, "The National Education-Recreation Council," *Recreation*, XXXIV (February 1941), 639–41; "Building Cooperation in Education-Recreation," *Recreation*, XXXIV (February 1941), 642, 693–94; Conrad Wirth to Wayne Coy, December 23, 1940, RG 79.7 "0–871," NPS, NA.

51. V. K. Brown to Alfred O. Anderson, March 2, 1938, HSB; Sommer, NRA Conference; ARS, *Early Years*, pp. 1–2.

52. Faust to Braucher, March 24, 1936, HSB. The most complete account of succeeding events is "American Recreation Society," January 14, 1962, NRA. My version below comes from both this document and the original sources, chiefly in HSB, which it used. Also NRA Board, May 27, 1936; Mathewson to author, June 10, 1970.

53. Braucher sent his letter in January 1937. Dorothy Enderis to Braucher, [January] and April 29, 1937, both in HSB.

54. Floyd A. Rowe to Braucher, January 11, 1937, HSB; Butler to author, November 3, 1970.

55. ARS, annual meeting, minutes, October 12, 1939, NRA.

56. Cremin, *School*, p. 323; Knight, *Education*, pp. 614–15, 622–24. NRA Board: April 21, 1937; January 11 and December 12, 1939. J. C. Walsh to Braucher, November 23, 1933, NRA; Susan Lee to Braucher, March 18, 1941, HSB; Carlson to author, July 23, 1970; Butler to author, November 3, 1970; Caulkins, interview; Meyer, interview.

57. The reports were U.S., National Park Service, *Recreational Use of Lands in the United States* (Washington, D.C., 1935), pt. 11 of U.S., National Resources Board, Land Planning Committee, *Report* (Washington, D.C., 1935) and U.S., Department of the Interior, National Park Service, *A Study of the Park and Recreation Problem of the United States* (Washington, D.C., 1941). Fitch and Shanklin, *Bureau*, pp. 46–53; Ise, *Park Policy*, pp. 364–67.

58. S. R. Tripp, memorandum to Arno Cammerer, October 10, 1939, and Wirth, memorandum to Cammerer, both in RG 79.7 "0–871," NPS, NA; James B. Williams to Braucher, October 27, 1939, and draft of memorandum for Cammerer, both in NRA; Braucher, notes of meeting with Wirth, November 8, 1939, NRA.

59. Harold Meyer to M. L. Wilson, October 3, 1947, HSB; Atkins and Welch, "Program," pp. 20–21, RG 69, WPA, NA.

60. U.S., Interdepartmental Committee to Coordinate Health and Welfare Activities, *Report of the Technical Committee on Recreation* (processed; Washington, D.C., 1937) copies available at Library of Congress and HSB. Fitch and Shanklin, *Bureau*, pp. 53–56.

61. NRA Board, March 13, 1940.

NOTES TO CHAPTER 7

1. Cutlip, *Fund Raising*, pp. 318–29. NRA Board: October 19, 1943; October 24, 1944.

2. File, HSB; Bernard Bellush, *He Walked Alone: A Biography of John Gilbert Winant* (The Hague, 1968), pp. 153–59. Braucher became president in June 1941. NRA Board, June 11, 1941.

3. Fitzgerald, *Organization*, pp. 69–70; Raymond B. Fosdick, "The Leisure Time of A Democratic Army," *Recreation*, XXXVI (September 1942), 319–25. "War Services of the NRA," HSB; NRA, *Proceedings*, 1946, p. 22; Butler, interview.

4. "Camp Community Service Defense Program," July 16, 1940, HSB; Braucher to Louis Kraft, October 25, 1940, NRA.

5. Braucher to Fosdick, June 4 and September 13, 1940, HSB; to Franklin D. Roosevelt, June 19, 1940, Roosevelt MSS.

6. "Recent Defense Developments in Norfolk, Virginia," HSB. By year's end fifty such towns had received NRA aid. NRA Board, January 14, 1941.

7. Braucher, notes of meeting with John E. Manley, September 19, 1940, HSB; Jay B. Nash to Braucher and enclosure, November 28, 1940, HSB. NRA Board, October 2, 1940. HSB has full details on the Manley committee. Braucher: memorandum of breakfast conference, October 18, 1940, HSB; to Kraft, October 25, 1940, HSB. *New York Times*, December 4 and 15, 1940.

8. NRA, *Proceedings*, 1941, p. 33. Braucher, notes of conferences: with Wayne Coy, December 12, 1940, HSB; with Fosdick, February 3, 1941, NRA. NRA Board, January 14, 1941.

9. NRA Board, February 18, 1941. Braucher, memoranda, February 18, 1941, HSB.

10. NRA Board, April 15, 1941; Hopkins, *YMCA*, p. 712; Cutlip, *Fund Raising*, pp. 399–401; G. Ott Romney, *Off the Job Living* (New York, 1945), pp. 73, 117–18; U.S., Federal Security Agency, Office of Community War Services, *Teamwork in Community Service, 1941–46—A Demonstration in Federal, State, and Local Cooperation* (Washington, D.C., 1946), p. 29.

11. "War Services," HSB; Rivers, "Report of Personnel Work Done for [FSA] Recreation Division," May 21, 1941, NRA; NRA Board, February 18, 1941. Both the USO and FSA Recreation Division have yet to be thoroughly studied.

12. U.S., FSA, OCWS, Teamwork, pp. 24, 37; Hartsoe, *"Brightbill,"* p. 7; FSA Recreation Division, director's memoranda nos. 105 and 268, RG 215.27, Office of Community War Services, NA; NRA Board, October 1, 1941; "The Defense Recreation Program," *Recreation*, XXXV (December 1941), 581; Braucher, notes of conference with Mark McCloskey, December 11, 1941, HSB.

13. Brightbill to McCloskey, telegram, August 3, 1942, RG 215.16, OCWS, NA; Butler, *Pioneers*, p. 136; Gates to Braucher, April 8, 1942, NRA; Charles E. Reed, memorandum, January 3, 1944, NRA; U.S., FSA, OCWS, Recreation Division, *Field Policy and Program: 1944* (Washington, D.C., 1944), copy in HSB.

14. Sidney Lutzin, Arthur Todd, Wayne Sommer, and Ott Romney at NRA Conference.

15. "After the War—NRA or FSA or USO?," HSB. Butler to author, November 3, 1970; Meyer interview, October 14, 1970; "From Lebert H. Weir," NRA. Braucher: notes of meeting with V. K. Brown, April 27, 1945, HSB; "Steps in the Attack on the NRA Which Ought To Be Remembered," November 18, 1948, HSB.

16. *NRA: What the NRA Has Done for Defense* (New York, n.d.); *Community Recreation and the War* (New York, n.d.); *Fitness for Victory* (New York, 1942). "Fun and More Fun," *Recreation*, XXXIX (November 1945), 423, 441.

17. Virginia Musselman, "Teen Trouble: What Can Recreation Do About It?," *Recreation*, XXXVII (April 1943), 6–10; Braucher to Frederic P. Keppel, October 9, 1941, HSB; Thomas Rivers, memorandum, January 9, 1942, NRA; NRA Board: May 27, 1942; October 24, 1944.

18. NRA Board: December 12, 1939; May 27, 1942; March 18, 1943; May 24, 1944. Braucher, notes of meeting with Floyd Eastwood, October 1, 1942, HSB; Butler, interview; Meyer interview; October 14, 1970; Cozens and Stumpf, *Sports*, pp. 212–13.

19. Hartsoe, "Brightbill," p. 59. NRA Board: December 3, 1930; October 19, 1943; April 12, 1944. George Braden to Braucher, December 12, 1940, HSB. Braucher to James B. Williams, April 15, 1943, HSB. FSA Recreation Division, "Report on State Recreation Committees," October 1944, copy in HSB.

20. Meyer to Braucher, October 13 and 18, 1944, NRA. NRA, "Field Department, Service to State Agencies, 1946," HSB. NRA Board: April 17 and December 18, 1945. Braucher: to district representatives, October 1944, HSB;

"The NRA and State Recreation," July 12, HSB. Fitzgerald, *Organization*, pp. 121–22, 145, 153.

21. Dulles, *Red Cross*, pp. 317–18, 397–411; Hartsoe, "Brightbill," p. 9; *Harold D. Meyer and Charles K. Brightbill, *Community Recreation: A Guide to Its Organization* (3 ed.; Englewood Cliffs, N.J., 1964), p. 313; S. W. Morris, "Sports Heal War Neuroses," *Recreation*, XXXIX (October 1945), 343–44.

22. Meyer: "Memorandum to Special Committee, Education-Recreation Council"; to Braucher, August 3, 1942; to Joe Hoffer, February 6, 1943, all in HSB. NRA Board: September 30, 1942; March 18, 1943. Robert Gamble, memorandum, January 22, 1943, and Arthur Williams, memorandum, May 17, 1943, both in HSB.

23. John Neasmith to Sherwood Gates, memorandum, May 20, 1944, and Stewart Woodward to Charles K. Brightbill, July 20, 1945, both in RG 215.31, OCWS, NA; Sidney Lutzin and Wayne Sommer, NRA Conference; Meyer, interview, October 14, 1970.

24. U.S., Congress, House, *A Bill to Make Available Specialized Services and Facilities to States, Areas, Counties, and Communities in Developing Recreation Programs . . .*, H.R. 5, 79th Cong., 1st sess., 1945, copy in HSB. This file also contains copies of successors to H.R. 5, including S. 2070, 79th Cong., 2d sess., 1946; S. 1229, 80th Cong., 1st sess., 1947; H.R. 5723, 80th Cong., 2d sess., 1948; and S. 250, H.R. 2025, H.R. 2026, H.R. 2284, and H.R. 2408, all 81st Cong., 1st sess., 1949. Fitch and Shanklin, *Bureau*, pp. 56–57; "Notes on FSA's Endorsement of H.R. 5," RG 215.17, Box 63, and Mark McCloskey to Braucher, April 19, 1945, RG 215.31, both in OCWS, NA; Wayne Sommer, NRA Conference; Meyer, interview, October 14, 1970. Thomas Rivers, memoranda: April 17, 1945, HSB; April 23, 1945, HSB.

25. V. K. Brown to Braucher, February 5, 1945, HSB; Braucher, notes of meeting with V. K. Brown, April 27–28, 1945, HSB.

26. Braucher to recreation executives, January 30, 1945, HSB; to NRA staff, March 27, 1945, HSB. NRA Board: February 7, April 17, and May 23, 1945. Sherwood Gates, memorandum, March 17, 1945, NRA; William G. Robinson to Gates, March 26, 1945, RG 215.17, Box 63, OCWS, NA; "Dope on H.R. 5 as of March 15, 1945," HSB.

27. U.S., FSA, OCWS, *Teamwork*, pp. 76–77; Doell and Fitzgerald, *Parks*, pp. 97–98. V. K. Brown to J. E. Sproul, March 21, 1945, and Thomas Rivers, report, April 11, 1945, both in HSB. NRA Board: April 11 and December 18, 1945.

28. Thomas Rivers, memorandum, December 13, 1945, HSB; "A Memorandum of How Federal Responsibility for Recreation Should Be Organized," HSB; Brightbill to Harold Meyer, December 5, 1945, RG 215.31, OCWS, NA.

29. Brown to author; Carlson to author; Sally Taylor to C. E. Reed, May 13, 1946, HSB. Braucher notes, February 3, 1945, HSB; notes of meeting with Robert Garrett, February 21, 1945, NRA. Downing E. Proctor to Brightbill, March 26, 1945, RG 215.17, Box 66, OCWS, NA; T. O. Hoagland to Brightbill, September 24, 1945, RG 215.31, OCWS, NA.

30. Meyer to Brightbill, July 4, 1945; "Plans for Federal Recreation Legislation," July 12, 1945; Stewart Woodward to Brightbill, July 20, 1945, all in RG 215.31, OCWS, NA. The Woman's Foundation, *The Road to Community Reorganization* (New York, 1945).

31. Hartsoe, "Brightbill," p. 66; Caulkins, interview, Durham, North Carolina, April 5, 1970; Butler, interview; Meyer, interview, October 10, 1970; Lutzin and Sommer at NRA Conference.

32. NRA, *Proceedings*, 1946, pp. 111–12; ARS, *Early Years*, p. 63; ARS annual meeting minutes, January 31, 1946, NRA; Milo Christiansen to Braucher, March 16 and May 17, 1946, HSB. Reports of Mathewson committee meetings: March 15, May 3, June 26, and October 17, 1946, HSB. Braucher, notes of meetings with Caulkins and Christiansen, February 15, 1946; with Mathewson, March 26, 1946, HSB. Mathewson to Braucher, July 12, 1946, HSB.

33. NRA Board, January 15 and March 19, 1946. Braucher to George Braden, n.d., HSB; notes of meeting with Kirby, February 28, 1946, NRA; to recreation executives, October 25, 1945, RG 215.31, OCWS, NA. Wayne Sommer to Braucher, December 6, 1948, NRA; Brown to Milo Christiansen, July 8, 1946. RG 215.31, OCWS, NA; "Outline of Study . . .," HSB; Arthur Williams, memorandum, March 22, 1946, HSB.

34. U.S., Congress, Senate, *A Bill to Authorize the Federal Security Administrator to Assist the States in the Development of Community Recreation Programs for the People of the United States and for Other Purposes*, S. 2070, 79th Cong., 2d sess., 1946, copy in HSB; Hartsoe, "Brightbill," p. 66; Watson Miller to Thomas Rivers, (April 1946), NRA.

35. Arthur Williams, memorandum, May 3, 1946, HSB; Thomas Rivers to Ralph Gwinn, June 4, 1946, HSB; U.S., Congress, Senate, Committee on Education and Labor, *Development of Community Recreation Programs for People of the United States, Hearings*, before a subcommittee of the Committee on Education and Labor, Senate, on S. 2070, 79th Cong., 2d sess., 1946.

36. U.S., Congress . . . *Hearings* . . . on S. 2070 . . . pp. 156–63; "Some Comments on Senate Bill 2070," HSB; "The NRA and H.R. 5," HSB; Williams, memorandum, March 6, 1948, HSB; "HSB Reasons . . . ."

37. Lutzin, NRA Conference; Meyer, interview, October 14, 1970; George Hjelte to James E. Murray, May 8, 1946, HSB; NRA Board, January 28, 1942; Braucher, notes of meeting with Raymond B. Fosdick, March 8, 1945, NRA; Romney, *Off the Job*, pp. 71–72; U.S., Congress . . . *Hearings* . . . on S. 2070 . . ., pp. 26–34, 57–58. U.S., Department of Commerce, Bureau of the Census, *Historical Statistics*, p. 139.

38. Braucher to NRA staff, June 20, 1945, HSB. NRA Board: October 16, 1946; January 21 and February 17, 1947; May 26, 1948; February 9 and April 2, 1949. R. J. Schwartz to Paul Moore, May 17, 1948, NRA. U.S., Congress, Senate, *Authorizing the Federal Security Administrator to Assist the States in the Development of Community Recreation Programs for the People of the United States*, S. Rept. 1648 to Accompany S. 2070, 79th Cong., 2d sess., 1946.

39. Fitch and Shanklin, *Bureau*, p. 57; NRA Board, October 16, 1946; notes of meeting, September 6, 1946, NRA. Braucher, notes of meetings with: J. W. Studebaker, January 16, 1946, NRA; Conrad Wirth, August 19, 1946, HSB; J. A. Krug, August 7, 1946, HSB. Braucher to Robert Garrett, August 21, 1946, and Walter Scott, November 4, 1946, both in NRA 12 3 6. Milo Christiansen to Braucher, November 1, 1946, HSB C 2 15.

40. George E. Dickie of the NRA was secretary of the committee for thirteen years. *The Role of the Federal Government in the Field of Public Recreation* (New York, 1949). Butler, *Pioneers*, p. 54; Fitch and Shanklin, *Bureau*,

pp. 57–59; "Interagency Committee," HSB; Meyer, interview, October 14, 1970; NRA Board, February 17, 1948; Braucher, notes of meeting with Conrad Wirth, March 11, 1947, NRA.

41. ARS, *Early Years*, pp. 26–27, 34–35, 64; ARS administrative council, minutes, November 19, 1946, HSB; Thomas Rivers, memorandum, September 23, 1946, HSB; Arthur Williams, memorandum, November 4, 1946, HSB; George Nesbitt to Braucher: October 8, 1946, HSB; April 15, 1947, NRA.

42. The conferences were in December 1947 and March 1948. "Recreation: An Essential Community Service," *Recreation*, XL (November 1946), 374, 393; ARS, *Early Years*, pp. 33–34, 42–43; Lutzin, NRA Conference; ARS administrative council, minutes, September 26, 1948, NRA; Arthur Williams, reports, January 16–17 and May 22, 1948, HSB; Doell and Fitzgerald, *Parks*, pp. 103–05.

43. Sommer and Romney, NRA Conference; Butler, interview; Williams, memorandum, November 19, 1946, HSB.

44. NRA Board: January 21, March 18, and May 28, 1947. ARS executive committee, minutes, March 28, 1947; Thomas Rivers, memorandum, February 17, 1947; report of the ARS meetings, October 13–17, 1947; all in HSB. Homer C. Wadsworth, "Continue to Seek a Federal Recreation Service Is Plea," ARS *Quarterly Bulletin*, II (October 1947), 15–16. The new bill was H.R. 5723, 80th Cong., 2d sess., 1948.

45. NRA Board: January 5 and December 14, 1948. Arthur Williams, memoranda: January 5, 1948, HSB; April 4, 1949, HSB.

46. NRA Board, October 19, 1948; Braucher, notes of meeting with Brown, January 4, 1949, NRA; "Committee on Cooperation," HSB; Milo Christiansen to Braucher, January 19, 1949, HSB.

47. "Special Services . . . Which Have Been Discontinued . . .," NRA; NRA Board, March 15, 1949. Braucher, memoranda: February 18, 1949, NRA; May 4, 1949, HSB. Butler, *Pioneers*, p. 53.

NOTES TO CHAPTER 8

1. "Robert Garrett Retires," *Recreation*, v. XLIV (February 1951):470; Butler, *Pioneers*, pp. 169–70.

2. For more biographical data on selected NRA senior staff *see* "George Dickie—An Appreciation," *Recreation* v. LIV (February 1961):70. "George D. Butler," ibid., v. XLVI (February 1948):543. "George A. Nesbitt," ibid., v. XLVII (May 1948):85. "C. E. Reed," ibid., v. XLI (October 1947):351. "Thomas E. Rivers," ibid., v. XLVII (April 1948):37. "Willard C. Sutherland," ibid., v. XLVI (January 1948):499. "Rose Jay Swartz," ibid., v. XLIII (March 50):589. "Arthur Williams," ibid., v. XLIII (September 1963):305.

3. NRA Financial Statement for 1950, NRA-M; "National Recreation School Incorporated: 1931–1956," NRA-M.

4. NRA Board, May 25, 1949.

5. Interview, Susan M. Lee, Robert W. Crawford. During Braucher's illness, the board began gathering information about persons who might possibly be appointed to a central executive position with the probable title of executive secretary. Braucher, at that time was president; NRA Board, March 15, 1949.

6. NRA Ex Com, January 4, 1950; NRA Board, February 8, 1950; "Joseph Prendergast, new Executive Director," *Recreation*, v. XLIII (February 1950): 511; NRA, *Proceedings*, 1950, pp. 17–18.

7. NRA Board, May 24, 1950; November 29, 1950.

8. NRA Board, November 29, 1950; "Now You Can Belong," *Recreation*, v. XLIV (October 1950):235; Report of the Executive Director, May 28, 1952, NRA-M.

9. "Joint Membership Statement of the American Recreation Society and the National Recreation Association," *Recreation*, v. XLIV (February 1951): 473; ARS, *Early Years*, p. 5.

10. Ibid.

11. Ibid.

12. NRA Board, November 18, 1953; Report of the Executive Director, May 28, 1952; "District Advisory Committees," *Recreation*, v. XLV (June 1952):125; "The National Advisory Committee," *Recreation*, v. XLV (June 1952):126.

13. NRA Board, October 29, 1964.

14. NRA Board, January 27, 1954; December 1, 1954; Executive Director Working Paper No. 3, "Membership on the Board and Suggested New Members," May 1954, NRA-M.

15. Butler, *Pioneers*, pp. 83–87; "Otto Tod Mallery," *Recreation*, L (January 1957):4; "Grant Titsworth," *Recreation* v. LIII (June 1960):247. Evans became interested in the work of NRA through service on the NRA Chicago committee, a group of businessmen organized by board member Gaylord Donnelley.

16. Cutlip, *Fund Raising*, p. 501; NRA Board, September 29, 1953; "Recreation and the United Defence Fund," *Recreation* v. XLV (October 1951):245; "The National Recreation Association and the National Defence Program," February, 1951, NRA-M; "Special Defence—Related Services to Local Communities and For the Armed Forces," NRA-M.

17. Report of the John Price Jones Company, Inc., November, 1955, NRA-M; memorandum from Joseph Prendergast to fund-raising study committee, January 23, 1967, NRPA.

18. "Internationally Speaking," *Recreation*, v. XLII (September 1948):262–67; See November 1931 issue of *Recreation* devoted to international recreation. Prendergast, "An International Recreation Service," *Recreation*, v. XLVI (October 1952):254–55; "The International Recreation Service and the United Nations," *Recreation* v. XLVII (January 1954):8–9; Rivers, "World Service through Recreation," *Recreation* v. XLVIII (September 1955):320–21; "Around the World with Recreation," *Recreation* v. XLVIII (October 1955):362–63; "Cooperative Community Exchange Project," *Recreation* v. XLIX (September 1956):326.

19. Erna D. Bunke, "Serving Your Community Institutions," *Recreation* v. XXVI (June 1932):135–38, 161; Report of Beatrice H. Hill to NRA board, November 19, 1958, NRA-M.

20. Virginia Frye and Martha Peters, *Therapeutic Recreation: Its Theory, Philosophy and Practice* (Harrisburg, Pa., 1972):27; *Recreation* v. LIV (January 1961):9.

21. See golden anniversary issue of *Recreation* v. XLIX (June, 1956); Prendergast, "The Past is Prologue to the Future," *Recreation* v. XLIX (January 1956):4–5.

22. NRA Board finance committee, April 30, 1954; NRA Board, May 26, 1954; NRA news release, "National Recreation Association Building Dedication," January 22, 1956; "Dedication of New Headquarters," *Recreation* v. XLIX (March, 1956):116.

23. "International Advisory Committee for the International Recreation Congress," *Recreation* v. XLIX (May 1956):222; NRA Board, September 26, 1956; Rivers, "The Launching of the International Recreation Association," *Recreation*, v. L (January 1957):12.

24. NRA Board, February 6, 1957; memorandum, NRA Board special committee on NRA-IRA relationship, May 22, 1957; Rivers to Titsworth, January 13, 1960; Prendergast to staff, February 25, 1957; NRA international service annual reports 1958–64, NRA-M.

25. David J. DuBois, "A New Pattern for Recreation," *Recreation* v. XLIX (October 1956):382; W. C. Sutherland, "New National Internship Program," *Recreation* v. XLIX (September 1956):400–01.

26. Both Hjelte and Crawford were past-presidents of ARS and active in the advisory committee structure of NRA; "NRA Board Elections," *Recreation* v. LVII (September 1964):354.

27. NRA Financial Statement for 1963, NRA-M.

28. The National Budget and Consultation Committee, headquartered in New York City, was made up of one-hundred members representative of local community work who were chosen both by national agencies and by local chests and united funds.

29. NRA Ex. Com. Board, November 28, 1964; Prendergast, "The Establishment, Growth and Management of the Endowment Funds of the NRPA, 1906–1965," NRPA. The book value of the NRA endowment fund in December 1965 was $970,808. Of this amount, over $182,000 was in assets whose use was restricted by the donor and some $478,000 was designated by the board to be invested and administered as general endowment. The remainder of the endowment was in a special fund which included the purchase price equity in the headquarters building.

30. NRS Ex Com, October 29, 1964.

31. Ibid. NRS Board, May 28, 1958; NRA Board, January 22, 1965; May 26, 1965. At the January meeting, Evans emphasized that the assets and grant-making functions of the foundation were not a part of merger negotiations and that the foundation would remain an autonomous body.

32. Prendergast, "The National Recreation Association in 1965," NRA-M.

33. *This Is Your NRA*, 1964, a report on the work and services of the association based on 1963 figures, but typical of any current year, NRA-M.

34. Doell and Fitzgerald, *Parks*, p. 99.

35. The National Assembly was organized in 1923 as the National Social Work Council and changed its name in 1945 to the National Social Welfare Assembly; the current name is the National Assembly of National Voluntary Health and Social Welfare Organizations, Inc.

36. "The National Recreation Association and the National Cultural Center," *Recreation* v. LIII (June 1960):245; Prendergast, "The National Cultural Center" ibid., (September 1960):306–307, 335, continued in the October and November issue; "NRA Adds New Office in Washington, D.C.," ibid., (January 1965):6.

37. Ben Solomon, "Recreation's Greatest Need," *The American Recreation Society Bulletin*, v. 11 (August–September, 1959):1–5; Prendergast, "An Open Letter to Ben Solomon, Editor of Youth Leaders Digest," NRA-M.

38. Mallery to Braucher, September 8, 1933, NRA.

39. Robert Coughlin, "A $40 Billion Bill Just For Fun," *Life*, v. 47 (December 28, 1959):69.

40. Doell to Susan Lee, April 6, 1964, AIPE Executive Directors Report 56, p. c-9, NRPA.

NOTES TO CHAPTER 9

1. Evans became vice-president of Dun & Bradstreet after merger of the Reuben H. Donnelley Corporation into Dun & Bradstreet. He accepted the position of president of the Seamen's Bank for Savings in 1965 and was later elected chairman and chief executive officer of the Union Pacific Corporation.

2. The review commission (ORRRC) was composed of four U.S. senators, four representatives, six presidentially appointed commissioners and the chairman. Most of the congressmen were from the western states and most of the commission members had strong ties to conservation interests.

3. U.S., Outdoor Recreation Resources Review Commission, *Outdoor Recreation For America* (Washington, D.C., 1962), pp. 3–10. In addition to the basic report, the study included twenty-seven separately published supporting documents.

4. Harold D. Meyer to President Kennedy, March 27, 1962; ARS resolution 62–1, March 25, 1962; Prendergast to Meyer, March 30, 1962.

5. NRA Board, January 24, 1962.

6. Weir, *Parks*, pp. xx, xxi. *See also* Mary Virginia Frye, "The Historical Development of Municipal Parks in the United States: Concepts and Their Applications" (unpublished Ph.D. dissertation, University of Illinois, 1964): 227–234; Leslie M. Reid, "Parks and Recreation: Should They Separate?" *Park Maintenance* (April 1976):15–20.

7. See AIPE *"Report of the Growth Committee,"* September 1963; Warren W. Kershaw to Prendergast, November 6, 1961. The Maryland Recreation and Park Society was one of the first state groups to propose consolidation of national organizations.

8. Mabel Lee and Bruce L. Bennett, "This Is Our Heritage," *Journal of Health, Physical Education and Recreation*, Vol. 31 (April 1960):42–43; Gulick to Brancher, October 13, 1911; Gulick to Lee, April 5, 1912.

9. Lee to Gulick, April 23, 1912.

10. See discussion in Chapter 6; Prendergast, *The American Recreation Society*, January 14, 1962, NRA–M.

11. Doell and Fitzgerald, *Parks*, pp. 98–99; Arthur Williams, "Report of the Joint Meeting of the Executive Committees of the ARS and AIPE, March 5–6, 1948," NRA.

12. Milo F. Christiansen, Superintendent of Recreation for the District of Columbia and a past-president of the ARS, served as president of the federation during the period when NRA, ARS and AIPE discussed merger. Following consolidation, the federation became inactive.

13. For background information on NCSP see "Fifty Years: The Origin and Development of the National Conference on State Parks," *Parks and Recreation*, v. 5 (December 1970):18–21, 53. The National Industrial Recreation Association, headquartered in Chicago, was organized in 1941; its members are mainly directors of recreation programs in industry.

14. See *This Is Your NRA* included as an insert in the June, 1964 issue of *Recreation* magazine.

15. NRA, *Proceedings*, 1963, pp. 119–20.

16. Ibid., pp. 120–21; AIPE, "Report of Growth Committee," pp. 9–12.

17. NRA Board, January 24, 1962; "Report on ARS-NRA Relationships Study," *Recreation* v. LV (November 1962):439; "ARS-NRA Relationships," *Recreation* v. LVI (January 1963): 14–16.

18. "Progress Report of ARS-NRA Relationship Study Committee," *Recreation* v. LVI (December 1963):464, 469; NRA, *Proceedings*, 1963, pp. 129–35.

19. NRA Board, September 30, 1963; ARS Newsletter, December, 1963.

20. AIPE, "Report of Growth Committee," September, 1963, p. i.

21. AIPE, *"Executive Director's Report No. 55,"* January, 1964.

22. NRA Executive Committee, January 10, 1964; NRA Board, January 20, 1964.

23. Susan M. Lee to NRA board members, March 10, 1964.

24. Memorandum from NRA Executive Committee to ARS Administrative Council on Report No. 55, April, 1964; ARS, *Administrative Council Consolidation Report*, April 11, 1964; AIPE Board, June 27–28, 1964.

25. NRA Executive Committee, June 23, 1964.

26. Prendergast memorandum to NRA board members on future relationships between AIPE, ARS, NCSP and NRA, November 12, 1964, NRA-M.

27. Prendergast, "The Tax Exemption of the National Recreation and Park Association," March 10, 1965; NRA-M.

28. Prendergast memorandum, November 12, 1964.

29. NRA Executive Committee, November 20, 1964.

30. Howard Gregg and Kathryn Krieg, "Proposed Charters and Bylaws to Unite the National Professional Organizations," July 17, 1964; Edward H. Thacker to ARS members, September 15, 1964; Prendergast, "The Merger of AIPE-ARS without NRA," September, 1964; ARS president's annual report, September 17, 1964.

31. NRA Board, May 27, 1964; "New NRA Projects," *Recreation*, v. LVII (September 1964), 344; "NRA Adds New Office in Washington, D.C.," *Recreation*, v. LVIII (January 1965):6.

32. See AIPE, "Executive Directors Report No. 60;" Prendergast newsletters, "To Keep the Record Straight," July 1964 and "The Unification and/or Federation of AIPE-ARS-NRA," August 1964, NRA-M.

33. Conrad L. Wirth to James H. Evans, Edward Thacker and Norman S. Johnson, June 28, 1964.

34. NRA Executive Committee, June 23, 1964.

35. Charles K. Brightbill to James H. Evans, August 12, 1964. Identical letters were sent to the presidents of AIPE and ARS and to the executive directors of NRA, AIPE and ARS.

36. NRA Board, October 5, 1964; ARS Administrative Council, October 2, 1964; AIPE Board, October 17, 1964.

37. NRA Executive Committee, May 13, 1964.

38. Alfred B. LaGasse to Frank Vaydik, November 25, 1964; AIPE, "Executive Directors Report No. 60."

39. Many professional supporters of NRA were primarily interested in the services they received rather than in the governance structure.

40. Stewart G. Case and Frank Vaydik to James H. Evans, October 22, 1964.

41. Robert W. Ruhe to officers of AIPE, ARS, NCSP and NRA, December 7, 1964; minutes of joint meeting by officers of AIPE, ARS, NCSP and NRA, December 5, 1964; NRA Executive Committee, December 11, 1964.

42. Joint meeting minutes, December 5, 1964.

43. James H. Evans to Laurance S. Rockefeller, June 23, 1965.

44. "Proposal for Merger. Statement of Implementation," March 1, 1965; NRPA, Board of Governors, May 23, 1965; Prendergast to NRA board members, August 18, 1965.

45. NRPA, Administrative Board, December 2, 1965.

46. NRPA news release, August 18, 1965; "New Organization Now A Reality," *Recreation*, v. LVIII (September 1965):315–17.

Selected Bibliography

SPECIAL BIBLIOGRAPHICAL AIDS

> Of the various bibliographies available on recreation and related topics, only a few, chiefly those by Meyersohn and Van der Smissen, are readily useful to historians of recreation.

American Association for Health, Physical Education, and Recreation. *Recreation Bibliography*. Washington, D.C., 1953. *N.V.*

Cureton, Thomas K. *Doctorate Theses Reported by Graduate Departments of Health, Physical Education, and Recreation, 1930–1946*. Washington, D.C., 1949. *N.V.*

———. *Masters Theses in Health, Physical Education, and Recreation*. Washington, D.C., 1952. *N.V.*

Denny, Reuel, and Meyersohn, Mary Lea. "A Preliminary Bibliography on Leisure," *American Journal of Sociology*, LXII (May 1957), 602–15.

Doty, William G. *Meaningful Leisure, an Interpretative Bibliographical Essay*. New York, 1963.

Gloss, George M. "Bibliography of Master's Theses and Doctoral Studies in the Field of Recreation," *Research Quarterly*, XI (March 1940), 150–63.

———. *Recreational Research*. Baton Route, 1940.

McCurdy, James H. *A Bibliography of Physical Training*. Springfield, Mass., 1905. *N.V.*

Menefee, Louise A., and Chambers, Merritt M. *American Youth, an Annotated Bibliography*. Washington, D.C., 1938.

Meyersohn, Rolf. "A Comprehensive Bibliography on Leisure, 1900–1958." Pages 389–419 of Larrabee, Eric, and Rolf Meyersohn, eds., *Mass Leisure*. Glencoe, Ill., 1958.

National Recreation and Park Association. *Research in Recreation*, 1965. New York, 1965.

————. *Journal of Leisure Research*, Arlington, Virginia, 1969 on. Listing of dissertations and thesis in leisure and recreation reported annually.

National Recreation Association. *A Guide to Books on Recreation*. New York, 1956 on. Published by the National Recreation and Park Association from 1966 on. Title changed in 1973 to *Publications on Parks, Recreation, & Leisure*.

Neumeyer, Martin H. "Areas for Research in Leisure and Recreation," *Sociology and Social Research*, XLIII (November 1958), 90–96.

Pinkerton, James R., and Pinkerton, Marjorie J. *Outdoor Recreation and Leisure: A Reference Guide and Selected Bibliography*. Columbia, Mo., 1969.

Sapora, Allen V. *Index to the Literature of Leisure, Recreation, Parks, and other Recreational Resources . . . .* New York, 1965. *N.V.*

U.S. Department of the Interior, Bureau of Outdoor Recreation. *Outdoor Recreation Research: A Reference Catalog*. Washington, D.C., 1967 on.

U.S. Outdoor Recreation Resources Review Commission. *Outdoor Recreation Literature: A Survey*. Outdoor Recreation Resources Review Commission Study Report 27. Washington, D.C., 1962.

Van der Smissen, Margaret E. *A Bibliography of Research Related to Recreation*. Iowa City, Iowa, 1962.

————, ed. *Bibliography of Theses and Dissertations in Recreation, Parks, Camping, and Outdoor Education*. Washington, D.C., 1970, 1979.

War Camp Community Service. *Community Service in Periodical Literature*. New York, 1920.

Williams, Marguerita P. *Sources of Information on Play and Recreation*. New York, 1920, 1927.

ARCHIVAL RECORDS

National Archives, Washington, D.C.
  Commission on Training Camp Activities. RG 165.
  Federal Security Agency, RG 235.
  National Conference on Outdoor Recreation. RG 220.
  National Park Service. RG 79.
  National Youth Administration. RG 119.
  Office of Community War Services. RG 215.
  Works Progress Administration. RG 69.
National Recreation and Park Association. Arlington, Va.
  Howard S. Braucher professional files.
  American Institute of Park Executives records.
  American Recreation Society records.
  National Recreation Association records.

University of Minnesota. Social Welfare History Archives Center. Minneapolis, Minn.
National Recreation Association records.

U.S. GOVERNMENT DOCUMENTS

U.S., Congress, House. *A Bill to Make Available Specialized Services and Facilities to States, Areas, Counties, and Communities in Developing Recreation Programs for the People of the United States.* . . . H.R. 5, 79th Cong., 1st sess., 1945.
U.S., Congress, Senate. Committee on Education and Labor. *Development of Community Recreation Programs for the People of the United States.* Hearings before a subcommittee of the Committee on Education and Labor, Senate, on S. 2070, 79th Cong., 2d sess., 1946.
U.S. Department of Commerce, Bureau of the Census. *Historical Statistics of the United States: Colonial Times to 1957.* Washington, D.C., 1960.
U.S. Department of Interior, Bureau of Outoor Recreation. *America's Park and Recreation Heritage: a Chronology,* by Carlton S. VanDoren and Louis Hodges. Washington, D.C., 1975.
U.S. Department of the Interior, National Park Service. *Recreational Use of Lands in the United States.* Washington, D.C., 1935. Pt. 11 of U.S., National Resources Board, Land Planning Committee, *Report.* Washington, D.C., 1935.
————. *A Study of the Park and Recreation Problem in the United States.* Washington, D.C., 1941.
U.S. Department of Labor, Bureau of Labor Statistics. *Park Recreation Areas in the United States.* Bulletin No. 462. Washington, D.C., 1928.
U.S. Federal Security Agency. Office of Community War Services. *Teamwork in Community Service, 1941–1946—A Demonstration in Federal, State, and Local Cooperation.* Washington, D.C., 1946.
U.S. Interdepartmental Committee to Coordinate Health and Welfare Activities. *Report of the Technical Committee on Recreation.* Washington, D.C., 1937.
U.S. Outdoor Recreation Resources Review Commission. *Outdoor Recreation for America.* Washington, D.C., 1962.
————. *Trends in American Living and Outdoor Recreation.* Outdoor Recreation Resources Review Commission Study Report 22. Washington, D.C., 1962.

PUBLICATIONS OF THE NRA

By 1965 NRA had published over 2,000 books, pamphlets, reprints, and bulletins as well as the periodical *Recreation.* Several hundred of these items are listed in the printed catalogs of the Library of Congress. The list that follows contains representative publications authored by the Association.

NRA. *Arts and Crafts for the Recreation Leader.* . . . New York, 1943.
————. *Charges and Fees for Community Recreation Facilities and Activities of Public Park, Recreation, and School Systems.* New York, 1932.
————. *Community Drama.* New York, 1926.
————. *Community Music.* New York, 1926.
————. *County Parks: A Report of a Study of County Parks in the United States.* New York, 1930.
————. *County Parks and Recreation,* published jointly with the National Association of Counties, 1964.
————. *Games for Children.* New York, 1943.
————. *Guidelines for the Organization and Administration of a Cultural Program in Community Recreation,* New York, 1965.
————. *Home Play.* New York, 1945.
————. *Howard Braucher Memorial Booklet.* New York, 1949.
————. *In-service Education for Community Center Leadership,* New York, 1955.
————. *Recreation and the Church: A Manual for Leaders.* New York, 1946.
————. *Recreation and Psychiatry,* New York, 1960.
————. *Recreation for Men: A Guide to the Planning and Conducting of Recreational Activities for Men's Groups.* New York, 1944.
————. *Recreation for Older People.* New York, 1947.
————. *Recreation for War Warkers: A Guide for Workers in Charge of Recreation in War Plants.* New York, 1943.
————. *Recreation Leadership Standards: Standards of Training, Experience, and Compensation for Positions in Community Recreation.* New York, 1944.
————. *Schedule for the Appraisal of Community Recreation,* New York, 1951.
————. *Standards for Neighborhood Recreation Areas and Facilities.* New York, 1943.
————. *Starting a Recreation Program in a Civilian Hospital,* New York, 1952.
————. *The Performing Arts as Recreation,* pamphlet series, New York, 1962–65.
————. *The Role of the Federal Government in the Field of Public Recreation.* New York, 1949.
————. *Training Volunteers for Recreation Service.* . . . New York, 1946.

BOOKS AND PAMPHLETS

Books written by people with experience on the staff of the NRA are marked (NRA). Items of special interest are indicated with an asterisk (*).

Allen, Edward F., and Fosdick, Raymond B. *Keeping Our Fighters Fit: For War and After.* . . . New York, 1918.

American Recreation Society. *The American Recreation Society: Its Early Years (1937–1952).* Washington, D.C., 1953.

Anderson, Jackson M. *Industrial Recreation.* New York, 1955.

Atkinson, Henry A. *The Church and the People's Play.* Boston, 1915.

Bremner, Robert H. *American Philanthropy.* The Chicago History of American Civilization Series. Chicago, 1960.

Butler, George D. *Introduction to Community Recreation.* 5th ed. New York, 1976. (NRA)

———. *Pioneers in Public Recreation.* Minneapolis, 1965. (NRA)*

———. Municipal Recreation Administration, Chicago, 1960. (NRA)

Carlson, Reynold E.; MacLean, Janet R.; Deppe, Theodore R.; and Peterson, James A. *Recreation and Leisure: The Changing Scene,* 3rd ed. Belmont, California, 1978.

Chambers, Clarke A. *Seedtime of Reform.* Ann Arbor, 1967.

Cohen, Sol. *Progressives and Urban School Reform.* New York, 1964.

Cozens, Frederick W., and Stumpf, Florence. *Sports in American Life.* Chicago, 1953.

Cremin, Lawrence A. *The Transformation of the School.* New York, 1961.

Curtis, Henry S. *Play and Recreation for the Open Country.* New York, 1914. (NRA)

———. *The Play Movement and Its Significance.* New York, 1917. (NRA)

Cutlip, Scott M. *Fund Raising in the United States.* New Brunswick, N.J., 1965.*

Cutten, George B. *The Threat of Leisure.* New Haven, 1926.

Davis, Allen F. *Spearheads for Freedom.* New York, 1967.

Davis, Helen E. *The YMCA and Public Recreation.* New York, 1946.

Davis, Michael M. *The Exploitation of Pleasure.* New York, 1911.

de Grazia, Sebastian. *Of Time, Work, and Leisure.* New York, 1962.

Diehl, Leonard J., and Eastwood, Floyd R. *Industrial Recreation.* Lafayette, Ind., 1940.

Dillick, Sidney. *Community Organization for Neighborhood Development.* New York, 1953.

Doell, Charles, E., and Fitzgerald, Gerald B. *A Brief History of Parks and Recreation in the United States.* Chicago, 1954.*

Dorgan, Ethel J. *Luther Halsey Gulick, 1865–1918.* New York, 1934.*

Dulles, Foster R. *The American Red Cross: A History.* New York, 1950.

———. *A History of Recreation: America Learns to Play.* 2d ed. New York, 1965.*

Dyer, Donald B., and Lichtig, J. G. *Liability in Public Recreation.* Appleton, Wisc., 1949.

Edwards, Richard H. *Popular Amusements.* New York, 1915.

Ekirch, Arthur A. *Man and Nature in America.* New York, 1963.

Fitch, Edwin M., and Shanklin, John F. *The Bureau of Outdoor Recreation.* New York, 1970.*

Fitzgerald, Gerald B. *Community Organization for Recreation.* New York, 1948.

Follett, Mary. *The New State*. New York, 1918.

Fosdick, Raymond B. *Chronicle of a Generation: An Autobiography*. New York, 1958.

Frye, Virginia, and Peters, Martha. *Therapeutic Recreation: Its Theory, Philosophy, and Practice*. Harrisburg, PA, 1972.

Fulk, Joseph R. *The Municipalization of Play and Recreation*. Lincoln, Neb., 1922.

Gates, Herbert W. *Recreation and the Church*. Chicago, 1917.

Glaser, William A., and Sills, David L., eds. *The Government of Associations*. Totowa, N.J., 1966.

Glenn, John M.; Brandt, Lillian; and Andrews, F. Emerson. *Russell Sage Foundation, 1907–1946*. 2 vols. New York, 1947.

Green, Arnold W. *Recreation, Leisure, and Politics*. New York, 1964.*

Gulick, Luther H. *A Philosophy of Play*. New York, 1920. (NRA)

Hanmer, Lee F., ed. *Recreation Legislation*. New York, 1915.

Hjelte, George. *The Administration of Public Recreation*. New York, 1940.

Hopkins, Charles H. *History of the YMCA in North America*. New York, 1951.

———. *The Rise of the Social Gospel in American Protestantism, 1865–1915*. New Haven, 1940.

Huth, Hans. *Nature and the American*. Berkeley, 1957.

Ise, John. *Our National Park Policy: A Critical History*. Baltimore, 1961.

Jacks, Lawrence P. *Education Through Recreation*. New York, 1932. (NRA)

King, C. Wendell. *Social Movements in the United States*. New York, 1956.

Konopka, Gisela. *Eduard C. Lindeman and Social Work Philosophy*. Minneapolis, 1958.

Kraus, Richard G. *Recreation and Leisure in Modern Society*. 2nd ed. Santa Monica, California, 1978.

Krout, John A. *Annals of American Sport*. New Haven, 1929.

Lee, Joseph. *Constructive and Preventive Philanthropy*. New York, 1902. (NRA)

———. *Play in Education*. New York, 1915. (NRA)

Lies, Eugene T. *The New Leisure Challenges the Schools*. New York, 1933. (NRA)

Lindeman, Eduard C. *Leisure—a National Issue: Planning for the Leisure of a Democratic People*. New York, 1939.

Lubove, Roy. *The Professional Altruist*. Cambridge, Mass., 1965.

Lundberg, George A.; Komarovsky, Mirra; and McInerny, Mary Alice. *Leisure: A Suburban Study*. New York, 1934.

Lutzin, Sidney G., and Storey, Edward H., eds. *Managing Municipal Leisure Services*. Washington, D.C., 1973.

McKelvey, Blake. *The Emergence of Metropolitan America, 1915–1966.* New Brunswick, N.J., 1968.

———. *The Urbanization of America, 1865–1915.* New Brunswick, N.J., 1963.

May, Herbert L., and Petgen, Dorothy. *Leisure and its Use: Some International Observations.* New York, 1928.

Mero, Everett B. *American Playgrounds.* Boston, 1908.

Meyer, Harold D., and Brightbill, Charles K. *State Recreation.* New York, 1950.

———, and Sessoms, H. Douglas. *Leisure Services: The Organized Recreation and Park System.* 5th ed. Englewood Cliffs, N.J., 1975.

Musselman, Virginia W. *The Day Camp Program Book.* New York, 1963. (NRA)

Nelson, Beatrice M. *State Recreation.* Washington, D.C., 1928.

Neumeyer, Martin H., and Neumeyer, Esther S. *Leisure and Recreation: A Study of Leisure and Recreation in Their Sociological Aspects.* 3rd ed. New York, 1958.

Nolen, John. *General Plan of a Park and Playground System for New London, Connecticut.* Boston, 1913.

Owen, John D. *The Price of Leisure.* The Hague, 1969.

Pangburn, Weaver W. *Adventures in Recreation.* New York, 1936. (NRA)

Patton, Clifford W. *The Battle for Municipal Reform: Mobilization and Attack, 1875–1900.* Washington, D.C., 1940.

Perry, Clarence A. *Ten Years of the Community Center Movement.* New York, 1921.

Pound, Arthur. *The Iron Man in Industry.* New York, 1922.

Rainwater, Clarence E. *The Play Movement in the United States.* Chicago, 1922.*

Reps, John. *Making of Urban America.* Princeton, N.J., 1965.

Romney, G. Ott. *Off the Job Living.* New York, 1945.

Sapora, Allen V., and Mitchell, Elmer D. *The Theory of Play and Recreation.* 3rd ed. New York, 1961.

Schwendener, Norma. *A History of Physical Education in the United States.* New York, 1942.

Scott, Mel. *American City Planning Since 1890.* Berkeley, 1969.

Shryock, Richard H. *National Tuberculosis Association (1904–1954).* New York, 1957.*

Sizer, James P. *The Commercialization of Leisure.* Boston, 1917.

Steiner, Jesse F. *Americans at Play.* New York, 1933.*

———. *Research Memorandum on Recreation in the Depression.* Social Science Research Council. Bulletin 32. New York, 1937.

Stewart, Frank Mann. *A Half Century of Municipal Reform: The National Municipal League.* Berkeley, 1950.*

Tilden, Freeman. *The State Parks.* New York, 1962.

Torrey, Raymond H. *State Parks and Recreational Use of State Forests in the United States.* Washington, D.C., 1926.
Truxal, Andrew G. *Outdoor Recreation Legislation and its Effectiveness.* New York, 1929.
Vinal, William G. *Nature Recreation.* New York, 1940. (NRA)
Weir, Lebert H., ed. *Camping Out: A Manual on Organized Camping.* New York, 1924. (NRA)
———. *Parks, A Manual of County and Municipal Parks.* New York, 1928. (NRA)
Wiemer, David L. *Foundation Philanthropy as Related to the Field of Municipal Parks.* Bloomington, Ind., 1967.
Wilcox, Delos F. *The American City.* New York, 1904.
Zanzig, Augustus D. *Music in American Life.* New York, 1932. (NRA)

PERIODICALS

> Among the periodicals most useful for this study was, of course, *Recreation.* Numerous other periodicals, including those that follow, contain material on parks, recreation, and related topics.

The American City (1909–date).
American Physical Education Review (1896–1929).
American Recreation Journal (1960–1965).
American Recreation Society *Quarterly Bulletin* (1940–1957).
Charities: A Weekly Review of Local and General Philanthropy (1897–1905).
Charities and the Commons (1905–1909).
Garden and Forest (1888–1897).
Journal of Health, Physical Education, and Recreation (1930–date).
Leisure (1933–1938).
Municipal Affairs (1897–1902).
Municipal Year Book (1934–date).
National Civic Review (1912–date).
National Conference of Charities and Corrections. *Proceedings.* See National Conference on Social Welfare.
National Conference on Social Welfare. *The Social Welfare Forum.* (1874–date).
National Municipal Review. See *National Civic Review.*
National Recreation Association. *Proceedings* of Annual Recreation Congresses. (1907–1965).
Parks and Recreation (1921–1965).
Parks and Recreation (1966–date).
The Playground. See *Recreation.*
Recreation (1907–1965).
The Survey (1897–1952).

Index

PHOTO CREDITS